TEXAS HUMORESQUE

AMERICAN HUMOR IS BASICALLY PROTEST HUMOR . . .

John Henry Faulk

FOR TEXAS WRITERS MAYBE COMEDY IS A FORM OF REALISM . . .

Tom Pilkington

TEXAS HUMORESQUE

Lone Star Humorists From Then Till Now

An Anthology
Collected and Arranged
by
C. L. Sonnichsen

Texas Christian University Press Fort Worth

Library of Congress Cataloging-in-Publication Data

Texas humoresque : Lone Star humorists from then till now / compiled
and edited by C.L. Sonnichsen.
    p. cm.
    Includes bibliographical references.
    ISBN 0-87565-046-5
    1. Texas—Humor. 2. American wit and humor—Texas—History and
criticism. I. Sonnichsen, C. L. (Charles Leland). 1901–
PN6231.T56T49 1990   89-37113
813'.010832764—dc20   CIP

All the drawings for this book were made by Charles Shaw.
Designed by A. Tracy Row.

THANKS

Most writers and editors, by choice or by necessity, work alone. The anthologist, however, operates in a crowd. He is surrounded by, and responsible to, librarians, editors, publishers, agents, copyright custodians, individual authors, and helpful friends. He is profoundly grateful to all, but some of his benefactors deserve special mention. For indispensable assistance of one kind or another I am greatly indebted to the following:

Bruce J. Dinges, editor, Julie Campbell, assistant editor, and Monica Wood, secretary, of the publications staff at the Arizona Historical Society, Tucson.

Bud Newman, Special Collections librarian, Professor John O. West of the University of Texas at El Paso, Dale L. Walker, director of Texas Western Press, UTEP, and Hugh Treadwell of El Paso, field representative for W. W. Norton, publishers of New York.

Professor James W. Lee of the University of North Texas, Professor Francis L. Abernethy of Stephen F. Austin State University, and Professor Tom Pilkington of John Tarleton State University. Tom's comment on the uses of comedy in Texas is from a letter to C. L. S. dated November 17, 1988.

Joyce Roach and Ann Gibson of Keller; Deolece Parmelee of Austin.

David Grossblatt of Dallas and Augusta Hemphill of Irving.

Librarians and library staffs at the University of Texas at El Paso, the Arizona Historical Society, and the Tucson Public Library, Nanini Branch.

Judy Alter, director, and Tracy Row, editor, at Texas Christian University Press.

There would have been no book without the encouragement, constructive criticism, and secretarial skill of my wife Carol. My greatest debt will always be to her.

CONTENTS

DEDICATION

To the humorists of Texas from Alex Sweet to Cactus Pryor who have lighted the way to truth and reason with the lamp of laughter.

TEXAS HUMORESQUE

C. L. Sonnichsen

Lone Star Humorists and How They Grew

Humor is alive and well in the Lone Star State. Texans are funny and have been laughed at and have laughed at themselves since the early days of settlement, and Texas humorists are in full cry today. They seem, in fact, to be more active than ever before—the annual crop of Texas stories is convincing evidence of that. Possibly it's because there is more to be humorous about.

There is some uncertainty, however, about what we mean when we talk about humor. To most of us "humorous" is the same as "funny" and all the other words that mean "laughable." This is a mistake. Humor is often funny or at least amusing, but it doesn't have to be.

To understand this, one has to look at a little etymological history. Doctors in the Middle Ages believed that the four bodily fluids—the "humors"—strongly influenced human health and human personality. A full-blooded man was sanguine. A man with an excess of yellow bile was bilious and irritable; of black bile was melancholy; of phlegm was phlegmatic. The words are familiar but the concepts behind them have been forgotten. A humorist, then, is or should be a man interested in the quirks of human personality and behavior and is amused by them. He keeps his balance and stays in the middle of the road. Otherwise he is something else. If he makes his men and women too ridiculous, he writes a farce. If he makes them disgusting or despicable, he is a satirist.

Larry McMurtry, for example, is often hilarious, but his funniest scenes, as has been accurately pointed out, are pure farce. Edna Ferber, on the other hand, deals convincingly with the foibles and foolishness of rich Texans and has every opportunity to play them for laughs, but she seldom does. Her mood might be described as one of quiet horror. When Leslie Benedict in *Giant*, a bride from the East totally unprepared for Texas, almost faints when presented with a roasted bull's eye at the barbecue in her honor, Ferber sees nothing funny in the scene and neither does the reader. Edna is not a humorist.

The way humor works is well illustrated by a scene in Judge Smart's Houston courtroom described by H. T. McCullen in *What's Going On?*, the 1976 publication of the Texas Folklore Society.

After hearing all the testimony, including the confession of an industrial magnate who had seduced a girl, Judge Smart rendered a verdict: "You will give this girl $10,000, establish a trust fund of $20,000 for her unborn child, and give her mother—a poor woman humiliated and crushed by this ordeal—$5,000." As the judge lifted his gavel to dismiss the case, the mother interrupted: "All the saints bless you! and may Our Lady always smile upon you! But, Your Honor, if my Virginia has a miscarriage, please order this man to give her another chance!"

There you have it. The mother does not behave as you and I would behave. So we laugh at her. Nobody knows why. We just do it, and two thousand years of speculation by philosophers has not brought forth a satisfactory explanation. The key word is "ridiculous." The mother in Judge Smart's courtroom might have been presented as pitiful or evil, but the humorist doesn't go that route, possibly because he knows he shares her weakness.

When the humorist gets hold of a suitable subject, a wide range of moods is available to him. He can be *good* humored like Laura V. Hamner depicting ranch people in *Light 'n Hitch*, or Ellen Bowie Holland in *Gay as Grig*, smiling at the special traits of her Scottish father—both excerpted in these pages. At the other end of the spectrum is serious social criticism. A DeWitt County schoolteacher, writing for the *Galveston News* about a multiple killing in 1867, smiles ironically but reacts negatively:

"Hit seems John Bell and Walt Edwards had words up on Sandies, and Bell sent Edwards word not to come stock hunting on his range. Well, they met out on Lower Hog Eye, hit's a branch of the Cabasas over in the edge of Karnes, and who begun it and shot first he couldn't ondertake to say, but hit was a very good fight and only four in it, there was old man Edwards and Walt agin John Bell and Charley Thee, two and two aside and a very good fight. Walt Edwards and Charley Thee was shot down directly, but Charley kept a shootin' at old man Edwards long as he could raise his weepin—it was a very good fight and John Bell emptied his six-shooter and never missed only one shot, Walt Edwards and Charley Thee fell in thar tracks and was killed on the ground, and old man Edwards is dead since, of a wound through his shoulder, and John Bell was the only one not hurted and hit was a very good fight." Was there no one to interfere and stop it? "Well, the boys was all round; they was on a stock hunt, and nigh the pen, but it come on suddint, and was all over in half a minute; only four in it; two and two aside, but it was very good fight; the best he had heerd on since the war." So much from the gentleman from Lower Hogeye, and nothing more—*a very good fight*. Three immortal souls gone to their account, a few children orphaned; but nevertheless, indisputably a "very good fight!"

"So that's what it is like in Texas!" your grandfather said when such stories were snatched up and retailed to Eastern readers. "What a horrible place!"

In most cases the humorist is reminding us of the difference between what is and what ought to be no matter how mild or severe his approach.

For some reason the nonconformists—the oddballs, the exceptions, the ones who are different—have always been fascinating to their conformist brothers and sisters. They may appeal to the rebel in us: we may envy them their freedom. Whatever the reason, they never fail to get our attention. From the time of Aristotle to the present, writers have featured them and readers have enjoyed them. The English have been especially fond of them and the great writers, beginning with Chaucer, have been character mongers. Britons were proud of their queer ducks and even had a name for them: "original genius," "original" for short. When they migrated to the New World, they brought their humors with them, and wonderful characters were celebrated all the way to the Pacific Ocean—Down-East Yankees, hard-living southerners, Forty-niners, Pike County mule-skinners, and a hundred more.

The humorists found specially good hunting in Texas. The enormous size of the state and the diversity of its population had much to do with it. Since each segment looked odd to all the rest, the possibilities for humorous observation were endless. At first country characters were favored, but as the cities expanded and absorbed more and more of the population, metropolitan types moved in and replaced the backwoodsmen and sandy-land farmers as grist for the humorist's mill. Leon Hale, the gentle, genial columnist for the *Houston Post,* says he has difficulty finding the old independent Texas characters in the Gulf Coast region northeast of Houston, where he is most at home (*Turn South at the Second Bridge*). Leon need not worry, however. Texas will never run out of serene independents like oil billionaire H. L. Hunt of Dallas who brown-bagged his lunch; Dr. John R. Brinkley of Del Rio, the goat-gland specialist who promised restored virility to aging Romeos; Billy Sol Estes of Pecos, a sincere and dedicated Christian on Sundays, and a purveyor of nonexistent drums of liquid fertilizer on weekdays. New vistas beckon all the time. Edwin Shrake opened up a promising one in *Peter Arbiter,* a novel which made hilarious and immodest capital of the gay subculture of Dallas.

Awed by the plethora of possibilities, the anthologist finds himself in the position of the proverbial blind dog in the meat house—forced to make difficult choices. Every reader will fault him for leaving out a favorite author. He can only plead that the book is a sampler—not a compendium.

Finally a reminder that humor is a civilized and civilizing product of the human mind. "Criticism of society, of human foibles, of man himself," says Tom Pilkington in *My Blood's Country,* "is implicit in the Comic Spirit" and "it demands a certain amount of taste and perspective." It puts the fear of ridicule in the heart of the potential transgressor and helps to keep the tissues of society healthy. In Texas it is a precious resource, just under cattle and oil in importance, and should be treated with respect as well as with laughter. Let us rejoice and be glad in it.

Appetizers

Evidence that Humor
Is Alive and Well in Texas

Alex Burton

Just One Kiss, Baby!

ALEX BURTON, a Dallas institution for a good many years, entertained Dallasites on their way to work with his morning monologues on radio station KRLD with almost religious regularity. Alex covered every imaginable subject from garage sales to grandmothers, often bringing his "child bride" into the discussion and sometimes introducing a philosophical pigeon whose opinions he respected. He has been described as a combination of H. Allen Smith and Andy Rooney. Like them, he was original, inexhaustible, and consistently humorous.

From *Just One Kiss, Baby!* Austin: Eakin Press, 1983, pp. 83–84.

"Science cannot define the light in a firefly's behind. I can think of nothing eerier than flying about with an unidentified glow in one's posterior."

Those lines from Ogden Nash flashed through my head, if you'll pardon the pun, the other night during the rain and thunderstorm. The reason was, we had a firefly, or lightning bug, flying around in the bedroom. I had thought it was the flashes of lightning that woke me, but it turned out to be the firefly.

Now according to my encyclopedia, the fireflies attract each other in a sexual way by flashing their back ends at one another. It is a whitish green light, for those of you who have never seen it. And there is something about counting the number of times it flashes to determine the temperature or something.

The firefly in our bedroom was in a frenzy of desire, as near as I could figure, from the way he kept the room alight with his flasher. There was lightning outside which was lighting up the world at about the same rate as the lightning bug was lighting up the room. He flew over to the window and watched the lightning.

"Just one kiss, Baby," I heard him holler into the night.

I chose to ignore it as an intemperate remark. So the firefly flashed around for about fifteen minutes and then went to visit a night light we have in another room. He was back pretty quickly.

"All of them city girls are alike," I heard him mutter, "all good looks and flash clothes, nothing for character or conversation."

Finally he took up residence in the ceiling light fixture where he flashed fitfully for a minute or so, and at last went to sleep.

"What was that all about?" said the Child Bride sleepily, and I explained about the firefly and why he lights up like that. "You mean," she said, "the way your eyes light up?"

"You got that straight, Baby!" I told her as she put on her sun glasses.

Leon Hale

Aunt Lizzie's Snuff

LEON HALE, long-time columnist for the *Houston Post,* is best known for his vignettes of small-town and country people of the Gulf Coast region north of Houston. He has a sharp eye for the off-beat but his humor is warm and refreshing. He gives his characters credit for their gifts, even if his subject is only the champion long-distance spitter, like Miss Lizzie Thompson.

From *Turn South at the Second Bridge*. College Station: Texas A&M University Press, 1985, pp. 64–67.

"Everything should be natural." —Teodora Saenz

Aunt Lizzie Thornton was born in the Piney Woods near Trinity. She is eighty-six years old now and the farthest she's ever been from home is Crockett, twenty-eight miles away.

Still, she gained her measure of fame. Around Trinity she is noted as an expert snuff dipper and spitter. She used to come to town every Saturday and bring along her favorite rope-bottomed chair. She'd park that chair out front of the feed store, watch the people, dip snuff with an elm twig and spit with remarkable skill. She could drown a fly at twelve feet.

Trinity folks walking on the street always gave Aunt Lizzie a wide berth when they went by the feed store. At the end of the day she'd leave behind her a solid brown snuff-juice stain, extending from her chair in a broad arc twelve to fifteen feet in diameter.

Aunt Lizzie hasn't been into town for a long time, so I got a friend to steer me out to her house to find out why. She was at home and feeling pretty well. It was a hot afternoon and she came out on her front porch, barefoot, to do her talking. She's a little thing. Likely doesn't weight eighty-five pounds. The years have etched a thousand lines in her face and stooped her narrow shoulders, but they haven't dulled her tongue or her wits.

Now you used to hear a great deal of talk about people still hidden deep in the East Texas woods who've never been to school, never seen a train, never seen a city, never even ridden in a car. Perhaps they exist. I've not found them. Well, sure, there are a good many who've not been to school, or at least not enough to learn to read and write. And many more who can read and write like sixty who've not seen a city.

Aunt Lizzie just never did recognize any necessity for seeing a city. Once a week she went into Trinity, which has eighteen hundred people. And then she traveled twenty-eight miles that time all the way to Crockett, which is a county seat town and has more than five thousand folks and a courthouse and a county fair, and if she saw a city it'd just be the same things only more of them. So she stayed home. Except on Saturdays.

Aunt Lizzie still has her rope-bottomed chair. She pulled it out on the porch and we had a question-and-answer session.

Does she still dip snuff?

"Yessirboss," she said, using an old country expression. And saying it just that way, without any commas or spaces between the words. The "boss" part of the expression doesn't imply that she is recognizing a better. It's just a way of giving an emphatic answer.

How long has she dipped snuff now?

"I don't know. Started when I was a little girl. Ten, maybe. Used to steal snuff from my mother."

Does she think seventy-five years of snuff dipping ever hurt her?
"Naw."

Can she still spit good? Could she hit that washtub yonder by the chinaberry tree, twelve feet away?

"Could if I hadn't lost my teeth. Can't spit good without my teeth."

What would she do if the doctor told her to quit dipping?

"I'd have a dip when I wanted it. People are gonna have what they want, it don't matter what. I'm gonna have my snuff."

Why doesn't she go into town on Saturdays as she used to?

"The reason I don't," and Aunt Lizzie's eyes fired a little at the question, "I can't stand the sight of these women, wearin' pants and smokin' cigarettes. And I don't think women ought to vote either."

Why shouldn't women vote?

"Because they're out of place at the polls. Women ought to stay in their place."

And where is that?

"At home."

How about women who work, in offices and stores?

"I don't think they ought to, but I guess it's none of my business."

Has Aunt Lizzie ever voted, even one time?

"Nosirboss."

Wouldn't she like to vote?

"Nosirboss."

Has she ever watched television?

"Saw one once. Didn't like it. That's what's makin' these children so bad, watchin' all that stuff on television."

Is Aunt Lizzie aware that men are now getting ready to fly into space and land on the moon?

"I've heard about it."

What does she think about it?

"They oughtn't to do it. That's God's moon. God put that moon there."

Does she think men will ever land on the moon?

"Naw. There's a man up there already, burnin' brush."

There's a man on the moon burning brush? How does she know that?

"Well, I can see him."

Is that what makes the moon shine, the brush burning?

"Yes."

Is that a real man up there on the moon?

"Well, I don't know. I haven't been up there to see." Aunt Lizzie thought that was a good joke and ducked her head and laughed.

But does she believe it's a real man?

"Well, it looks like a real man."

Wouldn't Aunt Lizzie like to travel? See the ocean, go to Houston, fly in an airplane?

"Nosirboss."

Does she have any particular ambition? Anything she'd especially like to do that she's never done?

"Nosirboss. I just wanta keep on doin' just what I'ma doin'."

I drove away then, and Aunt Lizzie Thornton went back to doing what she wanted to do, which was dipping snuff.

Cactus Pryor

The Ballad of Billie Sol

RICHARD ("CACTUS") PRYOR was born in Austin and never got over
it. He is passionate about Texas, though he admits that the times are
changing and Texas is not was it was. In the 1940s he began a career in
radio which took him into the Age of Television. At the same time he
carried on a second vocation as a public entertainer. He was in demand
as an after-dinner speaker and he provided entertainment at parties
given by such bigwigs as Lyndon Johnson. In his book *Inside Texas* he
recounts his adventures and misadventures in his two specialties. He is
a true humorist and describes his vicissitudes with bounce and flair.

From *Inside Texas*. Bryan, Texas: Shoal Creek Publishers, 1982,
pp. 37–38.

I never won a free weekend in Ruidoso because of my horse sense.
My best grades in school were in non-intellectual subjects such as phys-
ical education. My talent is athletic, as I have proven many times by
excelling in my favorite sport—putting foot in mouth. If this sport ever
became an Olympic event I would be the modern Jesse Owens. My best
performance in my chosen event occurred at the ranch of one Lyndon
B. Johnson on the heretofore-"that day" placid waters of the Pedernales
River.

Senate Majority Leader Johnson was having a little party on the
front lawn for some of his good old boy and girl friends. Nothing
fancy—just burgers and beer and Cutty and branch water. And to
further demonstrate the casualness of the get-together, I was invited to
present a program of entertainment. My price was right—one burger
and two Lone Stars, and I knew a group of musicians who would work

for the same wages. Texas VIPs were strewn across the ranch house lawn like the herefords feeding across the river.

Towards sundown we rang the ranch bell and the group assembled in folding chairs before the public address microphone for a little entertainment. I introduced some folk singers (Bohemians—hippies hadn't yet been invented) and a fiddle band. They seemed to be doing the right numbers, because the guests' feet were tapping in collective rhythm, and the ranch owner seemed right pleased with the proceedings.

As a matter of fact, things were going so swimmingly that I decided this would be a good opportunity to introduce my latest ballad. A horse would have had more sense.

A factor in my decision to do this particular number was the fact that the Billie Sol Estes scandal (the first one) was at its juiciest climax. And the attorney who was representing Estes, Austin lawyer Hume Cofer, was one of the guests. My song was "The Ballad of Billie Sol Estes," done as a parody on our state song, "Texas, Our Texas." It was like blaspheming bluebonnets.

So I began to regale my audience with my "hilarious" (that's a direct quote from me) lyrics. There was encouraging laughter at first. But then it dwindled to a deafening silence. I read what was happening. They were all watching their host to see his reaction to this jester's audacity, and they immediately determined from the smoky nostrils and fiery eyes that LBJ was vastly unamused.

I knew what I was doing. I was standing there singing myself to death for a burger and two Lone Stars. But there was no retreat so I continued my swan song in the key of C—as in *c*omplete panic. I came to a verse that played on Governor John Connally, who was also in the audience. When the lyrics came from my trembling mouth like blood dripping from my jugular, Governor Connally broke out in a large, gorgeous, magnificent, stupendous, colossal, fantastic guffaw!

The audience, thus released from guilt, joined brother John and soon all were rocking in uproarious laughter. Johnson, always a believer in the will of the majority, decided to join the throng and was soon holding his sides in joyous mirth. Hallelujah! I'd been saved.

I tell you this so you will understand that if John Connally should run for pope or king or even coach of the Dallas Cowboys, he will have my unwavering support and undying loyalty.

Joe Bob Briggs

Is The National Geographic in Zambooli Land?

JOE BOB BRIGGS (right name John Bloom) burst upon a startled Texas in the early 1980s as a reviewer and critic of drive-in movies, the farther out, the better. He assumed the persona of a nineteen-year-old sub-literate redneck from Rockwell, Texas, with no illusions or inhibitions and a viewing record of over 800 drive-in films. His outrageous humor and some lapses in taste lost him his job with a Dallas newspaper, and he boasts that he has been "banned" in several southwestern cities, but he kept his delighted fans and made new ones. As his reputation ex-panded, his coverage did likewise, and he felt free to comment on national and even international affairs. He even wrote a book purport-ing to be an autobiography. His claim to public interest, however, rests solidly on his preposterously funny movie reviews.

From the *Dallas Times Herald,* August 31, 1984.

This week I want to take time out for something we forget about in this hustle-bustle world of ours. It's something we take for granted after a while because we forget we're in America. Of course, you know what I'm talking about.

I'm talking about Tanya Roberts' boobies.

Now I don't want any snickers there, you hear me? I *know* she's the first bimbo to pop her top on the big screen and still get a "PG." I *know* we got problems in the tape-measure department.

But some actresses have the raw talent to overcome a few profile limitations, if you know what I mean and I think you do, and Tanya is one of 'em. Let's talk "Sheena, Queen of the Jungle." Let's see what happens when you take a bunch of wild savages from Malibu and stick 'em in the jungle and see if they'll eat each other. Let's talk Attack of the Stupid White People. Let's talk National Geographic in Zambooli Land. But mostly let's talk Tanya's hooters.

It starts off with some plot about how Sheena's parents were turned into Mrs. Paul's fish sticks by getting stuck inside a volcano, but Sheena runs the heck out of that stewpot and ends up with some people with bones in their noses. These are Zamboolis. Their idea of going to the doctor is they stick people in the ground up to their neck and then run around kicking dirt in their teeth until they're well.

Then Sheena takes a bath. It's better than the bath she took in "Beastmaster," and about the same as the bath Bo Derek took in "Tarzan the Ape Man," but it's no "Gas Pump Girls." While Sheena's taking the bath, this reporter is flying over in his airplane and he sees her down there and decides he'd like to sign up for African water polo. Then this old woman who's Sheena's stepmother heads off to the city to tell the king that he's about to get killed by the evil prince who used to play for the NFL, but before she gets there this moon-face American drinks poison and drowns in his oatmeal.

Then Sheena rides a zebra for a while. Sheena does a lot of zebra stuff in the flick.

Then the king makes this toast to the Super Bowl, and while he's talking a Zambooli shoots him with a poison arrow and he falls in the potato salad, and they arrest Sheena's mama for the crime. The reporter gets all hot and starts talking reporter talk.

Then Sheena sends some brainwaves to this elephant, and the elephant crashes through some trees and breaks down a fence and gets Sheena's mama out of jail. Then they use some more elephant ESP to get away, and the general of the army says "None of this women's lip stuff around here," and he sends the marines after 'em through the jungle. There's a lot of exploding bamboo like in Nam movies, and then all the animals come running out to save Sheena and keep the reporters in their Bronco.

Next thing, we got one of the most touching scenes in the history of drive-ins, and that's when Sheena's mom cashes in her chips, lays down on the ground, and starts dying while the elephant digs her grave with his trunk. I get all choked up just thinking about it.

Once the ugly old woman is out of the way, we get some Monkey Fu some Rhino Fu, some Snake fu and some monkey bidness between Sheena and the reporter in a tree house.

Then Sheena takes a bath again. Then she tries to talk. Like she says, "Remove those strange skins you wear." (The turkey put on a Haggar suit to go in the forest.)

Then the army starts blowing up everything and the reporter gets scared shirtless he won't live long enough to get an Emmy. The leader of the army keeps saying stuff like "Eez good psychology," but he never can catch Sheena, even when she's feeding fermented buffalo milk to Mr. Macho and shooting flaming arrows at gasoline trucks and dodging machine gun bullets. Then Sheena gets a little p.o.ed and she concentrates real hard and puts her fist on her head and starts talking to the animals and the zebras and antelopes all start running to make the machine-gun helicopter go in the other direction.

Finally, the evil prince football player's girlfriend decides she'll take Sheena up in the copter and drop her buns over the holy waterfall, but once they get up in the air Sheena talks to the animals again and this time we got results: killer flamingo attack. *The flamingos peck the copter to death.*

Now the army is *really* p.o.ed and so in the big final scene we got machine guns, flame-throwers, tanks, copters, trucks, and soldiers on one side. On the other side we got zoo animals. I won't tell you exactly what happens, but I'll give you a clue: it's feeding time.

Straight to Numero Uno on the 1984 Joe Bob Briggs list. We got 20 breasts. Half gallon blood. Twenty-two on the vomit meter. Fourteen beasts. Exploding bamboo. Twenty-five dead bodies. Kung fu. Bimbo fu. Zoo fu. National Geographical tribal dancing. Three baths. One heart attack. Animal ESP. One fist fight. Three motor vehicle chases. Three crash-and-burns. One killer flamingo attack. One stampede. One village destroyed like in Nam. One zebra massacre. Sheena gets slapped around. Two spears through the body. One cure for cancer. Drive-In Academy Award nomination for Sheena, who has a wimp boyfriend who says "How much I love you Sheena, so much it busts my heart." We're talking movie here. Four stars.

Joe Bob says check it out.

On the Frontier

For John C. Duval's "The Wild Texan Comes Home"

According to people who ought to know, including Larry L. King and Tom Pilkington, Texans have never got over their frontier past. The myth of the frontiersman begins with great-grandfather migrating from Tennessee in a covered wagon, bringing with him his cattle, his slaves, and the bones of his ancestors. It continues with the fight at the Alamo, the great plantations, Hood's Texas Brigade, ten thousand cattle on the Chisholm Trail, and the Texas Rangers. Its final expression is "Don't Mess with Texas."

The reality was much different.

Pioneer Texans were short on education, religion, and good manners. Their chief concern was survival and their difficulties and hardships were great. Travelers and newcomers who reported on those early settlers found them a new and striking breed and they sometimes played them for laughs. The woman from Mississippi encountered by Captain Randolph B. Marcy in 1850 had no idea that she was funny, but the captain played her for laughs, made her appear funny, exaggerating her dialect and poking fun at her lifestyle, including bedtime arrangements. His eastern readers expected and enjoyed his little caricature. Sometimes a frontiersman added to the amusement. When Bigfoot Wallace went back to his old home in Virginia, he was received with wide-eyed wonder as the "Wild Texan," and he took considerable pleasure in giving his old neighbors what they anticipated. Fortunately, the Texas pioneers could laugh at themselves. It helped them endure a perilous life.

Randolph B. Marcy

Frontier Settlers

CAPTAIN (LATER GENERAL) RANDOLPH B. MARCY spent many years
before the Civil War in the early west, sometimes on the edge of civilization or beyond it. He wrote two books about his adventures, *Thirty
Years of Army Life on the Border* (1866) and *Border Reminiscences* (1872).
His lively style and fine sense of humor won him a wide audience in his
own time and entitle him to attention in ours.

From *Thirty Years of Army Life on the Border*. New York: Harper &
Brothers, 1866, pp. 319–324.

The ideas, habits, and language of the population upon the borders of
Arkansas and Texas are eminently peculiar, and very different from
those of any other people I have ever before met with in my travels;
they seem to constitute an anomalous and detached element in our
social structure. Their sparsely scattered forest habitations, being far
removed from towns or villages, and seldom visited by travelers, almost
entirely exclude them from intercouse with the civilized world, and they
are nearly as ignorant of what is transpiring outside their own immediate sphere as the savages themselves. They seldom or never see a
newspaper, and could not read it if they did; and I honestly believe that
many of them could not tell whether General Jackson, Mr. Lincoln, or
Mr. Johnson is President of the United States at the present time.

Some of the most salient traits in the character of this singular type
of the Anglo-Saxon race have been exhibited in a conspicuous light
among the specimens I have encountered upon the frontier, and I now
propose to introduce some of them to the notice of the reader.

I remember, upon one occasion, after riding all day through a dense forest region in Northwestern Texas, in the winter of 1850–1, without the slightest indication of a road or even trail to guide me, and during a severe storm of snow and rain, and without having met with a single human being during the entire day, that I suddenly came out into a small clearing in the centre of which was a very diminutive log cabin, from whence arose a cheerful smoke, indicating the presence of occupants. This was a very pleasant surprise to me, as I had confidently calculated on being obliged to bivouac for the night alone in the woods, and this, during such a cold storm, would have been any thing but agreeable. I therefore gladly turned my jaded horse toward the hut, and, on my approach, a woman, some half a dozen children, and about as many dogs emerged therefrom.

After passing the customary salutations of the country, and exchanging particular inquiries as to the past and present condition of each other's health, I begged to inquire if I could be accommodated with lodgings for the night, to which the woman very obligingly replied, "Wall, now, stranger, my ole man he ar out on a bar track, but I sort-o-reckon maybe you mought git to stay"; she, however, for my consideration, added "that thar war narry show of vittles in the house barrin some sweet taters and a small chance of corn." As I was very hungry, and did not feel disposed to put up with such meagre fare, I dismounted, tied my horse, took my rifle, and went out into the woods in quest of something more substantial for supper, and fortunately had not gone far before I succeeded in killing a deer, which I *packed* to the house, and, by the aid of my *"couteau de chasse,"* soon had nicely dressed. My hostess and the children seemed highly delighted at my success, as they had seen no meat for several days, and the old lady complimented me by asking "what my name mought be"; and upon my informing her that it was Marcy, she said "she knowd a heap o' Massys down in *ole* Massasip," and that "me an him (Davy, her husband) allers 'lowed that them thar Massys was considdible on bar and other varmints." She then told me, if I would grind some corn in a coffee-mill which was fastened against the corner of the house, that she would bake a pone for me. Accordingly, I set to work, and, after about half an hour's steady application, succeeded in producing from the rickety old machine about a quart of meal, which was speedily converted into a cake. This, with some of the ribs of the fat venison well roasted, and a

cup of good coffee produced from my saddlebags, made a most substantial and excellent supper. After this was over I lighted my pipe, and,
seating myself before the cheerful log fire, for the first time since my
arrival took a survey of the establishment.

It consisted of one room about fourteen feet square, with the
intervals between the logs not *chinked,* and wide enough in places to
allow the dogs to pass in and out at their pleasure. There was an
opening for the door, which was closed with a greasy old beef's hide,
but there were no windows, and no floor excepting the native earth.
The household furniture consisted of two small benches of the most
primitive construction imaginable, and two bedsteads, each made by
driving four forked stakes into the ground, across which poles were
placed, and then covered transversely by flour-barrel staves, the whole
structure surmounted by a sack of prairie hay, upon which I observed
the remains of an antiquated coverlid that had evidently seen much
service. The table furniture consisted of one tin milk-pan, three tin
cups, two knives and three forks, two of the latter having but one prong
each. The *tout ensemble* gave every indication of the most abject desti-
tution and poverty; indeed, the hostess informed me that she had not,
previous to my arrival, tasted sugar, tea, or coffee for three months; yet,
as strange as it may appear, she seemed contented with her situation,
and considered herself about as well to do in the world as the most of
her neighbors. She had emigrated to this remote and solitary spot from
Mississippi about two years previously, and not the slightest trace of a
road or trail had since been made leading to the locality from any
direction, and she informed me that her nearest neighbor was some
fifteen miles distant.

Upon her remarking that her husband was occasionally absent for
several days at a time, I inquired if she was not afraid to stay alone in
this wild, out-of-the-way place. She said "No; that when Davy was
away the dogs kept the varmints off, and that mighty few humans ever
com'd that-a-way."

After finishing my pipe, and getting my clothes well dried, and
feeling quite fatigued and sleepy, I asked the woman where I should
sleep. She replied, "Stranger, you take that thar bed with the boys, and
I'll take this yere with the gals."

Now the width of the bed indicated for my use was measured with a flour-barrel stave, and was already occupied by three boys, two on the back side and one at the foot. It therefore became a question of some considerable interest to me as to how I should manage to stow myself away in such contracted quarters, especially in view of the fact that my longitudinal meridian was some twelve inches greater than the space allotted me. Nevertheless, as I was not very exclusive or particular in my notions, I turned in, and for some time tried to sleep, but my position between the three bedfellows was so much cramped and distorted that I found it impossible to get any repose. I did not, however, like the idea of disturbing the boys, but the case seemed to be a desperate one: I must have some sleep, and the only alternative, under the circumstances, was to make the effort to secure a greater area; I therefore very quietly administered a pinch upon my nearest juvenile neighbor, who was sound asleep, which caused him to scream most lustily. His mother, probably thinking that he was dreaming, or suddenly taken with the nightmare, called out from the other bed, "Now Dave, ef yer don't get shut o' that thar yellin, yer'l wake up the stranger." This admonition quieted him for a while, but as soon as he was asleep again I gave him another sharp pinch, which made him cry out more vociferously than before, while at the same time I was exerting my utmost efforts in giving a good imitation of the loftiest pitch of snoring. The mother then got up, came to our bed, and shaking the boy, told him "ef he didn't dry up that hollerin she woodn't 'low him to sleep 'long with the stranger no more, no how." Another well-timed and vigorous pinch, as soon as he had fallen asleep the third time, accomplished my object. He was taken up; but, as his mother was lifting the pugnacious young gentleman out of the bed, he had become so fully sensible of what was passing that he began to suspect I had something to do with his disturbance, and hit me quite a severe blow in the side with his hard little fist. I, however, after this episode slept soundly till morning.

Before I left the house my hostess inquired of me if I knew how to write; and, upon learning that my education had extended that far, she desired me to act as her amanuensis, while she dictated a letter to a friend "way down in ole Massasip." Having a pencil and some old letters in my pocket, I told her I would take down what she desired to communicate, copy it in ink on my return to the fort, and send it for her through the post, which seemed to give her great pleasure; whereupon I seated myself, and asked her what she wished me to write. She said:

"Tell um, stranger, thar's narry fever-n'agur down this-a-way."

"Very well," I said, "that is down; what shall I say next?"

"Tell um, stranger, Davy he raised a powerful heap o' corn and taters this year."

"Yes, I said; "what next?"

"Tell um, stranger, thar's a mighty smart chance o'varmints in these yere diggins."

And thus she went on throughout the entire letter, which she "'lowed was a peart hand write." I transcribed it literally in her own words on my return home, and forwarded it to its destination in Mississippi, and I sincerely hope the good woman has received an answer ere this.

John C. Duval

The Wild Texan Comes Home

WILLIAM (BIGFOOT) WALLACE left his native Virginia in 1837 and developed into Texas' most famous frontiersman. He made his reputation as a hunter, Indian fighter, rancher, Texas Ranger and skirmisher in the Mexican War. His first biographer, John C. (Texas John) Duval was an equally salty character who made his living as a surveyor out west of the settlements where manners were primitive. His lifestyle was sometimes an embarrassment to his genteel relatives in Austin. After frontier times were more or less over, he spent two weeks with Bigfoot on his little ranch south of San Antonio and got permission to publish the story of Wallace's adventures. His humorous portrait did not please the old frontiersman, who considered himself at least half civilized. He much preferred the more sedate portrait by A. H. Sowell (*The Life of Bigfoot Wallace,* 1899). Everybody else liked Duval's version better. Wallace's Virginia relatives welcomed him as the Wild Texan and he amused himself by living up their expectations.

From *The Adventures of Bigfoot Wallace.* Austin: The Steck Company, 1935, pp. 292–299 (copyright, 1870).

From Richmond I went on to Lexington, where my relatives lived. They were all glad to see me, and did all they could to make my time pass pleasantly while I was with them; though I could see very plainly that they all looked upon me as a sort of half-civilized savage that never could be entirely tamed; and perhaps they were right. I had lived too long the free and independent life of a ranger, to be contented a great while with the steady habits and humdrum existence of the people of the "Old States." I longed for the excitement of the chase, an Indian foray, a buffalo-hunt or a bear-fight. However, everything for a time was new and strange to me, and I enjoyed myself as much as I could have expected.

A few weeks after my arrival I went to a "fandango" that was given for my especial benefit. There was a great crowd there, and everybody was anxious to see the "Wild Texan," as they called me. I was the "lion" of the evening, particularly with the young ladies, who never tired of asking me questions about Mexico, Texas, the Indians, prairies, etc. I at first answered truly all the questions they asked me; but when I found they evidently doubted some of the stories I told them which were facts, I branched out and gave them some "whoppers," which they swallowed without "gagging." For instance, one young woman wanted to know how many wild horses I had ever seen in a drove. I told her perhaps thirty or forty thousand.

"Oh! now! Mr. Wallace," said she, "don't try to make game of me in that way. Forty thousand horses in one drove! well, I declare you are a second 'Munchusen'!"

"Well, then," said I, "maybe you won't believe me when I tell you there is a sort of spider in Texas as big as a peck measure, the bite of which can only be cured by music."

"Oh, yes," she answered, "I believe that's all so, for I have read about them in a book."

Among other "whoppers," I told her there was a "varmint" in Texas, called the "Santa Fe," that was still worse than the tarantula, for the best brass band in the country couldn't cure their sting; that the creature had a hundred legs and a sting on every one of them, besides two large stings in its forked tail, and fangs as big as a rattlesnake's. When they sting you with their legs alone, you might possibly live an hour; when with all their stings, perhaps fifteen or twenty minutes; but when they sting and bite you at the same time, you first turn blue, then yellow, and then a beautiful bottle-green, when your hair all fell out and your finger nails dropped off, and you were as dead as a door-nail in five minutes, in spite of all the doctors in America.

"Oh! my! Mr. Wallace," said she, "how have you managed to live so long in that horrible country?"

"Why, you see," said I, "with my tarantula boots made of alligator-skin, and my centipede hunting-shirt made of tanned rattlesnakes' hides, I have escaped pretty well; but these don't protect you against the stinging scorpions, 'cow-killers,' and scaly-back chinches, that crawl about at night when you are asleep! The only way to keep them at a distance is to "chaw' tobacco and drink whisky, and that is the reason the Temperance Society never flourished much in Texas."

"Oh!" said she, "what a horrible country that must be, where the people have to be stung to death, or 'chaw' tobacco and drink whisky! I don't know which is the worst."

"Well," said I, "the people out there don't seem to mind it much; they get used to it after a while; in fact, they seem rather to like it, for they chaw tobacco and drink whisky even in the winter-time, when the 'cow-killers' and stinging-lizards are all frozen up!"

I had been introduced to one young woman by the name of Matilda, who was as pretty as a pink! Her teeth were as white as an alligator's, her eyes were as bright as two mesquite coals, and her mouth looked like a little gash cut in a juicy peach. She was a "dead-ener," I tell you, and a regular "kneeweakener," in the bargain; and I wanted to have a little talk with her the worst in the world; but somehow I felt a little afraid to venture. After a little while, however, she came up to me of her own accord, and began to ask me a great many questions about Texas and the Indians, wild horses, and the prairies, etc. Among other things, she asked me if young women were in great demand in Texas.

"I should think they were," said I. "The day the first young woman came into our settlement there were fourteen Spanish horses badly foundered on sedgegrass, by the young men who flocked in to see her, from forty miles around; and the next morning she had seventeen offers of marriage before breakfast! The young woman was a little confused by so many applications at once, and before she could make up her mind which one to take, one of the 'rancheros' watched his chance, and the first time she walked out he caught her up behind him on his horse, rode off full speed to San Patrico, drew his six-shooter on the padre, and forced him to marry them on the spot. This saved the woman all further trouble on the subject, and they are now living happily together on one of the finest cattle ranches in the Country of Karnes."

"Oh! I declare," said Miss Matilda, "that is delightful! How romantic to be run off with in that way by a handsome young 'ranchero.' I think, Mr. Wallace, I shall have to go to Texas."

"You might do worse," said I; "and besides, you would stand a chance of being run away with by some great Comanche or Tonkawa chief, with a bow and quiver on his back and eagle's feathers on his head, and nothing else to speak of in the way of clothes."

Miss Matilda didn't seem to hear the last part of my speech, for she jumped up and clapped her little hands: "Oh," said she, "wouldn't that be fine? To gallop over the flowery prairies, free as the wind, from morning till night, and listen to the feathered songsters pouring forth their untaught melodies from every grove and shady dell! Oh, it would be splendid, Mr. Wallace!"

"Yes," said I, "it would. One of the handsomest young women in our settlement was carried off, three or four years ago, by 'He-che-puck-sa-sa,' the 'Bellowing Bull,' and when I went on a visit to his tribe, not long ago, she was the favorite wife and head squaw of the wigwam, and had brass rings enough on her arms and legs to have made a pair of 'dog irons,' if they had been melted up, besides one in her nose as big as the palm of my hand."

"Why! how many wives did the Mormon have?" asked Miss Matilda, looking a little down in the mouth.

"Oh! I can't say exactly," I answered; "I only saw six; but he had another wigwam at the village below. But," said I, "Miss Matilda, after riding over the flowery prairies all day, and listening to the coyotes howling in every grove and dell, where will you *put up* at night; and how will you manage to get along without hot rolls for breakfast, and baked custard for dinner?"

"Oh," said she, "I don't care for them; I can do very well without them; all I want is a nice cup of coffee in the morning, and a biscuit or a slice of toast, and a little fresh butter, or a few fresh-laid eggs; and for dinner a few vegetables and wild fruits, and now and then a nice beef-steak or a saddle of venison roasted before the fire!"

"Yes," says I, "that's all reasonable enough, and you could get them, I suppose, at any time; but you see, the Indians don't cook their meat."

"The cannibals!" exclaimed Miss Matilda; "they certainly don't eat it raw, do they?"

"Yes," said I, "as a general thing; only sometimes, when a fellow feels a little squeamish, he fastens a beef or mule steak under his saddle, and after riding and jolting on it all day, he finds it nicely 'done' when he stops at night; and it's a very convenient way of cooking, too, especially when a fellow is in a hurry (which the Indians always are, for they are always after somebody or else somebody is after them); and besides, they say it is the best thing in the world for a sore-back horse!"

"Oh! dear," said Miss Matilda, "I don't believe I'll go to Texas, after all; or if I do, I must put up with a 'ranchero'—they don't eat their meat raw, do they?"

"No," said I, "except when they are out on the plains, and can't find bufalo-chips enough to cook it with."

"Oh! tell me, Mr. Wallace," said she, "did you ever see a 'mirage' on the plains?"

"A mirage?" said I, rather taken aback, for I hadn't the least idea what she meant, unless it was a drove of mustangs or a herd of buffalo; "why, certainly, I have seen a thousand of 'em."

"I didn't think they were so common," said she.

"Oh, yes," I answered; "the last one I saw was just back of Santa Fe, and it stampeded when we got in about a quarter of a mile of it; and such a dust as was kicked up you never saw, for there hadn't been a drop of rain there in six months."

"Well, I declare!" said Miss Matilda; "I always heard that the mirage would disappear as you approached it, but I never heard of one kicking up a dust before."

"No," said I; "they don't in other countries, where the ground is kept wet by constant rain; but in Texas, you see, it is different."

Just then a dapper-looking young fellow came up and asked Miss Matilda if he might have the pleasure of dancing with her that set, and she walked off with him. I took a dislike to that young fellow at once, and felt for "Old Butch," without knowing what I was about! The fact is, I rather fancied this young woman, and I determined, the next time I met up with her, to give her a better account of Texas, and leave out all about the centipedes and "raw meat."

Well sir! I staid with my kinsfolk in Old Virginny till I began to pine for prairies and woods once more. They were as kind to me as they could be, but feather beds, tight rooms, and three meals a day were too much for me, and, like old General Taylor, when he was taken from "camps" to the "White House," I fell away daily, and "went off my feed" entirely; and, like him, I suppose I should have gone up the spout, if I had staid much longer. I helped matters a little by taking a camp-hunt of a couple of weeks in the Blue Ridge Mountains, where I killed the last bear, I suppose, that was ever seen in that part of Old Virginny, for when his carcass was hauled in, people came from twenty miles around to have a look at it. But I never got entirely to rights again till I returned to Texas and got into an Indian "scrimmage," and lifted the hair off of one or two of them with the aid of "Old Butch." That night, for the first time, my appetite came back to me, and I ate six pounds of buffalo-hump, a side of ribs, and a roasted marrow-gut and ever since I have been "as well as could be expected."

Embattled Texans

For Alex E. Sweet's "The Typical Texan"

The worst times Texans have ever known were the fifteen years following the Civil War. Indians raided the western settlements and organized gangs of desperadoes engaged in wholesale stealing and violence farther east, forcing the settlers to take matters into their own hands. Shadowy brotherhoods, known in central Texas as "mobs" traded work with mobs in other communities. In the almost total absence of law and order, "self redress" was the rule, and it was generally believed that a man who was a man should right his own wrongs. Everyone, including preachers and schoolboys, carried arms and did not hesitate to use them. The result was a spate of bloody feuds in the seventies and eighties, perhaps a hundred of them great and small. The area between San Antonio and Houston was known as "The Pure Feud Belt." By the early eighties the Texas Rangers had matters pretty well in hand, but there were small feuds and "difficulties" in the nineties and early 1900s. Bill Brett describes one of them in "The Way It Was— Southeast Texas, 1915."

Humorists could hardly be expected to flourish in such violent times, but Texans have always been able to laugh at themselves. Alex Sweet smiled at the generally accepted image of the Texan and made ironic fun of John Wesley Hardin's terrorizing of the village of Cuervo. A Texas Ranger who signed himself "Pidge" wrote in a similar vein for the *Austin Democratic Statesman,* extracting grim humor out of the Sutton-Taylor vendetta. They saw the ridiculous side of these lethal games and showed that sanity and common sense were still present.

Alex E. Sweet

The Typical Texan

ALEXANDER E. SWEET was Texas' most important early-day humorist. Canadian born, he came to San Antonio with his well-do-do parents in 1849, studied law, became a newsman, and hit his stride as a columnist for the *Galveston News*. His "Siftings" column was widely read and syndicated, indicating that everybody wanted to know about Texas. In 1881 Alex took on as partner an Irishman named J. Armoy Knox. The enterprise grew and they bought an Austin weekly which they renamed *Texas Siftings*. It soon attained a circulation of 50,000 and attracted so much attention in the East that they moved it to New York. For a time they even printed an English edition in London. Sweet came back to Texas in 1895 and died in 1901. He recognized and made fun of the old stereotype of the uncurried Texan but he also made Texas look like a wonderful place to live. Virginia Eisenhour, Sweet's latest editor, says that the "Siftings" may have done more to stimulate immigration "than all the fairy tales" put out by railroads and land developers.

From *Texas Siftings,* May 9, 1886, reproduced in *Alex Sweet's Texas,* edited by Virginia Eisenhour. Austin: University of Texas Press, 1986, pp. 95–97.

Some man whose head was flat—probably ourselves—has said that the North had been hating an ideal Southerner, who never existed; that the South had been hating an ideal Yankee, who never existed; and the Americans generally had been worshipping an ideal Indian, who never existed, except in [James] Fenimore Cooper's novels. We may add to the list of mythical personages an ideal Texan who figures so largely in the Northern mind and dime novels, but otherwise is as hard to find as Charlie Ross. The typical Texan is a large sized Jabberwock, a hairy kind of gorilla, who is supposed to reside on a horse. He is half alligator, half human, who eats raw buffalo, and sleeps out on a prairie. He is expected to carry four or five revolvers at his belt, as if he were a sort of perambulating gunrack. He also carries a large assortment of cutlery in his boot. It is believed that a failure to invite him to drink is more dangerous than to kick a can of dynamite. The only time the typical Texan is supposed to be peaceable is after he has killed all his friends, and can find no fresh materials to practice on. It is also the belief in the North that all the Texans are typical Texans, it being utterly impossible for a Texan to be anything except a desperado. Now, we propose to knock this typical Texan, who is accused of being particularly numerous in Western Texas, right off his pins. We are prepared to prove a complete *alibi* for him. We will show that the typical Texan is as mild as picnic lemonade. It will be remembered that stage robbing had been carried on for some time in Western Texas. There are only nine stage robbers in Jail in San Antonio now, and the Lord knows how many on the outside. Why, at one time, the traveling public became so accustomed to going through the usual ceremonies that they complained to the stage company if they came through unmolested. Being robbed came to be regarded as a vested right. On one occasion the stage driver happened to stop his horses right in front of the old Alamo, that sacred Thermopylae that is now being used to store cabbages and potatoes in, right in the heart of San Antonio, where most of the saloons are, in order to give a man on horseback a light for his pipe. As soon as the stage halted, the passengers tumbled out pell-mell, and falling into line, held up their hands, and called out: "Don't shoot!"

The point is this: Notwithstanding the stage was robbed so often when there were typical Texans in it, in no instance did any of them violate the law by discharging pistols, or even by using strong language. They never even said: "Why, damme, 'tis too bad!" until the robbers—probably missionaries from the North—had gone away. Does this look like rowdyism? The typical Texan acted more in accordance with the teachings of the New Testament, where it requires the plundered party, who has been robbed of his coat, to pull off his pants, and tender them also to the needy highwayman. It will be seen at once that great injustice has been done our people. There is, however, a world of consolation in the fact that in Missouri, where three crops of guerillas and bushwackers are raised every year, a bogus Jesse James and a few assistants rob a whole train. There is also much solid comfort to Texans in the fact that in Arkansaw, where the Arkansaw toothpick grows to be as big as a scythe, that lately four beardless boys collected four thousand dollars' worth of money, jewelry and pistols from a train full of passengers. But what has become of the typical Texan? Governor Roberts should offer a reward for a live specimen. Even the stage robbers are not as dangerous as a kerosene lamp to handle. When an officer of the law comes across a Texas stage robber, and says: "Oh, wake up, William Riley, and come along with me!" William invariably drops his little pop-gun and other playthings, and goes along with him.

Alexander Sweet and J. Armoy Knox

John Wesley Hardin at Cuero

ALEXANDER SWEET AND J. ARMOY KNOX traveled westward from Houston along the route of a proposed railroad as part of a promotional scheme. They stopped at towns along the way and established friendly relations with the local citizens. At Cuero in DeWitt County southeast of San Antonio they encountered the percussions and repercussions of the Sutton-Taylor feud, then in full swing. Characteristically, Sweet saw it from a humorous point of view.

From *On a Mexican Mustang through Texas*. Chicago: Rand, McNally, 1891, pp. 230–245.

We staid with Capt. Delane two days; and although we did not see as many rabbits caught as we expected, yet our visit was a very pleasant one.

Our conversation after supper gradually drifted into the subject of lawlessness in Texas.

"Yes," said the captain in a meditative tone, "things were rough around here once, and scenes were enacted within sight of where we sit that did more to give Texas a reputation for lawlessness than any thing else. At present DeWitt County is as orderly as any county in Texas, but only a few years ago almost the entire population was more or less involved in a *vendetta* that cost scores of men their lives. In fact, a regular *guerilla* warfare was carried on between the Taylors and the Suttons, in which most of the adult male population took sides. It reminded one of the way the rival Scotch clans used to engage in joint discussions. The son regarded it as his sacred duty to kill one or two of his neighbors, whose fathers had years before made him an orphan.

From their earliest age the boys devoted themselves to practicing with pistols, and nursing schemes of vengeance, in which latter occupation they were assisted by the relatives of the men against whom they entertained unfriendly feelings. In time some of the men, who at first were merely thirsting for vengeance, degenerated into ordinary cut-throats and highway robbers. Dominant among the DeWitt-county braves was John Wesley Hardin, who is now in the Texas penitentiary. It is believed that he has killed about twenty-one men. He inspired the whole community with dread. Nobody pretended to interfere with him. The officers of the law looked the other way when he passed. Unless a person had visited DeWitt County during the prevalence of that epidemic of lawlessness, he could not form the slightest idea of the homage that was paid to this outlaw. Not that the people liked him, but they were afraid to say or do any thing that might be construed into disapprobation of his course. I happened to be in the town of Cuero once during the 'reign of terror'; and, although the town was quiet, I was remarkably impressed with the scared looks of the respectable citizens when any reference was made to Hardin.

"In October, 1874, I first visited Cuero. I found the town comparatively quiet. Nearly a week had passed over without anybody having been murdered, and it was inevitable that the calm could not last much longer. There were a good many people in town, some local election being in progress. The first thing that I remarked, was the large number of armed men who patrolled the streets. I also found that there was an enthusiastic unwillingness, on the part of the natives, to be communicative on the subject of lawlessness; and as for 'Wes' Hardin,' as he was familiarly and even tenderly called, few would acknowledge being aware of the existence of such a person."

"Were they all so much afraid of him? and had he no friends?"

"Well, not many friends. He had some admirers; but they did not care to say any thing, even in his favor, because Wes' was too careless. He would hear that a man had been talking about him; and then, without inquiring what the man had said, he would fill him full of lead, and afterwards ask what lies the scoundrel had been telling about him. Then, when it was too late, he would find out that the deceased was really a friend of his, and had spoken kindly of him. Hardin would then apologize to the widow and orphans for his thoughtlessness, and make a solemn vow never again to shoot a man until satisfied that he really needed shooting. This course, however, made even his warmest friends appear cold and reticent."

"How did you manage to find out any thing about this bandit?" inquired the doctor.

"I met a man in the hotel who was very intimate with Hardin. He said that he and Wes' had been schoolmates, and that he was not afraid to talk about him. He volunteered to take a walk with me, and show me the principal points of interest in the town. As we strolled down the street, he said, pointing to a small store, 'Do you see that shanty that has "Oysters" painted on the gable? Well, sir, that's an historic spot. Right in that saloon is where Wes' Hardin shot an entire stranger—a man from Missouri—twenty minutes after the man had stepped off the stage that brought him to town. Wes' is the durndest fellow you ever set eyes on. Some people call him a murderer, when he ain't about to explain things to 'em. You see, the fellow came into the oyster-saloon, and began talking to a man who was with him about being on the ragged edge of civilization, and said as how he believed there was neither law nor justice in judge or jury; and he said he wouldn't be afraid to kill a man for he knew he could bribe the whole jury for two hundred dollars, bulldoze the judge for nothing, and fix the sheriff with a drink. Hardin, who was eating a dozen raw, back of the counter, asked the stranger if he was coming to stay in Texas. The stranger said he was. Then Wes' told him that he was the sort of immigrant that wasn't wanted in Texas. He told him that he lied when he said that a Texas judge or jury could be corrupted, and then (that temptation might be kept out of the jury-box, I suppose) he shot the stranger dead where he stood. Now, the idea of calling that a murder! He didn't even know the stranger's name; had never seen or heard of him before, and consequently couldn't have no malice. 'Tain't no murder unless there is malice, is it? Wes' was drunk, you see; and, when he's drunk, he's the durndest fellow you ever saw for law and order, and backing up the judiciary. When Wes' is sober, he wouldn't hurt a fly; but, just as soon as he gets whiskey, he's death on upholding the officers of the law, and he generally keeps at it till somebody gets hurt.'

"When I inquired why Hardin was not arrested, the friend of the outlaw was carried away by an uncontrollable fit of laughter at the idea of Wes' Hardin being arrested. He explained to me, that, when Hardin got into a difficulty, no one ever thought of arresting him. 'Getting into a difficulty' in Texas means killing a man. Out in some of the western counties the sheriffs had to reside in the brush for weeks, to keep from being themselves arrested. Let me tell you what I saw myself:—

"The Taylor crowd had about a dozen of the Suttons corralled in a house. The Suttons could not get out without being killed, and the Taylors dare not come within range of the house. After a siege of thirty-six hours, the hostile parties made a compromise, according to the terms of which they were to quit shooting each other, and to turn their attention to agricultural matters until after the cotton-picking season. This happened near Clinton, the county seat of DeWitt County. They all rode into town together. Court was in session, and the judge was very much surprised to see Wes' Hardin stalk into court with his gun on his shoulder. He showed a law-abiding disposition. If he had been a lawless character, he would have just cleaned up the docket of that court, and burnt the county records; but he wasn't that kind of reformer. He just said to the judge in his off-hand way, 'Old pard, me and my crowd have made up with the Suttons; and I called to inform you that, if you find any more indictments agin us, thar will be a vacancy in this judicial district.' Then, turning to the sheriff, he said, 'Me and the Suttons wants to draw up a sort of a treaty like, and I want you to sign it as a witness. I never want to do nothin' without the sanction of the law.' The sheriff was a little confused; because his breast-pocket was bulging out with some fifteen or twenty *capiases* from other counties, commanding him to arrest John Wesley Hardin, and to make due diligence in doing so. But he, and other prominent officials, willingly signed the document. After these formalities, Wes' gave the judge permission to go on with the circus, as he called it; and he and his crowd retired to a saloon to celebrate the armistice. Now, I saw all that myself."

"Did your friend show you any other historic points in Cuero?" said the doctor.

"Yes, replied the captain, "he did. We strolled out in the suburbs,—about a hundred yards from the business center of the town, where the saloons were,—and he pointed out an old live-oak covered with moss. I was anxious that he should talk about something else beside gory murders; so I took a lively interest in the old oak, and suggested that probably under its branches the pioneer fathers of Cuero formerly celebrated the anniversary of their arrival. He said that on that tree three of the Taylor crowd were hung last month. They were taken out of their beds and strung up in the night."

"Any more sacred spots?" asked the doctor.

"Oh, yes! plenty of them scattered about everywhere. He took me into a saloon; and pointing to a hole as big as a saucer, in the wall, as the next object of interest around which clustered tender and historic memories, he explained how it was caused by eighteen buckshot that Bowlegged Simpson desired to plant in the head of Mexican Mike, and how, by a providential interposition, Simpson's elbow was joggled as he pulled the trigger, and the buckshot missed Mike, and went through the wooden wall. Then my guide went on to give a long and mixed account of a battle between men with all sorts of barbarous nicknames, where all the participants were either killed, or perforated and carved beyond recognition, and where five or six spectators got severely winged. Finally, after inspecting a few more bullet-holes, and listening to some more history that sounded like a chapter from the life of the warrior saints of the Bible, we got back to the hotel, and I parted with my guide.

"While I was sitting in the hotel, musing about what an unhealthy place Cuero was, a man came in carrying two shotguns, a box of cartridges, and a rifle. He distributed the firearms around the room in convenient places. Presently another ammunition-wagon stepped in. He was loaded with six-shooters and metallic cartridges, which he deposited on a desk in the corner. Several other prominent citizens arrived, every one of them loaded to the muzzle, and ready to go off at a moment's notice, so to speak. Every once in a while a little fat man, who seemed to be chief of artillery, would pick up a shotgun, and, holding it in a line with my person, would lift the hammer of the weapon to see if the cap was all right. He did it in a careless way, that deprived me of any sense of enjoyment. I sought the landlord, and inquired the meaning of all this war-like preparation. He took me into a closet under the stairs, and, after swearing me to secrecy, informed me, with the aid of pantomime and whispers, that a crowd of the Taylors were in town; that the Suttons had threatened to come in, and clean the Taylors out;

and that the men now in the hotel were friends of the Taylors, preparing to hold the fort, should any attack be made that night."

"You didn't make Cuero your permanent residence?" queried the doctor.

"I reckon I would have, if I had staid there that night; but I started on the stage for San Antonio late in the evening. I had business there anyhow. I heard afterwards that there was a big fight in Cuero the night I left, and that the landlord of the hotel got killed by accident, besides having the whole gable end of his house shot full of holes. I did not come back to Cuero for two years afterwards. During these two years most of the murderers and robbers got killed off, and Hardin went to Florida, where he was caught about a year ago, brought back to Texas, tried, and sentenced to the penitentiary for twenty-one years."

"Captain, were you in Cuero when old Feehan was running the 'Weekly Clarion'?" said the red-haired man at the end of the table.

"I met him once," said the captain, "during my brief sojourn at Cuero. On the occasion I have just referred to, I found time to call on the editor of the 'Clarion.' I was once a newspaper man myself; and I always make it convenient, when I pass through such a town as Cuero, to call and pay my respects to the great man who wields the Archimedean lever that moves the world. During my visit to the 'Clarion' editor, I saw and heard what surprised me more than any thing I have ever seen or heard in the whole course of my life. You know how it is in the office of a little country paper. It consists of a suite of one room, which is composing-room, press-room, editorial sanctum, dining-room, and sleeping-apartment. The editorial tripod consists usually of an old candle-box or an empty nail-keg, in front of which is a decrepit old table upon which the thunderbolts are forged. The editor is a lank, hollow-eyed man, who looks as if he had been blighted by an unreasonable frost early in life. His clothes have the same blighted look, and his editorials show traces of dyspepsia and disappointment. Irregularity in taking his meals, and the mental wear and tear incident to his getting out a weekly paper, give him a pinched and careworn look. If he is particularly energetic, he can usually manage to raise enough money semi-occasionally to calm down the boy who sets up the paper and engineers the old Franklin press, and prevent him from going on a general strike."

"But the editor of the 'Clarion' was no such a slouch as that," said the red-haired man.

"No, he was not; and that is what surprised me. He must have weighed two hundred pounds, and he did not look as if he had missed a meal since he was born. Instead of wearing old clothes, he was dressed in a suit that a nabob or a drummer might have worn. Instead of an old cot to sleep on, he had a room all to himself, fixed up with an elegant set of furniture, 'Chimney-Corner' chromos on the wall, and other indications of extreme wealth on every side. I could hardly believe my senses, and even now the whole affair seems to be a kind of a vision. He asked me to step up to the sideboard, and setting out a whole box of cigars, desired information as to my preference in the way of tonics. He had bourbon and rye, dry sherry, burgundy, and port. He apologized for the absence of champagne, stating that his last shipment from his San Antonio wine-merchant had been unaccountably delayed on the way. I was acquainted with the circumstances of Texas editors in the large towns, but never had I witnessed such gorgeousness; and I wondered how that little country paper could support such a John Jacob Astor of an editor. Taking all the material that went to make up the 'Clarion,'—the type, presses, paper, and total outfit, including an average set of editorial brains,—the whole thing would have been extravagantly dear at two hundred dollars, on six month's time. Here was a mystery I determined to unravel if it took a week to do so.

"After we had discussed several kinds of beverages, and were in a somewhat advanced condition of mellowness, I brought the conversation around to the influences of the press, and expressed some surprise at the wonderful prosperity of the 'Clarion.' The editor and proprietor of the 'Clarion' opened a fresh bottle, and smiled a most significant smile. Said he, 'I owe all this fatness to Wes' Hardin.'

"'Do you mean to say that you give the moral support of your paper to lawlessness?'

"'Not a bit of it,' he responded. 'You know, Wes' and the boys are in the habit of coming to town and scaring the merchants out of their senses. There is no telling what Hardin and his crowd might do; and, when they hear of a man slandering them by intimating that they are not law-abiding citizens, just as likely as not they appoint a committee to forward the man to that bourn from which, etc. Now while the

"Clarion" is not a lawless organ, I did not purpose, for the sake of the miserable patronage it received from merchants, to pitch into the boys. Half of the merchants didn't advertise, and some did not even take the weekly at two dollars a year. They grumbled because I did not give them enough reading-matter, and because the editorials were not scholarly enough to suit them. If it had not been for Bill Jenkins, who keeps the Gently-Dreaming Saloon, I would have starved to death. My clothes needed repairs before they could have been fit to put on a scarecrow. The merchants treated me with contempt; and when I wanted to get a pair of trousers, or a few pounds of crackers, I had to come out and puff them, and call them merchant-princes. And now—well,' continued the editor of the 'Clarion,' as he passed the cigars and threw himself back in his armchair with the air of a man owning a silver-mine and a trotting-horse, 'you see yourself how I'm fixed.'

"'How in the name of all that is magnetic did you manage it?' said I.

"'Well, I'll tell you. These merchants here got into the habit of bullyragging me for not denouncing Wes' Hardin. They alleged, very truthfully too, that the town had a bad name; country customers were afraid to come here to trade: and they said that the "Clarion" ought to take a bold stand. I knew what the result would be if the "Clarion" were to hint that Col. J. Wesley Hardin was not one of the most respected citizens in DeWitt County. I would be—in short, shot; and I did not think the patronage the "Clarion" was getting justified any such sacrifice on my part. Now, sir, will you believe it? One morning about all the merchants in the town, including those who didn't subscribe, waited on me in a body. Said one, who was owing a year's subscription, "Vy ton't you shust dake a pold shtand, and give dem routies fits? So helb me grashers! I shtobs mine babers." He was one who used to take a bold stand by crawling under the store when Wes' Hardin came to town.

"'The drift of the matter was, that they had no use for a paper that did not sustain the good citizens by denouncing rowdyism; and they threatened to withdraw their support if I did not come out in the next issue, and denounce Hardin and his crowd. In their excitement, they called Col. Hardin every bad name they could think of. I offered them the use of columns of my paper. I agreed, that, if they would all sign a card denouncing the banditti, I would publish it free of charge. This threw a coldness over the delegation: the very idea scared them; for they knew, if they did such a thing they would be called to an unpleasant accountability as soon as Wes' would read the paper. A happy thought occurred to me. I would turn the tables on my unappreciative patrons. I asked them to wait, and I would write an editorial on the matter under discussion, and submit it to them. They smiled significantly at each other, as much as to say, "We knew we would bring him to terms." When I had finished writing my article, I read it to them. It was a simple statement of facts: it gave the name of each member of the delegation, the object of the visit, and the opprobrious terms each had used in speaking of Col. Hardin and his friends. It told how they sought to intimidate and coerce the "Clarion" into denouncing a man who had never yet been convicted of any crime. When I finished reading, that delegation was the sickest-looking set of mortals I ever set eyes on. At first they said they would withdraw their patronage if I published it. I told them I could better afford to lose such patronage as theirs than to suppress an article like this, that was bound to make a sensation, and run the "Clarion's" circulation up into the thousands. I asked their advice as to issuing it in the shape of an extra, and sending a marked copy to Wes' Hardin. I assured them that I would do justice to their memories when they were gone. I would be in attendance at their funerals, and publish a description of the obsequies in the columns of the "Clarion." But, to shorten my story, I collected two hundred and fifty dollars in cash on the spot for subscriptions and advertisements, having promised, at the earnest solicitation of the delegates, to say nothing of their visit. Since then I have had no trouble to get along. I am the only really prosperous editor in Texas. My credit is unlimited, and the "Clarion" is read with absorbing interest by our business men. They are all ready to endorse any thing I say. Here's to Col. Wes' Hardin, the friend of the press! God bless him!'

"Just as the editor was draining his goblet, we were interrupted by a prominent merchant sticking his head in at the door, and saying, 'Eggscuse me, mein frient, I chust stepped over to let you know dot my fall gootsh ash arrived. I hopes you comes over and picks yourself oud a new goat and bants for my birthday breshend.'

"I parted with the affluent editor, as he went off with the merchant to get the 'new goat and bants,' and for the first time I realized how completely we are all in the hands of the Archimedean lever."

T. T. Robinson

Pidge the Humorous Ranger

"PIDGE" was the pen name of T. T. Robinson, a young Virginian who came to Texas in 1870, probably because of a failed love affair with seventeen-year-old Page Mitchell, nicknamed "Pidgie," who lived on a neighboring farm. Her older brother Jesse violently opposed the match and somehow forced Robinson to leave the country. In Texas he found a place on the staff of the Austin *Democratic Statesman* to which he contributed prose and poetry.

When the Texas Rangers were reorganized, he joined L. H. Mc-Nelly's unit and became its first lieutenant. In 1874 McNelly and his men were stationed at Clinton in DeWitt County to break up the Sutton-Taylor trouble and Robinson described the action in letters to the *Democratic Statesman* using the "Pidge" pseudonym. Like Alex Sweet he viewed the tragic events in DeWitt County as high comedy, probably the only sensible way to approach anything so lacking in humanity and reason. According to Chuck Parsons, Robinson's biographer and editor, "Pidge" resigned his commission in 1876 and went back to Virginia "to fight a duel." The report came back that both he and his opponent were killed in the encounter.

From the Austin *Daily Democratic Statesman*, September 24, 1874. Quoted by Chuck Parsons in *"Pidge": A Texas Ranger from Virginia.* Wolfe City, Texas: Harrington Publishing Co., 1985, pp. 42–44.

Daily Democratic Statesman, September 24, 1874

Letter from "Pidge"
Clinton, DeWitt County,
Sept. 18, 1874.
Editors Democratic Statesman:

> "It was an ancient farmer man,
>   And he stoppeth one of three:
> 'By thy Colt's improved and Henry gun
>   I pray thee tell to me
> If you belong to the Sutton gang
>   or the Taylor companie?'"

Such is the momentous question asked of every resident in, or traveler through DeWitt. All things hinge on this, and the end, from appearances, will necessarily be a war of extermination. The people of both factions are men accustomed to righting their own wrongs, and they object decidedly to any interference, even should that interference be lawful. In any new difference which may arise between two men not previously connected with the *vendetta,* each takes his place with one or the other party, and in this manner recruits are gathered in the protecting *aegis* of a band which will defend them to death, if need be. The leaders of each party make large calculations on the rising generation; they turn the cylinder of a revolver as a rattle for the infants of this country, and give them empty cartridge cases for teething rings; they are weaned on gunpowder and brandy, and learn to shoot before they can talk. A few days ago two men belonging to the opposing factions had some words in Cuero, and appointed the bridge over the river three miles distant, as the place to argue the question, each member of the debating society to occupy the floor as long as he could pump fire from a repeating gun, and the decision to be left to the god of war; Capt. McNelly got wind of the affair and sent me a courier to have a dozen men mounted and in readiness by the time he got to camp; with some difficulty I mounted them, for every one wished to know where they were going, and for what purpose; I told them the time had come at last for them to strike for their *halters* and their fires and that, to use the words of the Father of his Country, I wanted them to remember for what they were about to fight for; an answering shout of "scrip and glory, and more glory than scrip," greeted me and it was with great difficulty that I restrained them [from] going alone. "We'll follow you; we will not wait for the Captain; a dollar a day in scrip nerves our spirits to deeds of daring, and a thirst for blood permeates our gizzards, which a holocaust of Taylors and Suttons will scarcely allay." I prevailed on them to hold in for a slight while, and when the Captain arrived, we started in a full gallop. That race I will ever remember, for it was far more exciting than any fox chase in which I had ever participated; a sensation of rapture, which is indescribable, came over me during that wild ride across the prairie, soon to be changed for one not quite so "rapturous." On a parallel line, and nearer the river, I could see a small body of men in single file, making desperate strides towards the bridges; and they had the advantage of us, for they were on a nearer road; but we beat them—as we swept past the point at which they would *debouche* into the main road, they were about a hundred yards distant. Although personally acquainted with most of them, I did not recognize any of the party, and supposed that the Captain wished to prevent them from effecting a junction with a larger force on the other side of the river. When near the bridge he ordered me to halt and keep these men from crossing; I waited with an anxious heart to hear him tell some of the men to assist me in this labor of love, but I waited in vain. "Well," thought I, "he is compelled to sacrifice some one, and he has resolved it shall be the sleeping partner of this concern, and I will take my last *siesta* this afternoon. Here is an end to my rations and aspirations also; at the entrance of this bridge I make my exit and leave DeWitt, I hope for a more peaceful state of existence. "I dismounted from my horse; he reeled as he walked; "Good-bye, Bucky!" said I, "I have the con-solation of knowing that if you are a source of as much trouble and annoyance to your capturer as you have been to me, he will shortly follow me for you will very soon aggravate the life out of him." I shoved a cartridge in my gun—it carries one about the size and length of a rolling pin and outkicks a Spanish mule. I never fired it but once, and then I carried my arm in a sling for three weeks. I brought it to bear on the foremost horseman. I knew I was good for him—at least I had a lingering ray of hope that it might kick me to the other side of the river. Splashed from head to heel with mud he rode rapidly toward me, and I discovered him to be a resident of Clinton, with whom I was well acquainted—felt as happy as when I left my creditors in Virginia. Napoleon, on the bridge of Lodi, never felt better or braver than I did then, and I trod the floor like it was the quarter deck of a line-of-battle ship, and I was the skipper.

By the time we got to camp I was perfectly reckless, and remained so for four days; and during this time we received advices as to where we could find Wes. Hardin. This has cooled me down considerably, for I had heard of him before I ever came to Texas. He kills men just to see them kick, and on one occasion charged Cuero alone with a yell of "rats to your holes!" and such a shutting up of shops has not been seen since the panic! He can take two six shooters and turn them like wheels in his hands and fire a shot from each at every revolution. There is a reward of eighteen hundred dollars for him, and it will be well earned when he is captured. He is said to have killed thirty men and is a dead shot. We started with twelve men for the settlement in which he was reported to be, with two guides who knew the country; they *did* know it too. They took a bee line, and we floundered through the bogs during that miserable night, which I will never forget as long as I live; bog, bog, at every step, until I thought that perhaps Hardin was in Asia, and the guides were looking for a short cut through. About daybreak we arrived at our destination, where Capt. McNelly divided the party, giving your correspondent one half, with orders to surround a certain house, while he, with the other half, surrounded another. The two were situated about the distance of a mile from each other, and Wes. Hardin was said to be in one or the other certain. It was the first time I ever made a call so early in the morning, and a long ride to pay a visit; but I would not have been at home—in fact, I believe I would have preferred his absence, for I did not wish to see him particularly. I thought of sending in to him my card, marked "P. P. C.—Mr. Hardin, if you will give me a half minute to do it in." We drew near the silent house; the ghostly looking moss, trailing from the trees, swept across my head, making me think of Wes. reaching for my scalp. We dismounted and cautiously approached the building, which was as silent as an Austin hotel in August. Sending part of the men to the rear of the house, I advanced in front. I had orders to wait until nearly sunrise before making myself known, and to fire a gun if I saw Mr. Hardin, in which case the Captain would come down from the other station. I did not have to wait five minutes, for I had my usual luck, and was discovered by the time I had reached the fence. Forty-nine dogs—from poodles to Spanish blood hounds, from rat terriers to British bull-dogs—charged me as I crouched behind some old lumber, and it was as much as I could do to prevent them from tearing me into strings like jerked beef. The next thing I saw was a faint light, and the next was a bearded Texan, shading his eyes with his hand, and gazing very earnestly on the lumber pile. Then I heard him speak: "Bill" said he, "I think I see his bulk; look behind the door and bring out the patent DeWitt protector"; this was a murderous looking gun, the barrel of which would almost reach to where I lay. Then he encouraged his canine brigade to find out my exact position, called them off again out of range, and prepared for business. "Is she well loaded, sonny?" "Sartin, dad; a heaping pint cup full in each barrel, not counting the slugs." Slowly he brought her to bear upon me, and the barrels yawned like two Hoosac tunnels; "Hold on mister," I shouted "don't shoot; you might bring the Captain down here on a false alarm and then—you might hit *me;* besides I think I see Mr. Hardin asleep in the left hand barrel of that fowling piece, and I do not wish him waked up." "What do you all want around my house this time of day?" "We are looking for a situation for a grocery, school house, cotton-gin, tan-yard, or any great industry calculated to develope the resources of a live State like Texas; we would like to discover a good mill site, or dam site" (of foolishness ever to go into this business) I added mentally. By this time the men had gathered around and I was as bold as brass again. The female population of the ranche were almost in hysterics, but I quieted their fears by assuring them that John Wesley was the divine we were following on this occasion. But oh! how touching was the meeting between the guide, a Sutton man, and the owner of the doubled barreled Columbiad, who belonged to the Taylor party. David and Jonathan could not have loved each other more; Damon and Pythias, after having been parted for a thousand years, would not have been half as glad to see each other; we could only stand and gaze upon this ebullition of affection. We were all deeply moved, but the time for marching had arrived and we must tear them from each other although we were fearful that it would break their hearts. Oh! it was a scene calculated to move the heart of a Stone or any other man; silently we parted them "from each other and their hearts are lonely now." One of the strangest things about these two parties is the good will exhibited when they meet where there is no chance for a fight; they have nothing against each other; oh no, "go home *mon ami,* and you shall not be disturbed," the individual who listens to these cheering and peaceful words, rates them at exactly what they are worth and remains in the brush. He lacks faith in these assertions, but he does not lack ammunition; he has no confidence in these premises, but he has in his Henry rifle, and he is right, for the lessons of experience are never forgotten. The trial of William Taylor commences Monday, and the Houston *Telegraph* of a late date has an account of rescuing a party of Taylor men on the way armed with "large sized, ivory-handled, silver plated, breech-loading, cartridge-shooting, double-sighted, central-fire, Colt's improved and still improving revolvers; "Sweet spirit! hear my prayer."

The folks of Indianola are grown up if they can get pistols like these over the bar. However the Houston people discovered this well-armed party of Taylors to be a few cowboys returning from Kansas, and all is serene again. John Taylor, who has just reached camp from Indianola, having gone down to the trial of his nephew, tells me that he wishes they *were* his men for with such pistols they ought to be able to kill men clear out of sight. He returns to court Monday and we will then hear the result of the trial.

Buenos noches,
"Pidge."

P.S. When I first wrote to you from here, I was not acquainted with the geography of the country; I have since been told by an old citizen of Clinton that it takes five large counties to bound DeWitt, and it is an awful strain on them to hold it all.

P.

Bill Brett

The Way It Was: Southeast Texas, 1915

BILL BRETT, postmaster at Hull, Texas, is an authentic country Texan who writes about the people he has known—dirt farmers, ranchmen, hunters, loggers, cowboys and kids. Author of two previous volumes of reminiscent stories, he devotes *This Here's a Good'un* to his growing-up time and the characters he remembers. They are mostly good people, but they live by the codes and customs of the country, and sometimes they shoot people, just as their grandfathers did. The victims, of course, need shooting.

From *This Here's a Good'un*. College Station: Texas A&M University Press, 1983, pp. 67–69.

Oh hell, yes, there used to be some bad men in this country. Some of 'em meaner than ten miles of blackland road after a three-day rain. But there wasn't many killers here, 'cept some of the law officers. Imagine them old sheriffs and their deputies was one reason there wasn't no more killings than there was. I've seen in the moving pictures law officers go up against some bad man and draw against him out in the street, but them shootouts didn't happen around here. Generally if the sheriff wanted to see a man, he'd just send him word and that man'd have sense enough to come in. If the man didn't, and the sheriff went after him, he'd take a deputy or several to back him up and they'd go with their wherewithal in their hands and get him. Easy or hard, whichever way he wanted.

The way lots of killings happened was accidental during a fight, or two men would have a falling out and start toting guns for each other and when they'd meet one'd kill the other'n. If all things was pretty equal in them cases, they was generally turned loose on a self-defense plea.

I guess, though, the most common killings was just cold-blooded. A feller would decide another'n had done something he couldn't live with, and he'd just go kill him. I've known several men go to the penitentiary for that, but I never knowed one to get the death penalty.

There was a few bad men passed through this country years ago before my time, but I never heard of any that was raised here. My grandmother said one time when she was a small girl she was walking to the store with my Great-aunt Ellen and their mother (they lived just west of Walter—that's part of Hardin now), and they met a man on horseback, and their mother seemed to know him and they talked a few minutes. He gave each of the girls a half-dime before he rode off, and later my great-grandmother told them he was John Wesley Hardin. They both kept the coins long as they lived. But John Wesley didn't live here; he just had lots of kinfolk here and was hiding out amongst them for something he'd done elsewhere.

I did know one feller that had killed three men, though, but he was an exception. Bud Knolles, it was. He killed his first one up at Batson during the oil boom, but there was so many killed up there that if it wasn't a plain case of murder, the authorities didn't even arrest them for it. That's what happened to Bud.

The next one he killed was when they was building the Missouri Pacific railroad from Beaumont to Houston. Him and another mule-skinner got in a argument, and that evening after they come in and tended to their teams, they each got a singletree and got after each other. Bud got beat up some but finally split the feller's head open and then finished him off on the ground. They took that one to the grand jury, but they no-billed him on self-defense.

The third one was at Liberty. Him and somebody—I can't remember his name right off—had a falling out at a saloon and just fell out in the street with their pocket knives and cut each other down and then laid side by side and kept cutting til they was drug apart. Bud finally got over it, but the other feller died. They no-billed him on that'un, too.

Well, after that lots of folks was skeered of Bud, and he knowed it and got pretty overbearing, 'specially when he'd had a few drinks. People would get out of his way and leave him alone all they could and try to get along any way they could, and he just got worse and worse.

Well, he come to town one day and hit several saloons and was coming out of one just as old Cap'n Nance was going in, and Bud just pushed the old man down on the porch and told him to get the hell out of the way and went on.

Now, if there ever was a mild man, it was the old captain. He'd fought from start to finish in the Civil War, and when he came back, he bought a place a mile or two out of town and settled down to minding his own business and leaving other folks alone, unless he was needed. He'd got too old to farm—he was ever' bit of eighty—but he'd walk into town ever' day, get the mail and one drink, and go back home. That's what he done after Bud pushed him down. Got his drink and went home.

Well, sir, I heard he got some water and cooled awhile and then took a bucket and some other things and went out next to the road and set down on the bucket in a little patch of brush under a big tree. Directly he got up and cut a sprout and set back down and whittled on it while he was waiting.

Just before sundown he heard a horse coming and leaned forward and jabbed the stick in the ground. It was forked, and he laid his old double-barrel on it, and when Bud Knolles got close on the road as he was coming, the captain cut him half in two with one barrel, and when Bud's horse run off and the dust settled, he took his time and walked over and give him the other barrel.

I learnt two things out of that. One is that when they said Colonel Colt made all men equal, they didn't give near enough credit to Mr. Remington's ole double-barrels, and the other'n was that old folks don't like to be pushed around any more than young ones do.

Early Times

For Shine Philips' "Put Your Little Foot"

Culture and the amenities came slowly to the Lone Star State, but
even in the worst of times Texans were not totally benighted. Immi-
grants from Europe, like Ellen Bowie Holland's Scottish father (who
fell in love and married a local girl) and German settlers at Fredericks-
burg, brought their cultures with them. Families with genteel southern
backgrounds who migrated to Texas cherished the manners and mores
of an orderly society. In the cities there was music, and the railroad
brought theatrical companies to the delight of citizens. Even in com-

munities as remote as El Paso, ladies and gentlemen dressed formally for parties. In country towns like Shine Philip's Big Spring an audience of puzzled cowboys was exposed to Shakespeare, and Ed Bateman tells of a group of roughnecks who couldn't get whiskey after Prohibition and settled for ice cream. Culture came a little faster to Texas with the advent of the Model T, and families like A. C. Greene's could taste the joys of travel and adventure.

The survivors of those uncurried early days liked to look back with humorous nostalgia on a time when things were, or seemed to be, simpler, happier and funnier than they are today.

Ed Bateman

The Old West Bows Out

THE PUBLISHER OF *Western Horseman* writes about this "Digression"
as follows:

This is taken from a rare old book, leather bound and printed on
handmade paper. Ed Bateman and my father were newspapermen together on the old *Houston Post Dispatch* in Texas, and Ed Bateman
wildcatted in oil. He hit it big when the Kilgore field opened up. The
book is called *The Instinct Never Dies*. Ed no longer had to write for a
living, but he had to write; and he was a powerful writer.

His instincts were still honed sharp, and his reflections of past
stories were as keen as ever. To quote from the opening of this book,
in part, he wrote: "Through great good fortune I can now sit down and
write all I please. More extraordinary, I can pay for printing it, as simply
or ornately as I like.

"This book is a first result. There is no necessity of selling a single
copy and any newpaper man can tell you that I do not require a reading
audience. I simply must write, and having written, put it to press.
Therefore those of you who now hold the volume in your hands have
two consoling thoughts for the boredom you may suffer; first, that it
cost you nothing, and second, that it is the concrete results of an old
newshound having a hell of a good time . . . ."

—Dick Spencer

From *Western Horseman*, May 1989, pp. 88–89.

This is not a story; just a word picture of one who belongs to a
vanished race. Thunder Mountain Bill is as truly anachronistic in
present-day society as a dinosaur would be in a modern zoo . . . he is
an ex-bartender too honest to turn bootlegger. In an all but deserted
"cow town" of New Mexico he keeps a gaunt and bare ex-bar that

shouts to you of the past doings of Titans. Over which he now peddles Volsteadian wares which a score of times each day turn him bitter with their joyless sterility.

Thunder Mountain earned his sobriquet quite honestly: that being another story in its entirety. Yet even a tenderfoot knows he is of the hard-bitten breed. Tourists recognize it in his sparing of words; in his voiceless contempt when they overstep the bar etiquette of 30 years ago . . . his ritual to the end. Only the news that I had driven in from Texas (imparted as I mused sadly over beer which was too evidently near) loosened Bill's tongue. He had fond recollections of San Antonio and El Paso, had Thunder Mountain. I refreshed those memories as best I could, and from that moment on I was a longhorn to him, and thence could do no wrong . . . not even with questions about his place. Carefully indifferent questions, though, as well I knew that the over-curious earn only the polite but biting rejoinder of the desert.

Musty Indian gear; ox-team yokes, mute testimony of prairie argonauts who pursued the West ill-fatedly; great pieces of yellow-threaded ore, rich enough to tempt a payroll bandit; magnificent hunting trophies; guns almost without number, eloquent of the Gunpowder Age of the West; all of it quite enough to break the heart of any antique collector who might have stumbled in.

"Oh, that?" he said, as I pointed to a jagged hole in the walnut upright of the handsome bar. "We had some lively times here twenty odd years ago, when the camp was going good. Some of the boys was pretty good with a six-gun. Me I never held with no six-shooter. I figgered it was up to me to keep things straight so I kinder kept the peace with this." From under the bar he drew a murderous looking sawed off shot gun. "I never had to argue much with'm when I brought out ol' Sary Ann." And indeed this very unfeminine bit of ordnance looked entirely capable of enforcing order. "She barked a few times, but generally once was plenty. She shore could bite wide and deep, and there wasn't no pistol pete could draw quicker'n I could grab her from under here.

"Naw, they ain't never coming back," said Bill, as we fell to discussing the changing order.

"A big mine in the hills now and then, maybe, and some cattle. But the old times? They ain't never coming back." His conviction was evident, without a tensity of hope.

"Why? Country has outgrowed it, I reckon.

"See that table over there? 'Bout two weeks ago I had the final verdict, and the jury was a bunch of train robbers and cattle thieves.

"Six of 'em sittin' there, playing stud. Oh, yes, we still have a few card games on the open. That was a big game for this country . . . dollar chips, and my old ceiling for the top.

"Brother, around that table was two men I knowed had help rob trains. Two more I knowed to be rustlers, and one more with two notches on his gun. Tough? You could of got any kind of action you wanted outa that bunch . . . maybe more than you'd wanted.

"Finally one of 'em says: 'Bill, what in the hell have you got to drink in that ol' broken down dump of yours?

"Some nice sodie pop, boys," I told 'em. "Or cold nighbeer, or maybe I can mix you a root beer. And listen, boys, somethin' special tonight . . . ice cream."

Any orator would have envied Thunder Mountain Bill the ultimate sarcasm of his dwelling on that phrase. One gathered that ice cream was the uttermost in banality.

"Well, they coulda been arrested for what they called me. I'm telling you if I hadn't been a old hand, I shore would have got mad. It took 'em five minutes to calm down, and I don't think a single one repeated once.

"It was plumb quiet for a little while more, and then one of them horse thieves turned round and said:

"Bill, you lousy old gin-hostlin' b——— you, bring me some of that damned ice cream!"

"Well, it shore was a sight. Them train robbers and rustlers and gun men set there at my poker table, with dollar chips on the table, and et ice cream . . . out of a dish, with a spoon. And the dirty punks liked it, too!

"That finished me, pardner. They liked it, just like any tourist! And I knowed as I stood there and watched 'em, that that was all . . . the old days was gone . . . and never was comin' back."

Shine Philips

Put Your Little Foot

SHINE PHILIPS spent his life in Big Spring, Texas, most of it as the town druggist. His store was a focal point of village affairs and also of the ranch country surrounding it. With kindly humor and a sharp insight into people and their affairs, he functioned as the town chronicler in *Big Spring*.

From *Big Spring*. New York: Prentice-Hall, 1942, pp. 177–182, 190–191.

"Didn't you ever have any fun out here?" my friend inquired. "People didn't just work all the time, did they?"

"Of course, we had fun," I snorted. "We had more fun than you young whippersnappers know how to have."

Nobody needs to think we didn't have a good time and social life out here in these parts. We didn't have any constant round of gaiety but when we did get to a party, durn if we weren't able to enjoy it and give it our all.

A cowboy dance isn't the most beautiful thing on earth but it sure is lively; and sometimes when you get to watching the sets and the sashaying and the do-ci-doing, and listen to that strange shuffling rhythm which makes a square dance and it is not possible to describe, along with the wild beckoning of the fiddle and the voice of the caller, then it is beautiful, in the way primitive expressions of happiness usually are.

Our ladies were lightfooted, even if they were the same ladies that stood over a washtub and a hot stove and could shoot down a coyote with one shot and no compunction. They were pretty too—and they never got tired.

Jim Winslow's four-piece band was in great demand out here. They played all over the plains. When the band started out to Lubbock, which was one hundred and twenty-five miles away, on horseback, they let folks along the way know they were coming and stopped off at Gail and Tahoka and made merry in the best barns and stables or anywhere else they could find a place big enough to shake a foot in.

They stopped overnight and played for a dance in every town. There was some kind of mental telepathy accompanying their progress through the country, because there weren't any telephones and the mail hack was the only means of communication between towns; but whenever the Winslow Band got to a wide place in the road the cowboys were there in large numbers, together with a few well-chaperoned girls and some old folks who were not too particular with their feet and still had a dancing spark left in their make-up. The floors were rough and full of splinters, and the surroundings were anything but decorative, but the fellowship and understanding was about perfect.

The square dances were still far and away the most popular, but waltzes were beginning to come in and the girls all swooned with joy when the fiddles struck up, "After the Ball Is Over." The "Blue Danube" was a great favorite too. We danced schottishe and many a lively polka. "Put Your Little Foot" was the best of all. Nothing is as pretty as a young girl in a wide lawn skirt, "putting her little foot."

The girls were outnumbered about five to one, so their popularity was legendary. Also their endurance. The men got to rest about four-fifths of the time but the girls danced every dance and the dances lasted all night—sometimes the next night too. The women had no chance to duck or sit one out. Five gallants were standing in line constantly begging the favor of the next one.

The main reason the dances lasted all night was because it was a long time between dances and then, too, the durn roads were so bad, where they were any roads, and snakes and skunks made traveling by night kind of undesirable. So they shuffled all night long and when dawn began to come up over the prairies and it got light enough for the cowboys to get going, they unhobbled their horses, pulled off their boots and rested their feet and the horses carried them back to the ranch. The ladies didn't fare so well. They had to soak their feet and doctor a few stone bruises where some gawky cowhand had stepped on them. These itinerant orchestra tours usually lasted about a week and were very profitable to the musicians and folks who sold medicine for sore pedal extremities.

The dances given by the big ranch outfits were planned affairs and we looked forward to them for weeks. Notice was given out in every way possible, because when an outfit had a dance, there was no re-stricted guest list. Everybody in the country who could get there was invited. They usually lasted two or three days and whole families came and brought their babies and children. The women and kids had the run of the ranch house, and the men slept in the bunkhouse or in their bedrolls on the ground in the yard, what time they had for sleeping. This wasn't much. The women always cooked up a bunch of hams and fried pies made from dried fruit and washtubs full of doughnuts, and the ranch owner barbecued a beef so there was plenty of food.

Everybody dressed up for these more formal affairs. Hands would ride thirty miles to town and thirty miles back to get a haircut, a bath, a new shirt, and their boots shined. The women all had their best dresses on—a new one if possible. They rode in the ranch hack and carried their ball dresses and dancing shoes, or else posted over on a sidesaddle with their clothes tied in a bundle behind. They had their hair all curled up on curl papers and had been putting buttermilk on their epidermis for days to bleach themselves.

The rancher who gave the dance had to put up the horses and feed them, along with the folks, and at these home affairs, the men were required to stay sober. If a cowhand got drunk at such a dance, he was disgraced. There were usually about thirty couples at these ranch dances, but Pa and Ma brought their daughters and the men came in a body, so there weren't any dates and no traveling of young folks forty miles to a dance together without strict chaperonage. During the danc-ing the older women sat in a group in a corner near the music, gos-siping with each other and watching the antics of the young girls with an eagle eye. If one got to holding on too tight they would all give her a look that broke the hold just like a referee in a modern wrestling match.

Everything was chaperoned up to the hilt but somehow the young folks must have got together in the dim light of the lanterns because we had a lot of weddings and such things can't exactly be arranged by remote control. Sometimes I think the girls themselves had to take the lead in courtship because the men were so shy. They didn't know anything about the fair sex and they used to blush as red as a turkey gobbler's neck when a girl would put her hand on one of their arms to walk off the dance floor. The little things looked so frail and sweet to a cowhand, he was afraid he would break one of them to pieces if he really started to hugging her the way he felt like.

The women usually wore flowered muslin dresses with rosettes and things on them and sometimes white dresses with ruffles made out of embroidery and beading with ribbons run through and a whole bunch of petticoats. Our ladies kept up with the styles the best way they could. They wore puffed sleeves and bustles and plenty of petticoats. Sometimes I think it is a good thing there were five men present to every girl. I don't think a dance could have lasted all night if one fellow had to carry five underskirts and a bustle through every dance. He would have pooped out long before daylight.

The men always managed to get on a coat and wear it during a dance, and they owned a blue serge suit if possible just for these occasions. This was about the only time you could get a necktie around their necks and they wore their pants legs tucked inside their boots and looked plum civilized. but every once in a while they would forget their decorum and let out a cowboy yell that would scare the bats out of the roof.

One old boy was warming his boots at the stove one cold night and burned a hole in the side of it. That was a real tragedy, of course, because he didn't have any more with him. But he made a deal with a friend of his—he and his pal took turns wearing the pal's boots, changing in regular shifts, whenever one had a partner. The boots were in every dance but the same man wasn't in the boots all the time.

Lots of times you couldn't hear Jim Winslow's fiddle or Bostick's guitar or the other members of the orchestra (usually four pieces), but you could always hear boots, boots, boots, and they kept time to the flop of the ladies' bustles in a way that is hard even to describe.

The drugstore was next to a saloon, and the boys always bought the girls some little something, usually some candy, and later on (after it was declared ladylike to chew it by the Emily Posts of the day) some chewing gum. Always before the dance, the boys gathered at the drugstore and the band gave a little free show for the Christians who, at that time, didn't dance and usually some cowhand would cut loose and sing some song and these boys could really sing (when you found one that could). I've been out here forty-three years and have never heard a cowboy yodel and believe that they would have shot him if he had tried just one time. I still want to shoot these movie cowhands who sing through their noses or yodel, and represent their sacred calling as yodeling. Cowhands hummed to quiet their cattle when they were going up the trail at night but there wasn't any damn yodeling.

☆ ☆ ☆ ☆

Along about 1905 the opera house was opened for its first show, and it was a gala event in the life of the village. Previous to that time, the cowhands hadn't patronized itinerant shows very much, but when *East Lynn* was blared over the billboards, the cowhands came in droves and bought the tickets at the drugstore, and the town was all set for its big premiere. The boys donned their best Sunday clothes, stormed the barbershops for their haircuts and spent the day getting all set for the evening performance.

East Lynn was a sad little ditty. Tears were streaming down the faces in spite of the fact that many bandanna handkerchiefs were wringing wet. The boys had never seen a show of any kind, and as the villain got rougher and rougher, finally it was too much for one of the boys who was taking the villain literally and who got filled up on the rough stuff being handed out to the fair maiden. He yelled right out loud in the middle of a very tense scene. "Hey there pardner, that's enough of that," and started for the stage. The combination of fighting whiskey and pent-up emotions was more than he could bear. The sheriff had to get him quiet and he finally got him to go outside, but the show was one grand flop because the villain couldn't do his stuff after that as villains should do.

Riding home through a rather stiff norther after the show was over, at the unearthly hour of ten-thirty, and still mad at the villain, didn't help the temper of the cowhands much, and for days and days afterwards, the stock gossip at the drugstore was, "That villain ought to be shot," or "I'll bet he is just as ornery as he was on the stage." Two or three posses collected, bent on tracking the actor down and investigating him, but nothing came of it.

The Woman's Club had nerve enough to bring *Romeo and Juliet,* which was showing to practically empty benches before it was half over. A few drunk cowhands in the balcony furnished more amusement than the scenes that took place on the stage, and were twice as funny and more interesting to most of the audience who were too proud to admit they didn't know what it was all about. Cowhands had a hard time getting acclimated to the opera. Theirs was the open range where there was no make-believe.

Ellen Bowie Holland

A Scotsman Comes Courting

ELLEN BOWIE HOLLAND'S FATHER was a Scotsman who paused in
Texas on his way to other parts of the world and never got away. He
married a Texas girl, became a prosperous businessman in Louisiana
and finally settled in Weatherford. Ellen's book is a combination of
family history and autobiography, brightly but simply written and full
of quiet humor. The story of her parents' courtship is typical.

From "Courtship and Marriage" in *Gay as a Grig: Memories of a
North Texas Girlhood.* Austin: University of Texas Press, 1963, pp. 23–
27.

According to Mother's diary her contacts with would-be sweethearts
were somewhat less exciting than the torrid affairs of today's movies.
She mentions having received three valentines, unsigned, as was the
custom then, and two letters, and having had a few young men callers.
She did not answer her mail because her mother did not approve of girls
writing to boys. Nor were the callers pressed to come again, which
moved Mother to write, "I guess I didn't care much."

But in January 1875 Mother notes that at church, "I met Mr.
Bowie, the new school teacher, who seems very pleasant, is good looking and a foreigner."

Mr. Bowie called the next day and carelessly forgot his gauntlets
when he left. She wrote, "I did not follow him to the gate to give them
back to him because I hope he will return for them." He had left them
on purpose anyway so their romance began with a pinging note of
subterfuge, and continued to be a crafty affair. Mr. Bowie had to return
often for articles he always "forgot." Mother knew before Mr. Bowie

did, that he was hooked, and she was keenly amused at his revealing behavior. He was looking for the pit in the cherry pie and he never found it. He was aware that his bright dreams of traveling the world over were, of late, less urgent and appealing. He no longer felt he must feel the winds of the seven seas. This was a caveat that he did not recognize.

In her diary, Mother shows great restraint over a lengthy period. Her references to Mr. Bowie are impersonal: "The school children have a little extra fun now because Mr. Bowie enters into their jokes and games at recess." But on the first of September restraint is thrown into the trash can. She writes, "I have brought my diary to the hilltop where, alone, I can have a good cry. I am so anxious, indeed miserable. Mr. Bowie is very sick with bilious fever. I would dearly love to go to see him but Ma says it would not do." Obviously the wishes of her parents were held in great respect. Ten days later she says, "Mr. Bowie came to-day, all the way on horseback (six miles) and he looks so pale and weak but he is determined to go back to teaching."

Well, it hardly seems fair for Love to take advantage of a man in a weakened condition from bilious fever but the next entry shows that Love did. On this call he left the following letter with her. The ink has turned brown and the paper has become fragile but I am glad it has lasted until I saw it.

10th of September 1875

Dear Maggie,

For sometime I have sought an opportunity to tell you of my love but I find it hard to express and yet harder to conceal. We cannot see the workings of one another's hearts and you probably are unacquainted with the feelings that, for sometime, have occupied mine. And now the strength of my attachment must be my excuse for presuming to write this way to you but I can conceal my love no longer. Let me tell you plainly that I love you. A word of encouragement, or a smile from you will make me the happiest fellow in existence, but I cannot be happy in this love without some hope of a return. The love I offer you will be unchangeable and if you can return it your happiness would be the object of my life. Your image is before me day and night but it is the image of one who gives me no hope. I am not writing sentamentalism [sic] to you, but fact and with the feelings of my heart. Do not be offended that I have written thus plainly. I am usually plain in all my dealings but pray, let me have an answer.

Ah, "the image of one who gives me no hope!" What an actress she was! He couldn't know that all the time she was up on that hill, so to speak, weeping to see him. I am taking a bit of a liberty in presenting this letter but it is so Victorian Gothic and so definitely has the dignity of the amorous epistles of that day. The Italians and French are reputed to come on very strong as lovers but this Scot with his shaky convictions was able to throw out a wistful quality that proved irresistible.

Of course being in love is a wretched state—unless it is reciprocated—but all wistfulness dissolved into roseate hours as the thoughts of the young couple took on the brisk air of decision. Father at once traded a ninety-dollar horse to a carpenter in exchange for the work of putting a wooden floor into his little house and for mending the roof and performing sundry requirements. If a new house could be built for eighty dollars this one must have been in a shabby state.

On October twelfth you can see Mother blush as she writes, "Today I am eighteen. Mr. Bowie, my intended, gave me some white kid gloves and enough white satin-finished brilliantine to make my wedding dress. Ma and Pa gave me a trunk and some white flowers for my hair and enough slate grey material for a traveling dress." In case you need a translation for "intended" it was early-day colloquialism for "betrothed." I rather like the light, indefinite quality of "intended"; there is no feeling of head-in-a-noose about it.

As Mother made these two important dresses the little sewing machine ran smoothly. Not bulky trousers today, not work shirts today, not men's underwear today, but instead something pretty. As she sewed Mother hummed a happy song.

Their wedding day was November 18, 1875, and from then on it was, "Ever thine, ever mine, ever for each other."

The house had been crowded before and after the wedding with ten guests staying overnight. The wedding must have taken place on Friday as Mother speaks of the necessity of only being away two days as Mr. Bowie had to be back for school on Monday morning. They took their first meal picnic fashion by the roadside. In the excitement of getting away Mr. Bowie forgot to take a knife of any kind and they had to eat ham, baked chicken, and cake in chunks.

November, in Texas, is perhaps the loveliest month in the year. Each red and golden leaf seemed to hang by the merest thread in the sharp shafts of sunlight. Bare trees, black and grave outlined themselves against the sky. The spongy earth muffled the measured tread of the horses as they drove away into the long adventure of marriage, leaving a wake of waving hands behind them.

Years later Father told us privately that actually each had married the other because of their worldly possessions. Mother owned a cow, a calf, a quilt, and a feather bed, and he had bought an eighty-acre farm with a log dwelling on it.

And the white kid gloves? They were laid away to discolor, but in a way they were a prophecy.

Skipping about among their old correspondence I find a poem (which I hasten to say I will spare you) written eighteen years after their marriage. Father's poems did not flow with sinuous grace, they were more like a huffle of wind in the chimney, but there is one verse which shows how the torrents of young love are beginning to spread and to run deeper and smoother:

> And now that the fires of youth have gone by
> We can meet age approaching with never a sigh
> For true to each other and true to the end
> The lover will sweetly combine in the friend.

And here is a last one. A letter that has been based on reason rather than emotion. It is phrased as if Father had just finished writing a sedate business letter, and while still in the same frame of mind turned his thoughts to their impending anniversary.

18th, November, 1905

Dear Maggie,

We commemorate to-day the thirtieth anniversary of the best deal I ever made and it seems only fitting for me to testify on this occasion as to my experience of married life.

Marriage is either a blessing or a dismal failure. But when a man secures such a life partner as I did, a helper in every way, uniting a pure and virtuous life with all the attributes of a good mother and a true heart with great housekeeping skill, then he is ready to acknowledge that marriage is the boon it is supposed to be.

After all these years the eye is not blinded by glamour or romance, and so I attest to the solid, downright goodness of the woman I married thirty years ago to-day.

I have been deeply touched by the beauty of many of these letters. If you ever write letters of this sort (Darling, you are wonderful!) see to it they are saved. It is a heart-warming experience for the child, or grandchild, who discovers their yellowed and sentimental existence. I don't believe people do much of this sort of thing today. Pity, isn't it?

A. C. Greene

The Ominous Journey

A. C. GREENE has become a legend among Texas readers and is regarded by his admirers as the dean of Texas letters. Born and educated
in Abilene, he has served Abilene and Dallas newspapers as reporter,
columnist, and book editor, and he has been a teacher of journalism and
owner of a bookstore. In his spare time he has been a persistent writer
of reminiscent and critical articles for Texas and national magazines. *A
Personal County,* a gently humorous book about A. C. and his Texas,
pleased a host of readers.

From *A Personal Country*. New York: Alfred A. Knopf, 1969, pp.
75–78, 80–81, 89–90.

The road between Cisco and Abilene is only forty-five miles in length,
but when I think of automobile travel this bit of highway makes the
first flash of recognition across my mind. We always seemed to have to
pass that way no matter what our destination.

Part of the passionate quality of travel with us came from the fact
that my father was usually the only adult male among three suspicious,
strong-minded women of his wife's family—my mother, my grandmother, and my great-grandmother.

For my grandmother a journey was an act of deliberate peril.
Everything contributed to fear. The clouds that came up from nowhere
to darken the land were but the face of some disparate god of personal
spite. This unlifted threat of disaster was bequeathed me by all three
female generations that nursed me to manhood. They reminded me by
word and act that man is never alone in his choices. As soon as God
leaves his side, or he leaves God's, in rushes the Devil. Hard work and
self-effacement were the only ways to thwart Beelzebub; sweat was the
holy water of purification. If you dare stand up to be seen, or leave your

house to perform some challenging act like moving across the face of the earth, then you are inviting divine testing—you are assuring yourself of it. So we seemed to undertake our departures by figurative candlelight so as to escape notice, for that short period of dawn grayness at least, of the moral responsibility which came from asserting our existence.

On the road we drove waiting for the next disaster, having escaped evil only from one mile to the next, never for good. The thanks we gave were more often for what we had missed than for what we had been given. My family could always find reasons to view a gift as a potential ticket to despair or dissolution.

Our vehicle, in the earliest days, was some kind of open touring model, but I can never recall the top being let down. It had side curtains with heavy glass panes sewn into the artificial leather fabric. Inside, with the curtains up, was dark and scary. The seats were firm and cold, and the rain was always coming down, making a drumhead of the fabric top stretched over the wooden bows—although this is plainly a specific memory of mine rather than any general condition because there is never that much rain in West Texas.

Luggage was carried wherever it could be tied, strapped, or sat on. One of my father's jobs was to locate, then attach, the expanding metal luggage carrier which fitted to the running boards. But even with this (you could only use one side of the car because these racks blocked the doors) there was not enough space, so I was usually given the honor of straddling an old brown leather suitcase belonging to an uncle but being used by my grandmother. Luggage was scarce and precious in our family and ownership was not so important as the circumstance of who was using it at any one time. Sometimes a particularly voluminous, costly piece of gear would be passed around from one journey to the next for a matter of years before its true owner broke the circle to reclaim its use.

My father always did the driving, although not without help from the various nondrivers such as my grandmother, who only learned how to operate an automobile after she was well into her fifties, and my great-grandmother who died at age eighty-four without ever understanding the basic usage of such items as brakes, steering wheel, horn, or gearshift. There is a family legend that my grandfather on my mother's side, a red-haired gentleman named Ambrose who had a notoriously short-fused temper, tried to give Granny a driving lesson in an EMF automobile back in the green years of personal motor ownership. But she was inclined to try and control the auto as one did a horse, and ended up almost immediately in a ditch, tugging at the steering wheel and shouting "Whoa!" This brought on a blast of polite obscenity from her son-in-law which alienated Granny from the auto forever. (The alienation from the son-in-law had preceded this by several years.) Nevertheless, when riding as a passenger she knew what her eyes told her, and she had an imperious kind of comment which verged on command when she espied a traffic danger that my father, the driver, was apt to overlook or not sufficiently to acknowledge in advance.

☆ ☆ ☆ ☆

Once on the road, my father faced other problems of travel. The matter of rivers and bridges was a severe one. My grandmother didn't want to cross any bridge when the creek or river was full because she had a theory that so much water was bound to be secretly eating away the supports. One might think, therefore, that in dry weather a bridge would be no obstacle. But this is overlooking the problem of quicksand.

I have never encountered quicksand and I am not sure my grandmother had, but she was an expert on it. Quicksand need not be wet to be deadly. Quicksand was quick sand. The name told everything. It was quick in the sense that it worked rapidly, engulfing a man (or woman) so swiftly that he (or she) hadn't time to extract a foot, much less an entire leg. And those unfortunate enough to sink to the waist were doomed, even though whole squads of would-be rescuers were standing nearby with all the standard quicksand rescue apparatus. It was the weight of the sand itself that gave it its awful sucking power, creating of the innocent natural element a beast with a cunning mind and lightning tongue. I could imagine it creeping up alongside some low bridge and pouncing hungrily on the first high-pressure tire that came within licking distance, pulling car and contents under.

So you were never safe around rivers. Floods were self-evident menace, known and understood to be instruments of judgment (and a flood, in my grandmother's nomenclature, was any running water). Despite the fact she spent a great many years in East Texas where deep rivers and springs are the normal rather than the unusual, her girlhood had cast her among people whose lives had been spent on the frontier where tanks and ponds were the only natural water, therefore running water was invariably dangerous, for the sudden downpours, the wet northers, the cloudbursts were great things for showing you how disastrously you had located your cabin, dugout, or stock pen.

For this reason, among a host of others, she also despised night travel. Her fear was not from collision with another vehicle (in fact, she welcomed the sight of another car because it showed her that someone else besides her son-in-law was foolish enough to be taking this forlorn route) but from the ever-present danger of unknowingly driving off the end of a demolished bridge—finding yourself and vehicle suddenly suspended in mid air, thoroughly conscious that in a twinkling of an eye you and yours would be plunged into eternity in the dark waters of the flood beneath you. (And about that time, as luck would have it, Thornton Wilder's novel *The Bridge of San Luis Rey* came out, a story which centers on the catastrophe of a bridge giving way, and my grandmother, who was a librarian, thrilled to have such high-level corroboration of something she had anticipated all her life.)

The bridges along the road were almost all narrow, spidery, and rattly, originally conducted for passage by wagon and buggy, laid with timber floors which rattled like bones or rumbled like kettledrums when any weight moved over them. In most cases, crossing was restricted to one vehicle at a time on account of width or fragility or both.

The main bridge over the Brazos, on the route we used, was located at the forgotten town of Brazos. It was a swinging bridge, a frightful span swung from cables about three inches thick, suspended between two pairs of towers and reaching across an impressive width of river. The bridge site was about a mile from the little town. You drove down a muddy lane, made a sharp turn around a hill, and just like that, the bridge was there. It had a remarkable tendency to sway, and the planking was not bolted down solid but was laid in flexibly so that the bridge could twist and turn without cracking. It was scary in broad daylight, and in the dark, or during a rain or flood, it could be hair-raising.

My grandmother refused to ride in a car across this devil, as she called it. She walked over, and did that only after the bridge was cleared of vehicles. As it was rather a long bridge, walking created its own traffic problem. Later, years later, a massive steel and concrete bridge was constructed over the Brazos a few miles south of that swinging one, but the first time she came to the new one she walked over it, too, just to be sure. It was so solid it seemed to have changed her whole outlook on bridges, and I never heard her voice her bridge fears again. But I must add, in her memory, that the swinging bridge over the Brazos eventually did collapse, dropping a bakery truck into the river which was at low water so that the driver was able to wade out, undrowned by the flood and unclaimed by the quicksand.

☆   ☆   ☆   ☆

From Cisco to Baird is a twenty-five mile stretch in which there was (and is) little habitation. For years the highway went by way of a T&P siding named Dothan where a monument informed you this was the route of the first military telegraph line into West Texas. Then the road passed the site where the grandiose city of Vigo had been planned at the turn of the century, went around an oil company tank farm which was almost a town in itself, and into Putnam, which had already faded badly from its brief days as a health resort (the mineral baths in the basement of the Mission Hotel now lie under twenty feet of Interstate Highway 20).

West of Putnam was the beginning of what I call the "Carl, stop" section. The filling stations of that day were mostly a single pump in front of a hardware store or some other masculine establishment. It was considered unladylike, in our family, for a woman to approach a man and ask where she could use the bathroom.

Baird, fifteen miles along the way, had one place which the women had spotted through experience, a simple two-holer of the period but marked LADIES so that no embarrassing questions were necessary. The fact that any female seen going off across the pasture in that direction caused all male eyes to "see where she was heading" was bad enough, but tolerable in comparison to a badly expanded bladder, which seemed to be an inherited weakness among the Coles and Dock-reys of my mother's line.

But Baird was far, and Putnam had an unfortunate reputation among our women, so as soon as the highway was empty of other cars, the cry went up, "Carl, stop." Usually it was mother or my grand-mother, but now and then it would be Granny, the tough old great-grandmother who had learned better control in the days of frontier travel. She could be even more insistent than the younger women, and she was not above cutting loose in the back seat of the car, attempting to use her snuff spit can for a receptacle. (With her layers of skirts and petticoats it amounted to a hidden undertaking, so far as delicacy was concerned, although not necessarily a successful one.)

So a stop was made, the car pulled over to the side of the road, a great deal of nervous looking around was done, to be sure no oncoming motorist would spot the inconvenienced women as they squatted be-hind mesquite bushes or in oak clumps, or would not see them crawling through the barbwire fence and know why they were heading for the bushes.

My father's idea of the best of all jokes was to honk the klaxon at what he had timed as the most inappropriate moment, bringing the women flocking in from the field in degrees of disarray. He would take on a serious look and apologize for having "accidentally hit the horn button," or say, solemnly, that he had seen a snake crawling across the road toward their roosting place. These occasions were the only ones on which I ever knew my mother to indulge in an indelicacy. "You caused us to wet all over ourselves with your honking," she would accuse him.

The breaking of the journey to accommodate the women plagued my father into modern times. Even with superhighways and super-service stations he would have to stop at least once on a trip to let my grandmother go outdoors because she claimed she had found all the commercial restrooms in a condition she called "filthy." This term, in her usage, defied definition. I think maybe she just liked nature.

Cow Country

For Elmer Kelton's "Hewey Arrives"

Texas was cow heaven from the beginning and cow people gave a special flavor to the state's humor. It could hardly have been otherwise, for life on the range with its loneliness, its dangers to life and limb, its demand for courage and endurance, produced men determined to be their special selves. Humorists loved their salty, vigorous personalities. You could dip down anywhere in the cattle country and come up with one. Humorous cowboys were common in the novels of the thirties and forties, bearing names like Rimfire Boggs and Wild Horse Shorty, Sundown Slim and Hell-for-Leather Jones, and the humorous sidekick and the ridiculous puncher were almost as common as the romanticized Hollywood version of the heroic horseman. Hopalong Cassidy in the early Bar-20 novels was wild and funny and makes for a fine example.

In the twilight of the western novel and western movie, however, the fun and romance are gone. In Larry McMurty's novel *Horseman Pass By* (1960), for example, Hud is a murderous rascal; in J. P. S. Brown's *Jim Kane* (1970), Jim is a victim, cheated by his employer; in Max Evans' *The Rounders* (1960), Wrangler Lewis and Dusty Rhodes are rural dead-end kids with no chance of success; in Edward Abbey's *The Brave Cowboy* (1957) and Elmer Kelton's *The Good Old Boys* (1978), the cowboy is out of step with modern times.

Today some historians see the cowboy as a rangeland dropout (see W. W. Savage's *Cowboy Life*, 1975), not intelligent or ambitious enough to become a cattleman. Cowboys aren't funny any more, though writers like Ben Capps (*Sam Chance*, 1965) and Robert Flynn (*North to Yesterday*, 1967) have done very well to keep the humorous side alive. Much of the best cowboy humor, however, belongs to yesterday.

Laura V. Hamner

Ellen Carter and the Black-Eyed Peas

LAURA V. HAMNER—Miss Laura—of Amarillo made herself the First
Lady of the Texas Panhandle through her newspaper articles and radio
programs. Her radio talks were directed at young people, but everybody listened. Her material was gathered from country people and
villagers throughout the High Plains region and she won their complete confidence. She sidestepped feuds and personal troubles and concentrated on the daily lives of pioneer settlers who survived when times
were hard and neighbors were many miles away. Some strange things
happened on those isolated ranches, however, and Miss Laura tells
about one of them with characteristic humor.

From *Light 'n Hitch*. Dallas: American Guild Press, 1943, pp.
145–147.

Ellen Carter was happy down on the Pecos, though one little article of food was a constant irritant to her. She hated black-eyed peas.
The cowboys never got enough of them and the cook preferred them to
any other food. The Carter outfit had peas for dinner, peas for supper,
and sometimes warmed up leftover peas for breakfast. They had them
on New Year's Day for good luck, then on every other day to satisfy
their liking. They were a long distance from market and had to buy
large quantities of provisions. Naturally they bought food that would
keep a long time. Beans, peas, dried fruit, cured meat, and always
black-eyed peas. Ellen grew so desperate that she wished a blight would
slay every black-eyed pea vine in the world. She groaned one winter day

when another wagon load of provisions was unloaded: two one-hundred-pound sacks of black-eyed peas were carried into the store room!

The boys would have said, if she had protested, "You don't have to eat peas if you don't want 'em Mrs. Carter; eat something else." They could not understand that the very sight of black-eyed peas turned her stomach.

Day after day, black-eyed peas were served until one sack was exhausted. The other sack was opened.

Unexpected relief came. One warm spring day, Ellen Carter was cleaning her bedroom. She looked up from what she was doing and there, right in the middle of the room, was a lovely black-and-white striped animal waving a beautiful plume-like tail. It was a polecat with two sure weapons of defense, sharp teeth and a pouch filled with a liquid having a terrible, almost everlasting scent. Ellen screamed.

Charlie, the Mexican cook, rushed in, and chased the animal into the store room. Mrs. Carter, still afraid, but wanting to see what happened, followed on Charlie's heels. The polecat took refuge behind a box and again Mrs. Carter screamed.

"Hush, Mees Carter. If he gets mad, he will ruin them peas. He is right on top of the sack thees minute."

Charlie moved quietly so as not to enrage the animal, not aware of its danger. Charlie searched for a small missile to toss at it and start it to moving toward the open door. As he stooped, his pistol protruded from his hip pocket. Ellen Carter thought fast. Now was her chance to rid the ranch of black-eyed peas for months. Of course, if she carried out her plan, the place would reek with a scent that would make it almost unbearable for a long time. Even that seemed preferable to peas, peas, peas, meal after meal. She snatched the gun, fired, then clapped her hand over her nose.

Her ruse worked. The sack of peas was ruined.

Charlie was disconsolate.

"Them so good peas, Mees Carter. He ees no *bueno* now . . . . No *bueno*." Charlie dragged the dead skunk to the yard, then returned, his face lighted with a new idea.

"I know, Mees Carter. I know. I take the sack to the reever and let it float in the water. Them peas, they come clean enough to eat."

Charlie trotted off toward the river with the large sack of peas on his back. Ellen watched him go.

Worse and worse, she thought. Not only peas, but peas that had been drenched in polecat spray!

It took more than Charlie to outwit Ellen Carter. She slipped out to the corrals, looking for a cowboy. All of them were devoted to her, so anyone would do to trust. She appealed to the first one she found.

"Sam, a polecat squirted his juice on that sack of black-eyed peas and Charlie has put them in the river to wash the scent off. If you'll slip down and cut a hole in the bottom of the sack, they will wash away and Charlie will think they swelled and burst the sack."

A few days later Charlie had a tale of distress to tell everyone who would listen to him. The peas had swelled and burst the sack and there would be no more peas to cook for a long time.

Early spring merged into summer and summer was waning. Ellen Carter had eaten red beans with gusto during all the weeks since she and Sam had conspired against Charlie, the cook. Then again her security of mind was destroyed.

One hot morning a cowboy rode up, an eager, excited look on his face. His slicker had been taken from the customary roll behind his saddle, and was now filled to bursting with something which the boy evidently considered a prize.

"Look, Mrs. Carter," he cried "look what I've found!"

It was black-eyed peas, young, tender, ready to snap for cooking.

"Where did you find those peas in this desert, Ben?" asked Ellen, suppressing a groan.

"You know that curve in the river, about seven miles down? You remember there's a rich flat at that curve, three or four acres of good land? Well, that whole flat is covered with black-eyed peas. There's enough for all the folks in the Pecos Valley for a year, I guess. How do you reckon they got there?"

Sam looked at Ellen. Ellen looked at Sam. They alone knew they were being paid back for robbing Charlie and the boys of their favorite food. The little seeds had washed down the river, had been spread over the flat in an overflow, and had produced a good crop, untended.

Charlie's face rounded with smiles.

"Peas. *Bueno* peas. I go every day to get some."

Ellen Carter knew when she was whipped. At Charlie's words, she looked into the future. Good luck or bad luck, New Year's Day or Sunday or any other day she was doomed to eat peas.

Elmer Kelton

Hewey Arrives

AFTER A START WRITING FORMULAIC WESTERNS, Elmer Kelton of San Angelo developed into a much-respected and successful novelist noted for his portrayal of ranch life in the cattle country of West Texas. Born on a ranch himself, he became a journalist after service in World War II, serving on the staffs of ranch and farm papers while writing novels on the side. His work has been analyzed in articles and books and even in academic theses and dissertations. He is a realist—not a pessimist— with a fine sense of humor, and even when he is dealing with potentially tragic situations (*The Time It Never Rained*, 1973, for instance), he can find something amusing to relieve the tension.

From *The Good Old Boys*. Garden City: Doubleday, 1978, pp. 1–13.

For the last five or six days Hewey Calloway had realized he needed a bath. Now, in the final miles of a long horseback trip, it was a necessity no longer to be denied. By nightfall he would be eating hot biscuits and brown gravy at his brother's table. Sister-in-law Eve Calloway was not inclined to generosity regarding the social graces.

Ahead of him the red wooden tower of an Eclipse windmill stood almost astraddle the wagon road which meandered casually among the gentle hills and skirted respectfully around the scattered stand of low-growing mesquite trees. The leaves were still the fresh pale green of early spring. Tall above those trees, the mill's white-painted cypress fan turned slowly in the warm west wind which had stuck Hewey's old blue shirt to his skin much of the morning. A vagrant white puff of cumulus cloud drifted over him, yielding a few minutes of pleasant shade before the sun broke free again in the full heat of early May.

The more he thought about it the more he began to look forward to that cool bath, but he didn't want to push Biscuit into a trot. The brown horse was favoring his right forefoot a little. If it got any worse Hewey would have to walk and lead him.

Hell of a note, going lame the last day out. But better here than where they had started the trip three weeks ago in the melting snows of New Mexico high country.

He had known this region for years, and the sight of the red and white windmill confused him a little. Those colors were the trademark of the Two C Land and Cattle Company, old C. C. Tarpley's outfit. Hewey would take a paralyzed oath that the place just ahead belonged to a four-section bachelor homesteader, a former cowboy who had always been glad to provide Hewey a meal or two and let him roll out his blankets on a hard and civilized wooden floor instead of the soft and uncivilized ground.

The red towers and white fans scattered from here halfway to Midland were sign to a traveler that he was crossing two Cs land, and welcome to it so long as he shut all the wire gates behind him and didn't run the cattle. He was welcome to camp a night anywhere but never two nights in the same place unless he had a broken wheel. One night was traveling; two nights was squatting.

Gradually Hewey realized he had been right about the homesteader. He recognized the layout of the place, the fallow field, some faded, rotting stalks where last year's hegari crop had grown, and last year's cane. By now a good farmer should have plowed it up and started planting anew. The crude shed stood where Hewey remembered it, but the little frame house was gone. Nothing remained but stubby cedar posts that had been its foundation, and a weather-bleached four-by-four privy thirty feet from what had been the back door, a short run on a cold wet night. Somebody had dismantled the house for the lumber, more than likely. By the windmill's color, that somebody had to be C. C. Tarpley.

Old C. C.'s still spreading out, Hewey thought idly, begrudging him nothing, curious as to why he hadn't taken the privy too. It looked lonesome standing there by itself.

C. C.'s water would be as wet as anybody's. Hewey looked up at the Two Cs brand painted in red on the mill's white tail, which automatically held the fan into the west wind to keep the maximum driving force on its angled wooden fins. The slow turning activated a sucker-rod which clanked and shuddered down the center of a pipe reaching deep into the ground. Each stroke brought rhythmic gushes of cool water, pumping it into a big dirt tank which long hours of man and mule sweat had scooped from the ground.

Hewey swung his right leg across Biscuit's rump, holding the leg to clear the rolled blankets and the "war bag" of miscellaneous cowboy accumulations tied behind the high cantle. Over that cantle was stretched a dried rattlesnake skin, supposed by many to ward off rheumatism, which became a mark of the trade for cowboys who survived the other hazards long enough to acquire it. Some said it also helped prevent hemorrhoids, another ailment common to the horseback pro--fession.

Hewey doubted that, because he had them.

He stretched himself and stamped his feet to stimulate the blood and to steady his saddle-cramped legs. He unbuckled the girth, slid the saddle from Biscuit's back, then led the horse down to the water's edge to let him drink. Not until Biscuit had taken his fill did Hewey tie him to one of the tower legs and prepare to get a drink of water himself. He laid down astraddle the heavy pipe which extended from windmill to tank. He pushed carefully out to the end of it. The pipe was pleasantly cool. He held on with both legs and his left hand, cupping his right hand as the water pumped out in time to the mill's even strokes.

It was good water, carrying only a faint suggestion of the gyp common to much of West Texas. Water was a thing to be cherished in dry country. A man prized a good sweet well the way he prized a fine horse. Hewey finally took some of the water up his nostrils and choked. He decided that was enough for a while.

He inched his way back along the pipe, misjudging where to step off and sinking his left boot into the mud. He talked to the boot the way he was accustomed to talking to his horse. "Won't hurt you none. Damn little mud you'll ever get on you in this country."

Inside a small plot which had been the homesteader's garden, green grass was coming up between last year's plowed rows and the fence. Hewey led Biscuit there and turned him loose, fastening the sagging wooden gate to keep him from straying off. He watched the horse roll in the soft dirt, taking up the sweat where the saddle and blanket had been.

Hewey was vaguely disappointed. He had counted on a noon meal from the homesteader, even if only some rewarmed red beans and hogbelly. Well, at least the horse could graze awhile. Hewey would make do with a cold biscuit and dried-out bacon brought from the Two Cs line camp where he had stayed last night with old cowpuncher friends. He might brew himself a can of coffee too, after a while. Right now he wanted to test the water in that tank.

He emptied his pockets and piled their contents on the bare tank dump. They didn't amount to much . . . a couple of silver dollars and some smaller change, a Barlow knife, a sack of Bull Durham smoking tobacco and a book of brown cigarette papers, a wallet containing his life's savings of twenty seven dollars. He set his boots beside his treasure. On them jingled a set of scandalous "gal-leg" spurs, the shank shaped like a woman's leg, silver mounted to show the high-heeled dancing shoe, the stocking, the garter on a plump thigh. It took a sport to wear such as that. He clutched his sweat-stained cotton socks in his hand and waded off into the tank with the rest of his clothes on.

The deepest part came up barely past his thighs. He took off his faded jeans and washed them out, then his shirt and finally his long-handled cotton underwear that once had been white. Naked except for the hat, he walked out with the wet clothing, squeezed as much water from it as he could, then hung it piece by piece to dry in the sun on the bottom bracer of the windmill tower. That done, he waded back into the tank until the water was at his knees, then sat himself down shoulder-deep.

If a bath always felt this good, he thought, *I would take one every week or two.*

He sat soaking, only his head and his battered old felt hat above the water. Bye and bye half a dozen cows and their calves came ambling out from a thicket, bound for a cool drink of water and then a long, lazy afternoon shaded up beneath the mesquites, chewing cud. The cow in the lead made it all the way to the top of the earthen dump before she noticed Hewey. She stopped abruptly, her head high in surprise. Her calf spotted him at about the same time and turned to run off a little way, its tail curled in alarm. The cow stood her ground but advanced no farther. The other cows came up even with her and joined her in consternation.

Hewey spoke gently, "Don't be afraid, girls. I'd scare you a lot worse if I was to come up out of here."

The voice was not reassuring. Hewey held still, and one cow's thirst overcame her timidity. She moved cautiously to the water, lowered her head for a few quick sips, then jerked it up again to study Hewey critically, the water drops clinging to the hair under her chin. Gradually she decided he posed no threat as serious as her thirst, and she settled down to drinking her fill. The other cows, followers all, took this for a clearance and moved on to water. Hewey watched, knowing that curiosity would sooner or later lead one of the cattle to investigate his boots and his pocket possessions. When a calf warily started toward them, Hewey brought up a handful of mud from the bottom and hurled it at him. All the cattle ran. But in a few minutes they trailed down to the water again. Hewey held still. It was a cardinal principle not to disturb cattle unnecessarily, especially when they were watering. A cow had to drink plenty of water to make milk. She had to make milk to wean off a healthy calf. Motherhood—human or bovine—was a sacred thing.

Eventually the cattle trailed away to the thicket and lay down in the shade to relax away the warm afternoon and rechew the grass they had packed into their paunches all morning. Hewey began to think he ought to be fixing himself a little coffee and moving on, but the water felt good. He sat lazily watching a hawk make slow circles above the thicket, screaming a vain protest at the cattle. She probably had a nest in one of those big granddaddy mesquites. The cattle ignored her.

Too late he heard the rattle of chains and then the clopping of hoofs and the sand-slicing sound of narrow iron rims along the wagon road. A desperate thought came to him: these might be womenfolks, and they were going to catch him in this tank barefoot all the way to his chin. He weighed his chances of making a dash for his clothes without being seen. They were poor. He sat where he was, stirring the muddy bottom with his hands to make sure nobody could see through the water. The move was unnecessary; there had never been a day when this tank was that clear.

Up to the windmill trotted two matched dappled gray horses pulling a buggy. Two men sat on the spring seat. Hewey's attention went to a gaunt old man with sagging shoulders and sagging mustache. Sawing on the lines to pull the horses to a stop, the old man stared at Hewey with about as much surprise as the cows had shown. He reached instinctively under the seat, where he probably carried a rifle.

Finally he found a brusque voice. "Are you alive out there, or have I got a drowned man on my hands?"

Hewey grinned, relieved that there were only the men. "How's the women folks, C. C.?"

"Just barely tolerable. That you, Hewey Calloway?"

"It's me. I'm comin' out C. C."

His surprise gone, the old rancher watched with a measure of tolerant humor. "Damn if you ain't a pretty sight! I don't believe I ever seen a man take a bath with his hat on."

"I sunburn easy, C. C."

Hewey waded out, following a patch of bermuda grass along the water pipe to keep his feet from getting muddy. He felt his clothes, found them mostly dry, then began putting them on over his wet skin. His body was almost white. His hands and neck and face were browned, but the rest was customarily never exposed to the sun. Even his loose collar would usually be buttoned to keep the sun out. The last thing he did was to rub the sand from his feet, then put on his socks and boots.

The other man had never spoken. Hewey decided he probably wouldn't. He was a generation and a half younger and fifty pounds heavier than C. C. Tarpley. His name was Frank Gervin. Behind his back, people referred to him by a boyhood nickname, "Fat," but the tactful and prudent never called him that to his round and ruddy face.

Hewey said, "Howdy, Fat."

Fat Gervin winced and slumped a little deeper in the buggy. He gave no more than a nod, a very small and tentative recognition of Hewey's existence, and then he looked away, his eyes resting in the direction of home, shade and cool water. Fat had worked as a cowboy on many West Texas ranches, usually for only a short time at each place. He tended always to be lost on drive or to be sitting his horse in the middle of the gate when other hands were trying to put cattle through. Evidently he was better as a lover than as a cowboy, for he had somehow swayed and won Tarpley's only daughter while the old man's attention had been directed to more important things. This gave him a hold on the Tarpley inheritance, provided the old man did not decide at the end to take it all with him.

Hewey gave Gervin no more of his attention. He said, "I had it in mind to fix me a little coffee. Join me C. C.?"

It would amount to nothing more than some water boiled with coffee grounds in the bottom of a smoke-blackened can and drunk directly out of that can. Hewey didn't even have a cup. But C. C. Tarpley, biggest cattleman this side of the Pecos River, said he wouldn't mind if he did, and he climbed down. Fat didn't say anything; he kept his seat in the buggy.

C. C. didn't look like a big cattleman was supposed to. If anything, in his frayed old clothes and run-over boots he appeared as if he might have a hard time holding down a swamper's job in a saloon. His wrinkled shirt was pockmarked by tiny tobacco burns. He didn't have to dress up to impress anyone; everybody in this country knew him. If he went somewhere else on business, nobody knew him, so he didn't dress up for them either.

The two men squatted on opposite sides of an economical fire and watched while the water stubbornly refused to boil. Tarpley said, "Boys at the Tule camp told me you spent the night there. I'd decided you left this country for good."

Hewey shrugged. "I've got kin here. Walter and Eve and their boys. I got lonesome to see them."

"How long since you left here, two years?"

"One year, ten months and twenty-odd days."

"I reckon you got lots of money, Hewey."

"Money?"

"I recollect you ridin' away on old Biscuit, leadin' a packhorse with all your stuff on it, sayin' you wasn't comin' back till you was rich and famous. I ain't heard a word about you since, so I don't reckon you're famous. How rich are you?"

Hewey grinned sheepishly. "Had twenty-somethin' dollars, last time I counted."

"What come of the packhorse?"

"Sold him."

C. C. turned his head and took a long look at the brown horse. Hewey was glad it wasn't apparent that Biscuit was trying to come up lame. Tarpley said, "Well, if you ain't famous, and you ain't rich, maybe you've come home two years smarter. Ain't you about worn the itch out of your feet, Hewey? Ain't you ready to light someplace?"

Hewey looked at the coffee. "I believe it's finally about to come to a boil."

"Ain't you ever found anywhere you wanted to stay?"

"Just about every place, at first. Then directly I get to thinkin' there might be somethin' better down the road."

"But it's never there, is it?"

It's always there, for a little while." Using two big sticks as a clamp, Hewey gingerly lifted the can from the fire and set it off onto the ground. "Ought to be ready to drink in a minute. You're company; you can have the first sip."

"No, you're company. This place is mine. I bought out Sam Gentry as soon as he got it proved up."

Sam Gentry. Hewey had been trying for an hour to remember the homesteader's name. Sad, how quickly a man's name got lost. It was hard to make a big-enough track that your name was long remembered.

People here would remember C. C. Tarpley for a long time, of course. He had done well for himself the last twenty-five years, since he had stretched a castoff army tent on the Pecos River in 1881 and had turned loose his thirty-three spotted cows and one droop-horned bull. If that bull hadn't made the first winter, C. C. wouldn't have survived either. But the cattle had been prolific. People used to say that on the Tarpley place even the bulls had twin calves. It was also said that C. C. Tarpley could find and put his brand on more unclaimed mavericks than any three men on the Pecos. In his prime he rode fast horses and carried an extra cinch ring tied to his saddle so he could stop and brand any animal he came across that didn't already have a claim burned on it. That sort of ambitious endeavor was occasionally fatal to other men, but C. C. was tough enough to make it stick.

Now, six years into a new century, if anyone were to gather the whole Two C herd from where it was scattered over four hundred square miles of mesquite and catclaw and greasewood country, he would probably tally out five or six thousand mother cows plus no telling how many yearlings and two-year-olds. All that in twenty-five years from thirty-three cows and a bull.

Hard work and attention to business were the key, C. C. had often preached. But he had always said he was not greedy. All he had ever wanted was that which rightfully belonged to him, and that which adjoined it.

The hard years of acquisition had not let him run to fat. He weighed no more now than when he had first come here. He rode in a buggy more than on horseback, a concession to rheumy bones, but the fire of ambition still glowed in coffee-brown eyes.

C. C. said, "I reckon Walter sent for you to help him out of his trouble?"

Hewey looked up quickly, surprised. 'Trouble! I never heard about no trouble."

C. C. had the coffee can, carefully holding his fingers high up near the rim where the heat was not enough to blister. The coffee was only a minute or so past a full boil, but he drank it without flinching. He had always been a man in a hurry.

Hewey waited impatiently for an explanation, but C. C. was busy with the coffee. Hewey demanded, "What kind of trouble is he in?"

"Same as all these nester operators . . . money. He's stretched thinner than a cotton shirt in a cold norther. Come fall, I figure he'll have to fold up and quit." C. C. stared quizzically at Hewey. "You sure he didn't send for you?"

"I ain't even heard from him since I left."

C. C. shrugged. "Not much good you'd do him anyway. You won't stay lit in one place long enough to wear out a change of socks." The statement was made matter-of-factly, not in an insulting way.

"I reckon you could help him, C. C., if you was of a mind to."

"I've tried. I offered to buy him out, same as I done with Sam Gentry. Walter ain't goin' to do any good on a little greasy-sack outfit like that. He'll just starve that good woman and them kids of his to death. I told him I had his old foreman's job waitin' for him any time he wants it back. When a man's been as good a cowboy as Walter is, it ought to be a penitentiary offense for him to ever take hold of a plow handle."

"What did he say to the offer?"

Fat Gervin had finally climbed down from the buggy. He put into the conversation, answering for Tarpley. "Said what all them shirttail nesters say, that he'll make it all right. But he won't. Best thing that can happen to this country will be when all them nesters starve out and leave it to people that know how to run it."

Hewey didn't look up at Fat. C. C. Tarpley gave him a sharp glance back over his shoulder, a look that told him to shut the hell up. He turned his attention back to Hewey, closing Fat out of the conversation. As if Fat had said nothing, Tarpley answered Hewey's question. "He said he'll make it."

Hewey frowned at the hot coffee. "But you hope he don't make it?"

"I got nothin' but his best interests at heart. I like Walter Calloway; I always did. I wouldn't do a thing to hurt him."

"But you wouldn't do anything to really help him."

Tarpley's eyes narrowed. "Best help for your brother would be to get him onto a steady job where he could do some good for himself and be of use to somebody else too. I never could understand what a man wants with one of them little old starve-out places."

"You started small, once."

"That was a long time ago. There was room in this country then. Now it's gettin' so crowded up that you can't breathe, hardly. You're apt to run into somebody's house every five or six miles. Nowadays everybody wants somethin' for nothin'. That's what's behind all these homesteaders, a hope they can get somethin' for nothin'. Everybody ought to pay his own way, is how I see it."

C. C. hadn't paid anybody for the use of the land here in his beginning years. Nobody else was claiming it, at least nobody as tough as C. C. It was too far from Austin for the state authorities to come out collecting. By the time they started charging lease, C. C. had had many years of free use and was strong enough financially that he could afford to pay. Even so, he had snorted and raised hell.

Hewey said, "Lots of people—I never was one myself—want to own somethin' even if it's small. They see honor in having a place they can stand on and say, 'This is mine.'"

"There's honor in bein' a Two Cs cowboy, too, if you're a good one." C. C. studied Hewey with keen brown eyes. "I've still got a place for you, too, if you're ready to settle down."

"Still payin' the same wages you used to?" C. C. had always advocated a high sense of morality among his ranch help. Too much money being a threat to that morality, he had seen to it that they were never seriously challenged.

Tarpley frowned. "Times've been a little tight. I've had to cut expenses. But I've always paid a fair wage."

Fair but not good, Hewey thought. He said nothing.

Fat Gervin took that silence as a challenge to C. C.'s generosity. He said righteously, "The man that's payin' the money is the one to say what's fair and what ain't. Trouble with the laborin' class is that it's always askin' for more than it's worth."

Fat had been born into that class, though he had labored little. He had started at the bottom and married up. He stood with his round shoulders back and his belly out, inviting Hewey to contest his studied judgment. To his disgust, Hewey ignored him. As the probable inheritor of the Tarpley power, Fat had tried diligently to copy C. C.'s gruff mannerisms, his toughness, his sureness of self. But he bore no more resemblance to the old man than the reflection in mossy water bears to the battle-scarred stallion.

C. C. turned on him irritably. "Fat, I wisht you'd take and water the horses."

Color flushed the big man's face. He turned and started to lead the horses to the tank, pulling the buggy. Tarpley said, in the same impatient tone he would use against an errant hound, "Unhook them first."

He and Hewey then hunkered in silence, passing the blackened can back and forth, offering none of it to Gervin. A stranger, if told one of them had six thousand cattle and the other had twenty-seven dollars, would have had a hard time deciding which was which. More than likely he would simply have doubted the statement. They were alike in as many ways as they were different. They had come from the same sun-warmed Texas soil. Though they had taken different forks on many roads, their roots gave them a kinship of sorts. They had a respect and a regard for each other that transcended the vast differences in their individual codes, their personal goals and their financial status.

C. C. Tarpley had been orphaned at an early age and cast out on his own in a world where orphans scratched or starved. A few years ago, in an uncharacteristic surge of emotion, he had contributed four hundred dollars toward the building of an orphans' home in Fort Worth. The word had spread and earned him a reputation as a philanthropist among those who did not know him well. Hewey Calloway, who had never owned more of the world's goods than he could tie on a horse, gave freely of whatever he had when he had it. Last fall he had given up a well-earned spree in town before it had fairly begun and contributed his only thirty dollars to a collection for a newly widowed nester woman and her four children. No one ever knew of it except Hewey and a half dozen other cowboys who had volunteered in like manner from their own pinched pockets. Reckoned on a percentage basis, Hewey was by far a more liberal philanthropist than C. C. Tarpley.

C. C. said, "You tell Walter I'd sure like to have him back. I miss him over at the ranch. God, Hewey, you've got no idea how hard it is anymore to find decent help. Just the other day I had to go all the way to Sweetwater to get me two good cowboys."

Remembering what C. C. paid, Hewey was not impressed. But he said a noncommittal, "Well, I'll swun," which C. C. could take for sympathy if he wanted to.

C. C. continued, "I miss that little woman of his too. When Eve was cookin' for the hands I used to like to go by there every so often and debauch myself on her cobbler pie. My wife never could cook worth doodly squat."

On the Two Cs Eve had been expected to cook for the regular bachelor cowboys, plus any extra help, plus any company that happened along. She wasn't paid for it; it was simply part of the honor of being the foreman's wife. That was one reason she had clung so tenaciously to the little homestead, poor as it was. She probably worked as hard or harder there than ever before. But she cooked for her own family and nobody else.

C. C.'s eyes narrowed. "You got an ugly mark across your jaw, Hewey. Fresh, too. Where'd it come from?"

Instinctively Hewey brought his fingers up. The place burned beneath his touch. He didn't look C. C. in the eye. "Horse," he said.

C. C. grunted. "How old are you, Hewey?"

Hewey had to figure; he hadn't thought about it in a while. "Thirty-eight. Thirty-eight the fourteenth day of last February."

Tarpley mused. "You sure ain't no valentine. I'll bet by now you're beginnin' to feel the arthritis settin' in. About time for the gray hair to start takin' over too. And all you've got is a brown horse past his prime, an old saddle and maybe twenty dollars. Ain't much to show for them many years, is it?"

Hewey thought before he answered. "I've left a lot of tracks and seen a lot of country. I've worked down to the border of Old Mexico. Been to Cuba for Uncle Sam. I've worked cows from the San Saba River plumb up to Wyoming and Montana. I even went north once into Canada and seen the glaciers. You ever seen a glacier, C. C.?"

The old man just stared at him. He probably didn't know what a glacier was. "What's it ever got for you?" he demanded. "Them places are too far from here to ever amount to anything. The man who gets ahead is the one who stays put and tends to business, not the one always fidgetin' around to go, like a horse in an antbed. You've seen all of that country, but how much of it do you own?"

Hewey pondered the question. "In a way, I own it all."

Old Tarpley didn't understand that. Hewey had found a long time ago that most people never did.

Paul Patterson

Best Old Feller You Ever Saw

BORN ON A WEST TEXAS RANCH, Paul Patterson spent most of his youth working as a cowboy in the country just east of the Pecos River. After service in World War II and a brief interlude as a disc jockey in Fort Worth, he became a high-school history teacher, settling finally at Crane, where he taught school for a living and wrote humorous tales about the cow country for fun. He is a legitimate humorist with a sharp eye for character and a keen ear for cowboy talk. His characters are authentic and are sometimes given their right names—a fact which makes him a historian as well as a humorist.

From *Pecos Tales*. Austin: Encino Press, 1967. Publications of the Texas Folklore Society, no. 31, pp. 17–18.

Joe Thorp's Daddy owned a little spread and a big family of little kids, all of which he ran out of Mertzon a ways. Even in those days of plenty of cowboys it was hard to get a good man, especially on a little spread. It seems that the good hands all gravitated to the OH Triangle, the Bar S or to where the big happenings were.

The help he managed to pick up were generally no 'count. Always their hands seemed too soft for a crowbar and too stiff for a cow's teat. And these cowboys were generally too hard on horses and too easy on post hole diggers.

Finally, in town old man Thorp picked up a hand, not young. He didn't look like much—shabby, scrawny, and run down at the heel. Old man Thorp worried at first, but as it turned out he had landed him a crackerjack good hand. There wasn't a lazy bone in his body, and, what's more, best old feller you ever saw. Easy on horses and kind to the milk cows, he knew how to take care of a team and could do anything there was to do around a ranch. He could even farm if it came to that. He was as handy inside the house as on the outside—he could cook, wash dishes, and scrub. And it wouldn't have surprised old man Thorp if this good old man had been able to knit.

On top of that the old man didn't use tobacco to excess, didn't cuss, was neat in all his habits, and patient with all the kids, which latter, to old man Thorp, was a miracle in itself. His wants were simple and his needs were few.

"Anything a-tall you might want from town?" was always Mr. Thorp's question when he went in.

"Nope, not a thang," was always the old man's reply.

"They's bound to be somethin' I can get for that good old man," Mr. Thorp repeated to himself one day on the way to town.

Eureka! He believed he had found it. Maybe that good old man might like a little toddy of a morning. That's it! "Never seen a feller yet—even some preachers—as wouldn't take a little nip of toddy of a mornin'. But I'm purt' near afraid to ask that good old man."

But by the time Mr. Thorp had gotten back to the ranch he was positive in his own mind that that good old man wouldn't be offended by his offering.

"Since you never want anythin a-tall for yoreself, I took it upon myself to bring you somethin' as might be good for you. I hope I ain't mistaken," he said, delivering a quart to that good old man.

It wasn't until that good old man had scared the chickens out of thirty days of laying, crippled a milk cow or two and chopped down the gallery posts, that old man Thorp realized he *was* mistaken.

Shortly thereafter Mr. Thorp was flogging it back to town with that quart of whiskey, most of which was surrounded by that good old man—the best old feller you ever saw—nearly.

Frank X. Tolbert

Cowboys: A Bunch of Sissies

DURING HIS LIFETIME Frank Tolbert probably met and enjoyed more people than anyone else in Texas. He reported on them in his column in the *Dallas Morning News* and included some of them in a handful of books which deserve to be reprinted and reread. He was probably best known, however, for his expertise in the uses and delights of chili and for his part in establishing a great Texas institution, the World Championship Chili Cookoff held annually at Terlingua in the Big Bend. Tolbert does not always come across as a humorist although he delights in far-out characters. His approach is usually serious and factual as he reports on incredible events and personages, such as Cap Warren of the Waggoner Ranch.

"Cowboys: A Bunch of Sissies" was first published in *A Bowl of Red*, Garden City: Doubleday, 1966. It is reprinted here from *Tolbert of Texas*, Evelyn Oppenheimer, ed. Fort Worth: Texas Christian University Press, 1986, pp. 292–296.

"Cowboys today is mostly a crowd of sissies."
                                                    —Cap Warren, range cook.

"If you do it right, grinding up them eye-watering peppers and dicing the beef, chili is lots of bother to make on the hind end of a chuck wagon," said Joseph Bailey (Cap) Warren. "Still, during cold weather I whip up a batch of chili about once every few weeks, and these new-style cowboys whine and blubber for it more often."

Cap Warren, a rangeland *cocinero* for more than fifty years, was once described by a rancher who was trying to lure him away from the Waggoner Ranch as "everything a chuck wagon cook ought to be, wrapped up in one snarling package."

When I knew him in the 1950s, Cap Warren was cooking on the

almost ceaseless cattle roundups of the half-million-acre Waggoner Ranch, which sprawls over six counties in northwestern Texas near the Red River and has its headquarters in Vernon.

Once when I was visiting with the Waggoner roundup crew I spent a whole day watching Cap Warren at his routine. The old boy became sort of bored with my presence and asked at the end of the day: "What you bird-dogging me fer?"

That morning, in early spring, Cap Warren arose from his bedroll at the usual time, four o'clock. As usual, he was in a bad humor, and for the usual reason. Mr. Warren had a low opinion of modern cowboys in general and the Waggoner Ranch punchers in particular, and the crew he was cooking for often had to listen to ill-tempered comment.

He was a tall man with the same athletic, 170-pound frame he'd had fifty years before when he quit cowboying to boss the chuck wagon. He hadn't had a haircut since spring roundup had started, and his thick white hair came down to a kind of duckbill in the back, giving him something of the look of an eighteenth-century gentleman with a powdered wig.

His "hood" (pronounced to rhyme with "rude"), or cook's assistant, was absent that morning. Normally the hood would build the cook fires. By lantern light, Cap ignited mesquite chunks in a square iron stove. He ignored me until I asked him how present-day cowhands compared with those he'd known in the old days. He surveyed the Waggoner Ranch riders, asleep in their bedrolls under the tent which also protected the chuck wagon and the portable stove. And he said:

"Cowboys today is mostly a crowd of sissies. In the olden days we could have made camp here with nothing but a wagon and four mules, and my Dutch oven and my frying pans and stewers in a cowhide sling under the rear axle, and fetching the bedrolls in the wagon. Then they et what I gave them and got wet when it rained.

"Now look at this danged camp with this big truck for a chuck wagon, and tons of other machinery, and this here big tent for them hands to sleep under. This don't seem like a cow camp to me. With that tent and all, it seems like we're holding a gospel camp meeting."

The Waggoner Ranch, often called the Three D because that is the cattle brand, has twenty-one divisions, each with a line camp. That morning forty-seven cowboys were to gather cow creatures on a division called The Harts. The tent was pitched on a little rise near a windmill and line camp, actually a dwelling occupied by the line rider's family.

The morning was tolerably windy with promise of a dust storm by midmorning. Off in the lifting darkness were the restless whistling and stamping sounds of the 325-horse remuda being brought in by the wrangler.

"Ain't many left that would make a wart on the hind cheek of a real cowpuncher," continued Cap. "Now, fellow, you stay here and don't slow-trail me. I'll be back in a few minutes." He picked up a lantern and a big butcher knife, and went off to a storage house near the line camp. He came back with a load of steaks, each about two and a half inches thick, which he'd sliced from a freshly killed beef. He had to make another trip before he had enough steaks for breakfast. Cap broiled or fried steaks for every meal after a beef had been butchered on the range.

"If I was cooking for real cowboys, I wouldn't have nothing but beef and bread and coffee this morning. Not with this bunch here, though. They got to have their fruit juices when they get up. And they got the gall to tell the cook how they want their eggs did."

Cap went to work making sourdough biscuits. He baked two big pans of biscuits before each meal. He made them in almost magician-like swiftness.

The Waggoner Ranch has a helicopter for many chores and errands. One of the plane's jobs was to fly over heavy brush and scare wild cattle into the open. This business of herding cattle with a helicopter came to the attention of a national television program and it sent some cameramen to the spring roundup that week. The day before, when Cap was making biscuits, he said one of the cameramen had asked him to pose over his dough with a rolling pin.

"I told that fuddy-grafter I didn't have no more use for a rolling pin than a hog has for a buggy whip. I roll out my biscuits by hand and choke them off into shape in the old style. Just like my mama taught me sixty-odd years ago."

The red truck chuck wagon had many steel compartments in the back of the bed, like those in a modern kitchen. The ingate doors dropped down to make a worktable. Cap could drive a truck, yet had such nostalgia for the old mule-drawn chuck wagons that he refused to be the truck's chauffeur and one of the young cowboys had to move it for him.

In one of the steel compartments he had a crock of yeast at work, the "starter" for his sourdough biscuits. Even when he joked, Cap's unwavering pale blue eyes kept serious. He said: "I got two young bullfrogs in that crock to keep my biscuit yeasts all worked up. Used to have an old bullfrog. But he got tired."

He put on an apron made of two flour sacks before he started broiling the steaks. The iron stove glowed red and took the chill off the air. When the biscuits and the steaks were almost ready, and coffee was boiling in a black pot, the cowboys began waking up, aroused by both the lovely smells and by Cap's whining, complaining baritone.

Cap prided himself on his biscuits, even more than on his proudest entree, son-of-a-bitch stew. He said it was his talent for biscuit making that shoved him, reluctantly he claimed, into a range cook's job back in 1912.

"Before that I was a cowboy and a danged good one. Everyone in that 1912 camp was tired of the old cook's biscuits. Ever' now and again we would find a cigarette butt in a biscuit. And them things baked out so heavy you could have took and th'owed one for over a hundred yards.

"Well it was known in camp that Mama had made me a pretty fair hand at baking. A passel of the boys teased me one morning to make up a couple of pans of biscuits. I done it.

"After that the wagon boss put the old cook back to driving a team. And I haven't been able to get shed of this cooking job since."

Humor of the Minorities

For James Lehrer's "Viva Max"

Texas minorities have contributed surprisingly little to the state's stock of humorous writings. Indians, Germans, Czechs, Swedes, Poles, Irishmen—all these and many more are part of the Texas scene and undoubtedly have their humorists, but their work does not seem to get into general circulation. Only black and Hispanic Texans come clearly into focus, but their humorists are few.

Blacks in the United States have created a special kind of humor based on their difficult situation in a white man's world. Beginning with Uncle Remus, black storytellers enjoyed poking fun at whites and Texan A. W. Eddins does the same in "Austin Wheeler's Dream," as does J. Mason Brewer in a few tales from *The Word on the Brazos*. They were published in the era of the black-face minstrel show, of *The Green Pastures* and *Scarlet Sister Mary*. Elizabeth Lee Wheaton followed the same path with her stereotypes in *Mr. George's Joint* (1941). Her stance would not, of course, be acceptable today. The Civil Rights movement changed all that forever.

The same taboos affected the Mexican-Americans, who demanded and got a respect denied to their forefathers, thereby putting a stop to laughter by and about them. But most of the existing material about Hispanics has been written or collected by Anglos. The Texas Folklore Society, for instance, has published many charming folktales about Hispanics, and the creator of the humorous classic *Viva Max* was James Lehrer, then a Texas newsman. It seemed that the Chicanos had found a humorous voice of their own when Amado Muro of El Paso published his short stories, but when he died in 1973, it was revealed that he was really Chester Seltzer of Ohio. He had altered his wife's name for a pseudonym.

BLACK TEXANS

A. W. Eddins

Austin Wheeler's Dream

A. W. EDDINS was a dedicated teacher in the San Antonio public schools. He loved folk stories and collected them from his black and Hispanic students, publishing them in the early issues of the collections of the Texas Folklore Society. He served as vice-president of the society in 1934 and 1935. Austin Wheeler's story is a fine illustration of the black man's ability to find amusement in the predicament of his race, struggling to survive in a white man's world—and in a white man's hereafter. Uncle Remus could not have done it better.

From "Brazos Bottom Philosophy" in *Southwestern Lore,* J. Frank Dobie, ed., Publications of the Texas Folklore Society, no. 9, 1931 (reprint edition, Hatboro, Pennsylvania: Folklore Associates, Inc., 1965), pp. 160–162.

One of the best carpetbag stories I have ever heard was told about Austin Wheeler, a leading negro politician in Falls County during the days of Reconstruction.

It is said that Austin dreamed he died and went straight up to heaven. Here he found a great city with towering high jasper walls and an immense golden gate which was closely shut and strictly guarded by the great Saint Peter. Recovering somewhat from his astonishment, Austin timidly approached the golden gate and knocked for admission.

From within came the pious voice of Saint Peter, "Who is this that dares to knock on the gates of high heaven?"

Austin, with fear and trembling, answered, "Hit's me, my Lord, Austin Wheeler, er member of de Texas Legislature, en er deacon in the Spring Hill Baptist church."

Saint Peter asked, "Are you mounted, Austin?"

To which Austin replied, "No, my lord, I's erfoot."

Then in solemn tones Saint Peter spoke, "Only mounted gentle-men can pass the portals of these golden gates. You are denied admis-sion."

Further knocking brought no response, and Austin in despair dragged himself over to the shade of some gourd vines and sat down. Presently he saw the governor of Texas approaching the golden gates. Full of confidence, he strode up to the portals and knocked loudly.

"Who is this that dares to knock on the gates of high heaven?" asked the stern voice of Saint Peter.

"It is I, Governor Davis of Texas, a true and tried Republican."

"Are you mounted, Governor?"

"No, my Lord, I am on foot."

"Only mounted men can pass the portals of these golden gates. You are denied admission."

Greatly discouraged when repeated knocking brought no further response, the governor turned and started back to earth. Just then he saw Austin under the gourd vine and hurried up for consolation.

"Austin, this is terrible. To think that we are right at the gates of heaven and can't get in because we have no horses!"

"Hit shore looks dat way, governor. I speck we is gwine ter wait er long time 'fore any hosses comes dis way."

Then the governor had a brilliant idea. "I'll tell how we will man-age, Austin. You be my horse. You get down on your hands and knees, and I will get on your back, and we will go up to the gate and when Saint Peter asks if I am mounted, I will say yes. Then he will tell me to ride in, and we will both be inside."

So Austin got down on his all-fours, the governor got on his back, and they again went up to the golden gate and knocked loudly.

"Who is this that dares to knock on the gates of high Heaven?" asked the stern voice.

"It is I, E. J. Davis, the governor of Texas a true and tried Repub-lican."

"Are you mounted, Governor?"

"Yes, my Lord, I am mounted."

"All right, Governor, just hitch your horse outside there and come in."

J. Mason Brewer

The Preacher and
His Farmer Brother

PREMIER COLLECTOR of Negro folklore in Texas, J. Mason Brewer had
roots deep in the soil of his native state. His grandfather was a freighter
in South Texas; his father was a cowboy. He himself had an aptitude for
languages and became a teacher of French and Spanish, spending most
of his active teaching career at Samuel Huston College, a black school
in Austin. In World War I he served as an interpreter. J. Frank Dobie
saw the manuscript which was published as "Juneteenth" in the Folklore Society's annual volume for 1932 and declared it to be "the best
collection of Negro folk tales to have come out since Uncle Remus."
"The Word on the Brazos" was first presented as a paper before the
Texas Folklore Society in 1934.

From *The Word on the Brazos: Negro Preacher Tales from the Brazos
Bottoms of Texas*. Austin: University of Texas Press, 1953, pp. 9–10.

Of occasion in de Bottoms, in de same fam'ly, you kin fin' some of de
bestes' preachuhs dat done evuh grace a pulpit, an' a brothuh of a sistuh
what ain't nevuh set foot in de chu'ch ez long ez dey live. Ah calls to
min' Revun Jeremiah Sol'mon what pastuh de Baptis' chu'ch down to
Egypt, on Caney Creek. He done put on de armuh of de Lawd when
he rech fo'teen; he come to be a deacon when he rech sixteen, an' dey'
dained'im for to preach de Word when he turnt to be eighteen. He one
of de mos' pow'ful preachuhs dat done evuh grace a Texas pulpit an' he
de moderatuh of de St. John's 'Sociation. But he hab a brothuh, what
go by de name of Sid, what ain't nevuh set foot in a chu'ch house in his
life.

Sid hab a good spot of lan' 'roun' 'bout Falls, on de Brazos, though; so one time Revun Jeremiah 'cide to pay Sid a visit. Hit been twenty yeah since he laid eyes on 'im; so he driv up to de house an' soon ez he gits thoo shakin' han's wid Sid's wife, Lulu Belle, an' de chilluns, he say, "Ah wants to see yo' fawm, Sid. Le's see what kinda fawmuh you is."

"Sho," say Sid. So he gits his hat on an' dey goes down to de cawn patch an' looks at de cawn Sid done planted an' what nelly 'bout grown, an' de Revun say, "Sid, youse got a putty good cawn crop by de he'p of the Lawd." Den dey goes on down to de cotton patch and de Revun looks at hit an' 'low, "Sid youse got a putty good cotton crop by de he'p of de Lawd." Den dey moseys on down to de sugah cane patch an' when de Revun eye dis, he say, "Sid, youse got a putty good cane patch, by de he'p of de Lawd."

An' when he say dis, Sid eye 'im kinda disgusted lack, an' say, "Yeah, but you oughta seed hit when de Lawd had it by Hisse'f."

Elizabeth Lee Wheaton

A Quiet Tuesday Night at Mr. George's Joint

ELIZABETH WHEATON's home territory was Texas City on the Gulf Coast and she was a diligent student of its people and its history. She wrote only two books, however: *Mr. George's Joint* (1941) and *Texas City Remembers* (1968). Her black neighbors and their lives interested her particularly. *Mr. George's Joint* is the story of a black entrepreneur who hopes to recoup his failing fortunes by opening a beer parlor—a rather fancy place for his neighborhood—with hostesses downstairs and gambling upstairs. His family and friends take advantage of him at every turn, however, and he is worse off at the end of the story than he was at the beginning.

Mrs. Wheaton's tale could not be published now. Her candid approach seems patronizing and stereotyped, especially for readers who have arrived on the scene since the Civil Rights movement began. To readers in 1941, however, her vision seemed to be true, sympathetic and amusing.

From *Mr. George's Joint*. New York: E. P. Dutton, 1941, pp. 265–280.

The Big Spoon was devoid of customers. George stood in the front doorway, glumly gazing up the street. Old Man Hall dozed in his chair on the porch. Flo and Magnolia moved about restlessly taking turns playing the phonograph. Annie sat in the front room, where Strong Man puttered about the bar. She seemed deep in thought, but as a matter of fact, she was "restin' her brains."

"Look lak all them pikah folks got their guts full," George said fretfully.

"This a Chuesday night," Annie reminded him. She shifted her weight, leaned back and stuck her stockinged feet out restfully. "Nothin' evah happen Chuesday night."

"Dat so," Strong Man agreed, automatically wiping the bar. "Don't sell off no slew uh nothin' on no Chuesday night, lessn we gots a boat in, uh some mens hits a payday uh sumpn."

It was nearly dark when the first patron arrived, and then it was only Gander. Few of his acquaintances knew that his real name was Andrew Jackson Williams. His nick-name had been bestowed in recognition of his long, lean neck.

George moved aside to let him enter.

"Evenin', Mistah Jawge," Gander grinned.

"Evenin', Gandah," George returned without interest. "Sho Hot."

"Yassuh, sho is," Gander mopped his face with a grimy handkerchief. He sauntered past the bar. "Miss Hall, Strong Man—" he murmured.

"Evenin'," Annie rejoined languidly. "How's you?"

"Hya, Gandah," Strong Man boomed with a friendly wave of his bar rag.

"Po'ly, po'ly," Gander called over his shoulder as he made for Magnolia.

"How 'bout you dancin' a set wid me?" he invited, a broad grin displaying his ugly teeth.

"We bettah git anothah reco'd on the reco'd machine," Magnolia temporized. "Set down an' wait tell that one runnin' play out."

Gander flopped into a chair and wiped his perspiring face again.

"Would you keer fuh sumpn to drink?" Annie called to him from her chair.

"No'm, thank you" he called back politely. "Ah'll jes set, uh else dance, efn Miss Mack-nolia wanna."

"Pass me a nickel fuh the machine, Gandah," Flo demanded, holding out her hand.

"Who gonna dance with Gandah?" Magnolia asked softly.

Flo looked surprised. "You the one he ast!"

"Efn Ah'm the one gonna dance, Ah'm sho gonna pick the reco'd. You allus picks them swingin'-hoppin pieces, an' Gandah ain't no wise limbah-laigged 'nough to dance 'em out."

Gander grinned sheepishly and ran the bandanna between his open shirt collar and his neck in a mopping motion.

"Which one you picks?" Flo asked sourly.

"Ah picks numbah nine."

Flo inserted the coin, pushed the ninth button, and the music blared. Magnolia and Gander danced.

While they were moving to the insinuations of the record, Caesar and Bill stumbled in, holding to each other solicitously. Uncertainly they made their way to a corner table and slumped into seats.

Flo took them two ice-filled glasses without wasting time to inquire what they wanted.

"Seem lak y'all drank a few fum y'all's bottle 'fo' y'all happen in to sip outn ma glasses," George called.

"We has," Bill agreed. "Hic! We rightly has."

"Does y'all want sumpn t'eat?" Flo inquired politely.

"Naw, baby," Caesar chortled. "Set down an' have a lil drink wid us all."

Astonished, Flo backed off, murmuring, "Ah ain't keer fuh nothin'," and departed hastily.

The phonograph stopped and Magnolia led Gander to a table.

"Ah wanna coke," she said. "What you picks to drink?"

Gander shoved his hand into his pocket and hastily counted his coins.

"Ah'll pick a coke, too" he answered.

Magnolia started for the drinks and met Edna, Luerline, and Petunia arriving without escorts. She nodded and eyed them curiously.

"Wheah at's y'all's comp'ny?" George greeted them jovially.

"Bee an' Tookey had to wuk," Edna replied, "an' ma frien' had to take his boss-man's truck to Houston."

"What'll y'all have?" George inquired.

"We seekin' fuh some body to haul us out to La Marque," Edna drawled, "to the Beer Barrel wheah they havin' a beer pahty an' dance." She turned to Magnolia. "Reckon will Fas' Black be in soon?"

"He gonna pass by sometime," Magnolia replied, "but Ah ain't know when."

"Does you wanna go with us all?" Luerline invited.

"No, thank you," Magnolia declined. "Ah ain't keer to go no-wheahs of a Chuesday. Chuesday too qui't fuh me."

Caesar lurched from his chair and reeled toward the girls. He stopped in front of Edna.

"Did Ah heah y'all guls say y'all wanna go out to La Marque an' ain' got no way?" he asked, grinning fatuously.

"Yeah, we wanna go," Edna admitted. "Will you rint us yo' ole piece uh cah to haul ouahse'ves?"

"Ah'll take y'all, free-hearted," Caesar chortled.

"Who gonna drive?"

"Me!" Caesar thumped his chest, staggering under the blow. "Hit ma cah an' Ah's drivin'."

"Ah hopes you ain't think Ah'd go behime yo' drivin'!" Edna sneered. "Drunk as you is now. An' drunk uh sobah, you sho ain't no GOOD drivah."

"Ah kin drive nice," Caesar protested thickly. "You thinks Ah kin drive nice, ain't you, Miss Lu'line?"

"Ah wouldn't go efn you drives," Luerline stated flatly.

Caesar looked injured. "Why not?" he asked in surprise.

"Ah jes ain't pick tonight to die."

"Whyn't you let Edna drive," Petunia suggested, "an' you go 'long an' set in the back?'

Caesar pondered the idea. "Us kin do dat," he agreed affably. "Ah'll let ya'll guls ride in ma cah free, but Ah'll have to pack ma pahdnah wid us all. Kin we carry him?"

"Dat O.K. with y'all?" Petunia asked her companions. "We all kin set in the front an' the mins in the back."

"It'll sho crowd us," Edna replied disdainfully, "but it's O.K. with me."

Caesar gathered his satchel of drinks and the party left.

A stranger staggered in. Arms crossed over his chest protected some treasure. He made his way over the rough floor with careful uncertainty, and sat down at a table. He shifted his burden into his lap and stared fixedly at it.

" 'Fo' Gawd efn that drunk man ain't packin' a kitten!" Annie exclaimed.

"Sho is," Flo agreed. "Now, reckon how he met up with that cat?"

Gingerly, Flo approached but before she got to him, the man's head fell forward on the table. With a frightened yowl, the kitten hopped from his lap and fled through the kitchen into the night.

"Go tote that drunk man out onto the back po'ch an stack him on them sacks," George instructed Strong Man. "Don't look nice to see folks sleepin' 'roun' on the tables an' thin's."

Strong Man gathered the bulky stranger up as if he had been a child and carried him from the room.

As Gander and Magnolia danced again, two more customers arrived, Ancestor Jones and George Washington Bryan. Ancestor was better known as "Duck" because of his dragging gait. His friend George bore the nickname of "Hog Jowl," descriptive of his large, oddly formed lower jaw. Both were in a genial mood. They made straight for the bar.

"Evahbody step up an' have a drink," loudly invited Hog Jowl. "Dis ma buffday, an' Ah gonna treat evahbody."

The women took soda water. Stong Man set beer before the men. Hog Jowl scowled at the amber-filled bottles, waved his hand airily.

"Ain't keer fuh none uh dat belly wash," he sneered. Pulling a pint bottle of whiskey from his pants pocket, he offered it to George. "Heah, Mistah Jawge, have a right drink."

George eyed the bottle with misgiving.

"That nice whiskey, Hawg Jow'" he declined politely, "but Ah ain't drink no strong drinks."

"You wrong, Mistah Jawge," Hog Jowl contradicted him pleasantly. "Dis cheap whiskey what sting yo' froat, but hit de kin' Ah wants whin Ah cel'brates. Ah laks to feel hit all de way down."

He took a long draught from the bottle, coughed; then smacked his thick lips appreciatively. He handed the bottle to Duck. Duck took a drink, coughed convulsively and passed the bottle back to Hog Jowl, who offered it to Strong Man.

"Ah thanks you, Hawg Jow'," Strong Man declined smiling. "Ah ain't nevah drink nothin' no mo'n pop."

Hog Jowl again offered the bottle to George.

"G'wan, take a lil drink," he urged. "One lil drink ain't gonna kill you. G'wan! Hit'll sho hu't me efn you ain't drink to ma buffday."

Reluctantly, George upended the bottle and took a swallow. He choked and a startled look came into his eyes. Hastily, he handed the bottle back to its owner. Hog Jowl fondled the bottle a moment then put it to his lips again. George sighed with relief as he saw the last of the liquor disappear down Hog Jowl's thick throat. Hog Jowl dropped it into his garbage can, then hastily wiped the bar. To George's horror, Hog Jowl produced a second bottle of the same cheap whiskey. He opened it expertly, moved to a near-by table and sat down, depositing the bottle before him.

"Come an' set down at dis table wid me an' let's y'all an' me git rightly drunk," Hog Jowl invited George and Duck.

Duck accepted with alacrity.

"C'mon, Mistah Jawge," Hog Jowl urged. "You ain't too good to drink a lil mo' wid me."

George accepted a seat at the table. Hog Jowl was a good patron. George could hardly afford to affront him by refusing to drink with him on his birthday.

Within a short time, the three had disposed of the second bottle. Hog Jowl produced a third. George shuddered. His eyes felt heavy and prone to wander independently. The room seemed to tilt and move around in quick shifts. George felt he had better sit still.

"You take one sip offn dis new bottle, Mistah Jawge, an' den me an' Duck gonna ma'ch on," Hog Jowl said expansively, handing George the newly opened bottle.

George felt his stomach heave, but he took the bottle, gulped a small drink, and unsteadily handed the bottle back to its owner.

"Ah's sho gonna prowl dis night," Hog Jowl proclaimed, rising to his feet. He slipped the bottle into his hip pocket, produced a razor and teetered precariously. "Evahbody Ah ain't lak bettah be in dey holes!" He waved the razor to emphasize his last remark. He slapped a pocket. "Heah a whole payday to take keer uh ma fine. C'mon, Duck, we gonna make tracks fuh somewheahs else."

As soon as they had left, George got to his feet uncertainly. He felt he was going to be sick. He lurched out through the kitchen and into the fresh evening air.

Maxie Bremer came in for a bottle of beer. Maxie was about half Mexican, with almost straight hair, an extremely light color and an arrogant air. It was rumored that he was quite a success with women;

rumor connected his name with that of Pressa, Hog Jowl's attractive wife.

"How you, Mistah Maxie?" Strong Man asked affably.

"O.K.," Maxie returned. "Pack me a bottle uh beer an' set an' talk wid me."

Maxie took a table near a window. Strong Man brought the beer and put it down in front of Maxie.

"Set down," Maxie repeated, handing Strong Man a dime.

"Ah ain't know efn Ah bettah," Strong Man said uneasily, glancing about and peering through the window into the darkness.

"Why?"

"Well—uh—ah—" Strong Man floundered.

"What you tryin' to tell me?"

"Mout be you'd oughta know. Hawg Jow' say he on de prowl, an' he packon' his razah an' full uh bad whiskey, an' he say anybody he ain't lak bettah be in dey holes."

Maxie set his bottle down and got up hastily.

"Wh-wh-which way he wint?"

Strong Man waved vaguely in the direction of the front door, and shrugged.

"D-d-don't y'all s-s-speak an' say Ah b-b-been heah," Maxie stuttered. "Ah'm g-g-goin' 'head on home. Efn he c-c-cut me, he g-g-gotta come to ma s-s-shack to do hit!"

He quitted the place hastily. Strong Man held his booming laugh until Maxie was well out of earshot.

"Ain't you a sight!" Annie chuckled admiringly. "How come you to think up that cute lil joke to play on Maxie?"

Stong Man shrugged modestly. "Hit jes come natchel to me. Ma pappy a big jokah, an' Ah notice how he done."

"Maxie ain't gonna close eye one this night," Annie laughed. "He think Hawg Jow' know all 'bout him an' Pressa, an' Ah bet he ain't even 'spicion 'em. Somebody oughta pull his coat 'bout that Pressa, but Ah sho ain't."

"Hawg Jow' got that bright gul in Galv'ston his ownse'f," Magnolia contributed. "Long Pressa keep his house clean an' his cloes wash an' his sumpn t'eat cook up, he ain't keer what she do with huh odd time."

Annie and Strong Man were still chuckling over Maxie's fright when Dick entered with a deep scowl on his yellow face.

"What the mattah with you, Dick?" Annie inquired, smiling.

"Ah's rightly hot," Dick spluttered.

"How come?"

"You knows dat O.B. tol' me an' you she gonna keep ma rum clean an' ma cloes wash jes fuh sleepin' in de flo' in ma rum?" Dick's voice shrilled with anger. It carried to May Lou in the kitchen, and she shuffled in to share in the excitement.

"Yeah?" Annie prompted, no longer smiling.

"Dat saddle-cullah slut ain't nevah tetch broom one to de flo', 'scusin' washin, ma cloes!"

"Ah knows Dick speakin' true, Miss Annie," May Lou put in. "Ah wint in he rum de yuthah mawnin' to let down de windahs whin de rain come up, an' you could rake feathahs fum unnah de baid. Dey mus' been fum de pillahs, sense de mattruss cotton."

"Yeah, an' Ah's damn tiahed uh huh layin' on ma daity flo'," Dick fumed. "Ah wants huh flang out, else Ah's gonna move."

"Whyn't you tell huh nice to git outn yo' rum?" Annie suggested.

"Ah did!" Dick snorted. "Ah tol' huh twict nice an' puhlite to git huh damn daity se'f outn ma rum, an' she ain't did hit. Efn you ain't git huh out, den Ah'll jes git me a rum somewheahs else, lak Ah say."

"O.K.," Annie sighed, rising. "Ah'll git huh out." She turned to May Lou. "Lou, in the mawnin', hop on ovah an' git Dick's rum clean up nice."

"Yassum, Miss Annie," May Lou grinned, as Dick and Annie left to oust the unwelcome parasite.

Before long, Annie returned.

"Git huh out?" May Lou inquired, smiling broadly.

"You knows Ah did! She sho a odd somebody, though."

"Ah jes sets an' looks at huh," Magnolia remarked. "A great big, strappin' nothin' with no chilluns uh nobody, an' what she makin' of huhse'f?"

"She sho triflin'," Annie agreed. "She sho slosh on the puhfumy to keep huhse'f sweetened up."

"She bettah of," Magnolia sneered. "She sho smell goatish. She smell wuss'n Lou do."

"She so dawg-lazy she won't wash up behime huh ownse'f whin she finish eatin'," May Lou sniffed, "less'n Ah tells huh."

A few customers drifted in and sat, spending little. The staff moved about desultorily. Fast Black came in and Magnolia led him to a table in one corner. She took him a bottle of beer, and sat down to talk with him while he drank it.

Black Bird and Flossie wandered in. Black Bird put a nickel into the phonograph and they danced. They were still dancing when Buckey Boy and Shorty entered. From the doorway, Buckey Boy called loudly to Flossie. She smiled at him over Black Bird's shoulder. Black Bird swung her around and scowled at Buckey Boy. Unabashed, Buckey Boy sauntered up and tapped Black Bird on the shoulder as a signal he was cutting in.

"Go 'long," Black Bird snarled up at the big fellow. "She ain't gonna dance wid you on ma nickel."

"O.K.," Buckey Boy grinned amiably, "den Ah'll sheve in a nickel an' dance de nes set."

"Buckey Boy bettah min' out how he meddle Black Bud's gul," Fast Black told Magnolia. "He been had dat same Flossie sense he come heah, an' he study cuttin' some man she roll huh big eyes at. Buckey oughta know dat by now."

"Buckey Boy so stout maybe he ain't studyin' no knife," Magnolia suggested.

"Efn he aint he kin learn lak Bill Jennin's did," Fast Black grinned. "Bill still packin' a scah what Black Bud whittle on his face, an' will tell he die."

When the music stopped, Buckey Boy put a nickel in the slot and punched a number. He held out his arms to Flossie. She floated toward him, but Black Bird's stiffened left arm stopped her. Black Bird's right hand was thrust deep in his trousers pocket.

"She ain't dancin' wid you, Buckey," Black Bird grated warningly.

"Sho she is," Buckey said easily, grinning broadly as he jerked the willing girl to him and started dancing.

Swiftly, Black Bird's hand came out of his pocket and he stepped in between the dancing pair, thrusting his weight against Buckey Boy, staggering him. Light glinted from a blade as Black Bird's arm whipped around. Black Bird stepped back, crouching slightly. Razor ready to slash again, he watched Buckey Boy warily. Flossie screamed. Blood was pouring from Buckey Boy's abdomen, over his trousers and spattering onto the floor. The horrified onlookers stared in frozen silence.

Buckey Boy gazed mutely at the razor; then looked down at the widening pool of blood on the floor. He patted his broad stomach gently, exploratorily, and raised his hand. It dripped blood. He viewed it with horror, his eyes widening in slow comprehension.

"Black Bud done kilt me!" he cried hoarsely. He staggered toward the door, clutching his abdomen with both hands. "Git de amberlanch! Ah gotta git to de hawspital! Git de Laws!"

Pandemonium broke loose. Flossie screamed again and sat down weakly. Shouts and confusion filled the Big Spoon. Chairs overturned as some of the few customers left unceremoniously. Shorty hurried to Buckey Boy's side.

"Set down in a cheah, Buckey," he advised, shoving his friend gently into a chair. He grabbed a paper napkin and dabbed ineffectually at the flowing blood.

Only Black Bird seemed calmly indifferent. A sneer on his face, he straightened up, pulled a handkerchief from his pocket and wiped his razor. He returned the handkerchief to one pocket and the razor to another. With exaggerated unconcern, he watched the excited group around Buckey Boy.

"Who gots a cah?" Shorty cried excitedly. "We gotta git him to de hawspital!"

"Fast Black edged away, pulling Magnolia with him. "Not in ma cah! Ah ain't gonna let Buckey dreen all dat blood on ma upholst'y."

Annie hurried to the door and looked out.

"They got a cah pahked in the front uh Bella's place," she called excitedly. "Look lak Randolph's cah, an' he study leave the keys in it. Whyn't y'all borrah it?"

"Catch a-holt uh me, Buckey," Shorty commanded. "Ah'll carry you to de hawspital in Randolph's cah."

Moving weakly, Buckey Boy staggered out, Shorty manfully trying to hold him upright.

Black Bird grabbed Flossie by the arm and jerked her to her feet.

"C'mon," he growled. "Ah's gonna carry you on home. You done staht 'nough trouble fuh one night, wid yo' womanish ways."

In a surprisingly short time, May Lou had cleaned up the blood and Annie and Strong Man had straightened the chairs. Only a damp spot on the floor remained as evidence of the excitement. Flo put a slug into the phonograph. Music and the hum of conversation filled the air.

An hour later, Shorty returned, pale and breathless. he rushed to the table where Fast Black and Magnolia sat talking.

"Buckey sho cut bad," he gasped, "an' Ah come to git you to ma'ch up to de hawspital an' spare Buckey some blood."

Fast Black's face turned a greenish gray.

"Me!" he exclaimed through quivering lips. "Me? Why, Ah can't spare Buckey no blood!"

"How come not?" Shorty asked, crestfallen.

Fast Black tried to marshal his slow wits.

"Uh—" he walled his eyes toward Magnolia, mutely beseeching her support, "well—uh—ah—you gotta have good, strong blood to give it to somebody—"

"Yo's is good an' strong, ain't hit?"

"Hit sho ain't! Ma bloods rightly weak. An' on top uh dat, ma bloods plumb bad. Mines is got de t.b.'s into hit, an' a lot uh yuthah stuff th'owed in."

"Healfy as you looks, Ah bet dey ain't thin' one de mattah wid yo' bloods," Shorty protested. "You had dem shots at de CCC camp an' at de Tran, too, an' Ah bet you got 'bout de stronges' blood in dis town."

Fast Black threw off the shock of Shorty's proposal and announced with firmness, "Ah tells you dry an' straight Ah ain't goin'. He yo' main frien'; you de one to ma'ch back an' lingah 'roun' dat hawspital an' spare him yo' bloods. Ah ain't no special fien' uh hisn' so dey ain't no call fuh me to strain an' spare him no bloods."

Wildly, Shorty looked around the room for a courageous friend. Averted eyes denied concern. Shorty shuffled out into the night, bowed with despair.

It was nearly midnight when Violet Williams and Waldo Horner came in. They were quarreling, with complete disregard for listeners. They chose a table by the door. Annie took their orders for two bottles of beer. They ignored her when she brought the beer, and they ignored the beer. Their voices grew louder. They screamed picturesque invectives at each other. A hush fell over the other tables. Everyone in the place watched and listened with amused curiosity. Suddenly, Violet reached across the table and gave Waldo's cheek a resounding smack with her open hand.

"Don't you call me no bitches an' thin's!" she shrieked.

Waldo rose, grabbed her by one arm and dragged her, screaming and clawing, outdoors. Heavy blows and more screams sounded. Then came silence.

A few minutes later, Violet returned behind a white policeman. Her clothes were in shreds. Two of her front teeth were missing.

"Where's George?" the policeman demanded.

"He—uh—ah—out in the back," Annie faltered.

"Get him for me," the officer ordered.

"Yassuh."

Annie sighed as she got to her feet and left the room. She paused in the kitchen.

"That lil busy Law in theah, astin' fuh Jawge," she muttered crossly to May Lou, "an' him drunk as he was when he lef', Ah knows he settin' out in the lavato'y tryin' to git sobahed up. Wheah that long knife? Ah gotta retch thu the crack in the doo' an' unlatch that hook an' feesh Jawgre out. That busy Law want to ast him a million ques'ons him uh nobody else can't ansah, but that's how them lil busy laws is."

"Heah de knife you uses, Miss Annie." May Lou handed her a long butcher knife.

"Efn it was Cap'n Wall," Annie muttered disgustedly, "he wouldn't say wo'd one 'bout that Vi'let. He done tol' huh he hope somebody whup huh down. But this lil busy Law ain't know she study tollin' off some woman's husban' an' ain't got no right to hop to the Laws."

"Yassum," May Lou yawned. "Vi'let sho a case."

Annie went out the back door. A few minutes later she returned with George. He walked uncertainly, holding tightly to his wife's fat arm. In the presence of the officer, he braced himself, blinking owlishly.

"How you, suh? Kin Ah help you?"

"What do you know about these fights?" the white man demanded, notebook in hand.

George shook his head to clear it. His wavering gaze rested on Violet's battered countenance.

"What fights you speakin' 'bout?" he asked, bewildered.

"Good Gawd! What fights? Don't try to tell me you don't know! A nigger in the hospital from getting cut here, I run into this woman on the way down to see about the cutting scrape, and you ask me what fights!"

"He ain't know nothin' 'bout 'em," Annie put in glibly. "He out in the back, sleepin' in the lavato'y."

"That's a hell of a place to sleep!"

"Yassuh," George agreed.

"Who does know something about that cutting?"

"Buckey?" Annie's voice was bland. "Ain't none us seen it, but he did say Black Bud cut him. Black Bud a nice boy. He'll be down in the mawnin' to pay his lil fine lak he allus do."

"Fine, hell! We got that nigger in jail. Looks like Buckey Boy might kick off."

"Say it do?" Annie's eyes rolled in alarm. "Ain't none us all seen nothin'!"

"How many of these niggers were in here when it happened?" he asked, with a wave of his hand toward the group then present.

Annie looked around the room and back at the officer.

"Ah ain't remembah none of 'em."

"You were here, weren't you?"

"Well—uh—ah—yassuh, but Ah ain't seen nothin'."

"These girls that work for you, what are their names?"

"Ain't none of them seen it. They was all in the kitchen."

"What are their names?"

"This Flo White, an' this Mack-nolia Beavah, an' May Lou Otman, in the kitchen, an' O.B.—wheah that lazy O.B.? Ah ain't know the las' paht uh huh name."

From table to table the officer went, asking questions of the few remaining patrons, writing down their names. At last he returned to George and Annie.

"What about this other fight?"

"Huh?" Annie pointed to Violet. "Ah ain't seen it neithah. Waldo step out with Vi'let an' we heah some hollerin', but we ain't able to ma'ch out in the streets an' dip into othah folkses' business, so we ain't to say know nothin' about it."

"You don't know anything about it?" the policeman asked George.

"Nawsuh." George grinned foolishly.

"Do you know where Waldo is?" the officer asked Violet.

The girl shook her head.

"I guess that's all, then," he told Violet. "Go on home; I'll look around and see if I can find him. Think you're able to make it?" he asked, viewing the girl's closing eyes.

"Yassuh," she mumbled, without conviction.

George watched them leave, then started for the stairs.

"It neah 'bout closin' time," Strong Man remarked. "Ah thinks Ah'll go 'head on home. Ah ain't sol' hahdly nothin'. Dis sho been a quit' night."

"Chuesdays mos'ly is," Annie yawned. "Onless we lucks up on a bunch of sailahs uh sumpn."

Bill Porterfield

Juneteenth with Sassmouth

THE TEXAS OIL FIELDS provided Bill Porterfield with his earliest recollections. His father was a rough-neck who went where there was
work, and his son came to know Texas from the bottom up. After
college he became a Houston journalist and worked for twenty-five
years as a reporter before he became a columnist for the *Dallas Times-
Herald*. In his column he continued reporting on the people he knew
best—the ones who have not made it—but his approach was upbeat
and cheerful. He left the vice and grime and misery for others to expose.

Porterfield could be called a sympathetic realist and is really not a
humorist at all, but sometimes he becomes one in spite of himself, as in
his account of the Juneteenth celebration on Dobie Creek presided over
by Jesse "Sassmouth" Cree.

From *Texas Rhapsody*. New York: Holt, Rinehart and Winston,
1971, pp. 55–59.

W e all knew that Deacon Sassmouth Jesse Cree wasn't old enough to
have been a slave, but one of the reasons we white kids slipped off and
crashed the big Juneteenth doin's down on Dobie Creek was to see
Sassmouth in all his black splendor and hear him tell of slavery days.

He was always the star of the festivities, he and his wife Corinna.
In fact, they always staged the holiday, and while they were careful to
start it out in the afternoon on a high sober note with appropriate
speeches by black leaders and one or two liberal white dignitaries, their
natural exuberance would start poking through the straitlaces along
about dark, and then the old campgrounds would rock and sway till the
wee hours.

For years I thought this annual root and toot to emancipation was exclusive to the blacks in Little Egypt, a kind of commemorative flare they sent up out of their own proud genius. If its origins proved to be as broad as Texas, it was no more a comedown to me than the realization that Sassmouth's stories were larger and older than his own experiences.

The Crees would print up handbills and distribute them throughout Froggy Bottom. The invitation was irresistible:

> Wear you dress above your knees
> And strut you stuff with who you please
> Juneteenth Picnic
> at
> Sassmouth and Corinna Cree's
> Dobie Creek Campground
> "Where the Living Dance and the Dead Lie."

The last allusion was to the departed members of Deacon Cree's congregation, who did indeed lie buried just a few yards away. Sassmouth was as nervy as his name. He played musical chairs with the furniture of heaven and hell, and everyone loved it.

Sassmouth would clear away the watermelon leftovers and get up on a picnic table. He would take off his black coat, loosen his tie, and hold you in the wonder of his tongue for as long as he wanted.

"Now you talk about hard times. I have had hard times. I started plowing at eight years old. I was barefooted as a duck. And I used to work in the tobacco patch catching worms off leaves. Marster would come behind me, and if he would find a worm I would have to bite off its head. I remember my sister broke old Marster's clock. He tied a rope round her neck and whipped her I don't know how long. There stood my father, and he could do nothing. But I seen the clod put on Marse after freedom come. We all knew that the children of Israel was four hundred years under bondage and God looked down and seen their suffering and brought them out, and that he would do the same for us. I am no mathematician, no biologist, neither grammarian. Like the song say,

> White man goes to college,
> Negro to the field,
> White man learn to read an' write
> Negro learn to steal.

But when it comes to handling the Bible, I knocks down verbs, breaks up prepositions, and jumps over adjectives. I am a God-sent man. All the education I got, it was out in the fields. The blade of my hoe was my pen, and my slate was the ground. Now the law says, 'Black and white shan't mix.' Who made that law? They made it. I made a law with my hoe, that all weeds must die that I hit . . ."

He would pause, for a long time, until it was so quiet you could hear minnows in Dobie Creek.

"One day I was in the public square when I met my old master. I had not seen him for nearly thirty years. He said to me,

'Jesse, do you remember me lacerating your back?'

'Yes,' I said.

'Have you forgiven me?'

'Yes, Mars,' I said, 'I have forgiven you.'

He held out his hand to me and said, 'Jesse come to see me and I will treat you nice. I'm sorry for what I did.'

I said, 'That's all right, Marster, I done left the past behind me.'

I had felt the power of God and had tasted his love, and this had killed all the hate in my heart."

Sometimes Sassmouth would tell stories for us kids. My favorite was the one about the snail, which he told in dialect.

"'What's the slowest thing you ever saw?'

'A snail was crossin' de road for seven years. Jus as he got across, a tree fell and barely missed him 'bout an inch or two. If he had been where he was six months before, it would er kilt him. De snail looked back at de tree and tole de people, 'See, it pay to be fast.'"

I need to explain something here. I have a good memory, but not total recall. I couldn't remember the particulars of everything Sassmouth said, since I was a kid the last time I heard him. But I was lucky. Twenty years later, I came across sermons and songs in Alan Lomax's *Folk Songs of North America* that were dead ringers of Sassmouth's palaver, making it possible for me to fill in the parts I had forgotten. Obviously, these traveler's tales had come down in an oral tradition that touched many a black American, and Sassmouth, inventive as he was, was happy to carry on the tradition. Fortunately for us, collectors like Lomax, J. Mason Brewer, O. S. Egypt, Charles S. Johnson, J. Masuoks, and Paul Radin came along to record that which might have been lost.

But what about Corinna Cree? Well, you'd have to see her to believe her. She couldn't have been a third of Sassmouth's age. She was so good looking it made you hurt to look at her, even if you were just a little kid and shy at being white. Every year they elected her June-teenth Queen. Everyone said she wouldn't be Sassmouth's woman past morning, that he couldn't hold her. But they lived together so long she was even old when he died.

And I'm sure, as Sassmouth would have put it, that they'll rejoice at the big Juneteenth in the sky. He always said he was fixed, pre-fixed, bought at the lamb sale, caught up in the election, and bound for glory. Hallelujah!

HISPANIC TEXANS

James Lehrer

General Max Takes the Alamo

THE HERO OF JIM LEHRER'S extraordinary novel *Viva Max* is a super-
patriotic Mexican general, Maximilian Rodríguez de Santos, commander of the Mexican garrison at Nuevo Laredo. He marches his
hundred soldiers to San Antonio and reclaims the Alamo for Mexico.
He could not have done it without the unwilling assistance of the San
Antonio police, the National Guard, the Texas Rangers and the United
States Army under General Barney LaComber, head of the Joint Chiefs
of Staff. Each organization wants to take charge, and as a result, no one
does. Max successfully withstands all attempts to oust him and finally
comes out a winner with the help of the presidents of the United States
and Mexico.

When the book was published in 1966, it did not get the attention
it deserved. When it was made into a moving picture in 1969, it got
more than it wanted. The Daughters of the Republic of Texas, who
came off badly in the book, succeeded in keeping the cast out of the
Alamo, but the picture was finally finished and released with Peter
Ustinov in the role of Max.

The last act of this hilarious drama begins with the arrival of "the
Chief" (LBJ) at Randolph Air Force Base, ready to invade the Alamo
by helicopter.

Lehrer is a Texas newsman and writer who migrated to the East
and became the co-anchor of the "McNeil-Lehrer News Hour."

From *Viva Max*. New York: Duell, Sloan & Pearce, 1966, pp.
192–197, 203–209.

R andolph Air Force Base just north of San Antonio was sealed off to
the press and the public, and no one but a few attending Air Force
personnel observed the landing of Air Force One at 2:33 P.M. News-

men, clustered beside the base's front gate, caught only a glimpse in the distance of the huge jet plane as it roared in.

The next thing they saw was the tiny speck of a helicopter taking off and disappearing into the sky toward downtown San Antonio.

Ten minutes later the olive-drab Army helicopter, with the blue-and-white Presidential seal on the side, appeared from the north bearing toward The Alamo. Everybody knew now who was in it, but nobody knew what he had in mind.

The chopper, roaring and bucking, now hovered high above the trees of The Alamo courtyard as a half-anxious, half-amused nation sat in front of their television sets watching.

Maximilian Rodríguez de Santos and his legion were also watching. Thinking the helicopter was the first wave of an extensive invasion by air, Max quickly ordered the men to their battle stations. The craft circled and hovered and tossed about overhead. It was apparent that the pilot was searching for a spot to land right in The Alamo courtyard!

There was only one possible place, near the tall cottonwood in the center of the back courtyard. Max saw this immediately and it was here that he stationed his antiaircraft force.

The helicopter finally began a slow descent through the trees and out of sight of the television cameras and the viewing nation.

It gradually came closer. Max's men, poised and ready, stood in a circle around the landing area.

Every third man held a water hose. Pointed skyward.

Closer. The roar of the engines. The wind force of the rotors blew leaves off the trees.

The Nuevo Laredo Garrison, Army of Mexico, tensed for combat. Max, their leader, turned to the men on the faucets. He raised his right arm.

The attack aircraft was twenty-five feet overhead, the pilot precariously nursing it downward as he tried to miss trees on one side and the tree on which the Mexican flag proudly waved on the other.

"*Tirar!*" Max screamed once again as he dropped his arm.

And for the second time in one day water was turned on an American invasion force.

The gushers splashed and popped over the helicopter. Water got caught in the rotating propeller blades and the plane looked like a monstrous lawn sprinkler spraying water over the courtyard.

The pilot shot the helicopter back up and out of water range.

The President was beside himself.

"Goddamn it! Goddamn it!" he screamed at the two Secret Service men in the passenger compartment with him. They were his only companions. "Why didn't some idiot think to have the water turned off in there?"

The two agents looked concerned, upset, as all Secret Service men do, but said nothing.

The Chief grabbed the telephone intercom to the helicopter pilot. "Go back down, there, damn it!"

"But, sir, I can't see when that water's all over the fuselage."

"Did you hear me?"

"Yes sir, but I'm concerned for your safety."

"You'd better start worrying about your own if you don't get this thing back down there. Those Mexicans don't know who is in this damned chopper or they wouldn't be doing this."

The helicopter glided back down into firing range and the water bombarded it again.

The Chief was furious. Over the protests of the two Secret Service men, he angrily threw open the door on the left side of the compartment and stuck his head out.

"Hey, you bastards . . . it's *me!* Goddamn it, turn off the water! It's me! You can't do this to me! I'm tellin—"

At that second a steady flow of water shot right into the Chief's face.

Max, who had thought this was a regular invasion force, now realized who his visitor was. He couldn't hear what the President was saying over the roar of the engine and the splash of water, but he did recognize him. Max was astounded.

"*Basta!*" he shouted, and the hoses went dry.

Unopposed, the helicopter now dropped the final twenty feet, scraping one palm tree and then pulling away into the cottonwood as it beat the rotor blade and hit the ground with a safe but jarring thud.

Max stood in awe as the rotors whined and circled slowly until they were still. A tall man clambered out of the cabin door. Max called his men to attention and ordered a salute.

Now Max stepped forward as the President, the two Secret Service men trotting behind, moved toward him. Max offered his hand.

In a quick move, the two agents stepped between Max and their leader.

"Goddamn it," said The Chief, pushing the two men aside. "Look around you. Your type of protection is out right now."

In a circle, soldiers of the Nuevo Laredo Garrison stood now with their rifles and hoses at the ready. All weapons were pointed in the direction of the President's party.

Confused, the two Secret Service men stepped farther aside, and Max and The Chief shook hands.

"Sorry if the hand's a bit wet, General. Your boys really let me have it."

Max felt true shame. Not only was this great man's hand wet, so was his shirt, his hair and his entire person. He was drenched.

"Please forgive us, your Excellency," Max said. "We had no idea who was aboard the plane. If we can step inside, I will have some dry clothes prepared."

Max was paralyzed by this entire turn of events. In his pre-invasion planning he thought that he had taken every possible eventuality into account. Everything but this. He never dreamed that the President would personally intervene. Now, as he stood there looking up at this tall man who was wringing wet, smiling and yet still awesome, General Maximilian Rodriguez de Santos, Army of Mexico, didn't know what to do next.

The Chief, a handkerchief in his hand, was wiping his brow and his head and mopping around his neck beneath his limp shirt collar.

"OK, General, don't you think it's time we talked this thing over—like reasonable men. I've come a long way . . . ."

Max nodded. He still couldn't think of anything to say. He was, in fact, still standing at rigid attention.

"Is there some place around here where we can talk—privately?" The Chief asked, looking around the courtyard. As he did, he spotted the captured men of the first invasion force, huddling under guard in a far corner. The Chief waved and grinned, but said nothing.

"Yes, sir. Oh yes, sir. We can go into the building there and talk while you change clothes."

"Never mind the clothes."

"Yes, sir."

"How about over there?" The Chief pointed toward the small gardener's shack where Max and Paula had sat and talked the night before.

"That will be fine, your Excellency."

"Call me Chief, General. Everyone else does."

"Yes, sir. Yes, sir, Chief."

The two men moved toward the shack, and the Secret Service men, operating by reflex, crowded in on either side of The Chief. "Goddamn it," he said. "Go help the pilot fix that damned airplane—do something. You're outnumbered, boys. Get lost."

The agents fell back, and Max and The Chief walked to the shack. They closed the door behind them. The two Secret Service men and five of Max's men, under the command of Sergeant Valdez, immediately took up positions in front of the door.

Five minutes passed. The looks of concern on the two agents' faces turned to deep, but controlled, panic.

One of the agents put an ear to the door. Sergeant Valdez moved up and pulled him away. The agent was angry, but remembering his situation, did nothing.

There was an uneasy silence for the next ten minutes. Valdez and the five Mexican soldiers, their rifles at the ready position, stood in careful, quiet watch over the two grim Americans.

When twenty minutes had passed, one of the agents held a whispered conversation with the other and suddenly knocked on the door. It happened so fast, Valdez' men were unable to prevent it.

The Chief opened the door.

"Is everything all right, sir?" asked the agent.

"Damn it, son, leave me alone. Sure, everything's all right. We're talking about the best way to barbecue a goat right now." He slammed the door shut.

It was another thirty-five minutes before the door opened again and Max and The Chief, chatting and laughing amiably, emerged. The Chief had one long arm around the shoulders of the smaller man and gestured broadly with the other as the two walked without explanation in the direction of the main Alamo building.

☆ ☆ ☆ ☆

The huge front gates of the Alamo slowly opened as the television cameras bore in. Ambulances were parked all along the side streets nearby on orders from the Red Cross. A standby helicopter had been keeping its motor warm as it waited in the middle of Houston Street on the north side of Woolworth's. Barney LaComber and the four companies of Laramie's National Guardsmen came to tense attention. Nobody on the outside knew what was coming, what had happened to The Chief—anything. The President's orders were for nobody to do anything until they heard from him. They hadn't heard anything and they hadn't done anything but wait during the hours that had passed since the helicopter disappeared behind The Alamo walls.

Hattie Longstreet Daniel was the first one out of the door. Following her at a brisk pace were the twenty-five American males who had spent forty-eight hours as prisoners of General Maximilian Rodríguez de Santos. Their trousers were wrinkled, and those wearing white shirts appeared particularly ruffled and dirty. Paula White brought up the rear.

Mrs. Polly Manley and her DTR sisters spied Hattie right off. "Hi, Hattie!" "Here we are, Hattie!" "We're proud of you, girl!" They swished their signs back and forth and sang, "For She's a Jolly Good Fellow."

Two minutes later Capt. Bob Harris, commander of B Company, 36th National Guard Division, walked out through the wooden door. He was bareheaded, his boots were muddy, and his hair was strung out in all directions. His green fatigues were still dark wet in spots, and where they had dried they looked as if they had been through several desert wars. He was not smiling.

The guardsmen, all of them in much the same state of appearance, slopped out behind the captain. Harris locked eyes with General LaComber, who had a just-wait-till-I-get-my-hands-on-you stare for the young company commander.

"A sadder bunch of soldiers I don't think has been seen anywhere," commented the CBS man to his national TV audience.

"Defeated, embarrassed, humiliated-those are the only words to describe the facial expressions of these men," said NBC.

"It seems unlikely that any of these National Guardsmen will be in any mood for any 'How was it at the front?' jokes any time soon," quipped ABC.

A fleet of six-by-six trucks pulled up in front of the Alamo, and the guardsmen were hustled aboard by regular soldiers from Fort Sam Houston wearing MP brassards on their sleeves.

Then, as if someone had given a signal, Alamo Plaza was filled with a loud whispering: "The Mexicans."

The other guardsmen standing by in front of Woolworth's turned to each other and smiled, winked, or frowned. Mrs. Manley's girls chattered anxiously among themselves. And various other groups who stood inside doorways, and on corners in and about the area began buzzing excitedly.

☆ ☆ ☆ ☆

Without warning, two columns of soldiers came marching out the wooden door. The plaza fell silent. Max's Legion, wearing green helmet liners and carrying rifles at right shoulder arms, hammered their heels against the stone-slabbed Alamo entranceway, two abreast, in perfect cadence.

The only noise heard was the clicking of heels and voices calling cadence in Spanish.

"*Un, dos, tres, cuatr'* —*un, dos, tres, cuatr'*—*un, dos, tres, cuatr'*—"

Suddenly a voice rang out, "*Columna a la izquierda—marchen!*"

The column cut a square military corner and proceeded parallel to the walls in front of The Alamo.

Another command was barked, and the column marked time, their heels clamping down on the sidewalk in unison.

While millions watched on television, the men of the Nuevo Laredo Garrison, Army of Mexico, formed a solid, perfectly dressed formation in front of The Alamo.

A soldier wearing several stripes on his sleeve strode out in front. It was Sergeant Valdez.

"*Alto!*" he yelled to his arch-backed soldiers. Not one missed his command. They stopped marching with the loud crash of their last step. Whop!

A scraping noise and another sharp crack of heels.

The Mexicans were now facing to the front at rigid attention.

Ten seconds passed. It seemed like one hundred and ten.

Then there was a silence-shattering blast from a bugle!

And then the clop-clop of a horse's hooves on the stone.

Pepe, her head high and tossed back proudly, appeared around the troops' right flank. Washed and scrubbed down by Moreno, her white coat glistened in the sun as she raised her hooves up and down like a show horse.

The President of the United States, the President of the Republic of Mexico, and Maximilian Rodríguez de Santos, holding the bridle, walked in front of the horse.

The Chief had one arm around Max's shoulders. The Mexican President was on his other side.

Together they approached the front rank of the Nuevo Laredo Garrison. Barney LaComber, uncertain as to what was going on, marched out gingerly to meet the trio.

They stopped face to face in the exact center of the plaza.

"Hi there, Barney," The Chief said. "I'd like for you to meet a fellow army man—General de Santos. General, this is Barney."

LaComber shook Max's hand, and, as an afterthought, the two exchanged salutes. Barney did it all with a frown. Max with a smile. There was also a quick introduction to the President of Mexico.

"OK, Chief, do I put the general under arrest now—take the rest of his soldiers prisoners? I'll give the word . . . ."

The Chief started to scowl and then grinned through clenched teeth as he remembered the television cameras trained on the group.

"No, you stupid bastard!" he said, slapping LaComber on the back—hard. "You don't do that! Just get those TV boys to get some microphones down here. All three networks. I want to make an announcement. The President and the General here and I do."

LaComber blinked. Then he turned to summon the microphones.

"We've got a few military geniuses in our country, too, General," The Chief reassured Max sarcastically. "Don't let them worry you too much. Just keep the water turned on . . . ."

"Look out!" somebody yelled.

LaComber turned to block Mrs. Polly Manley running toward them at full steam. She was headed right for Max, swinging her sign like a club and yelling. "You've desecrated our Alamo! You Red! You beast! Murderer! You're crazy!"

She slipped out of LaComber's hands spinning like a halfback, and he had all he could do to restrain her again, dodging her swinging sign as best he could.

With the rest of the membership of the Alamo Chapter of the Daughters of the Texas Revolution cheering her on from the sidelines, Polly then turned on the President.

"You sympathizer! Don't give him that deed! He's a Communist! How can you stand there like that with him?"

Screaming further insults, flaying her arms and kicking savagely, Polly Manley was transferred to the custody of a colonel and a brigadier general and escorted off the battlefield.

Max watched the elderly woman and the U.S. Army general in their nationally televised skirmish.

"It is interesting that she would accuse *me* of insanity," he said softly as Polly aimed one last glare at him.

"We've got some real emotional women in our country, General," The Chief assured Max. "Don't pay them no mind."

"If I find out who let those goddamn women in here in the first place, I'll have him court-martialed," LaComber muttered to The Chief as he picked up his helmet liner, knocked off during the scuffle, and called again for the microphones.

☆ ☆ ☆ ☆

A TV engineer yelled, "Ready!" and pointed toward The Chief and Max.

The Chief cleared his throat. He smiled.

His head tilted up toward the cameras on the top of Woolworth's. His remarks were to be directed to the cameras and thus to the nation—not to the throng of people in the immediate area.

"To all of you—my fellow Americans—within the sound and the sight of my voice and lips, I am happy to say that this incident is at its conclusion. General de Santos, the President of Mexico and I—" The cameras zoomed in on Max's face to give viewers a close-up of the little man who had defied the power of their country. They saw only the side of his head, however, for he was looking up admiringly at The Chief.

"—have knelt together and sought our God for a solution to this problem. He spoke to us—each of us—and we listened—"

To the television viewers—millions of them throughout the country—a tear became visible in The Chief's eye.

"—He told us that to settle differences with arms, with anger is wrong. He told us He did not want this to continue. He told us to seek peaceful solutions to conflicts that exist between peaceful men."

The Chief looked down again at Max, and the cameras again got only the tilted side view of Max's face.

"The people of the United States and Mexico are peaceful men. General de Santos, the President and I are peaceful men."

He paused.

"We listened when our God spoke to us there a minute ago within the walls of this great and sacred place, The Alamo—"

Another pause.

"—So we go from here now arm and arm, friend and friend, brother and brother, peaceful men having found a peaceful solution—"

A sober frown.

"—We leave this sacred ground, where many have died before us, both Mexicans and Americans, because our forefathers could not or would not do what we do here today—"

A smile grew full of warmth, kindness.

"—We leave here now, General de Santos, his men, the President of Mexico and I . . . there will be no more anger, only peace."

The two men, the tall one and the short one, gazed at one another for a full five seconds as the cameras held for a close-up.

Then the other President joined them and they walked away together toward Woolworth's.

Amado Muro

Cecilia Rosas

AMADO MURO, prize-winning short-story writer, focused his best work on *Chihuahuita* (Little Chihuahua), a poor but proud section of South El Paso on the border at the tail end of Texas. At the time of his death in 1973, Chicano critics were hailing him as the coming Mexican-American writer. Ironically, he was *puro gringo,* an American from Cleveland, Ohio, where his father was a prominent newspaper publisher. His name was Chester Seltzer, but when he married Amada Muro in El Paso, she provided him with a pen name. Unconventional and rebellious, he became a wanderer after imprisonment as a conscientious objector in World War II and made a precarious living as a sailor, newsman, field hand, and hobo. His heart was with his wife and son in El Paso, however, and with the Hispanic-Americans he came to know and love. He invented a Mexican background for himself and wrote industriously about it, presenting his Latinos with sympathy, understanding and gentle humor.

From *The Collected Stories of Amado Muro*. Austin: Thorp Springs Press, 1979, pp. 70–83.

When I was in the ninth grade at Bowie High School in El Paso, I got a job hanging up women's coats at La Feria Department Store on Saturdays. It wasn't hard . . . only boring. Wearing a smock, I stood around the Ladies' Wear Department all day long waiting for women customers to finish trying on coats so I could hang them up.

Having to wear a smock was worse than the work itself. It was an agonizing ordeal. To me it was a loathsome stigma of unmanly toil that made an already degrading job even more so. The work itself I looked on as onerous and effeminate for a boy from a family of miners, shepherds, and ditchdiggers. But working in Ladies' Wear had two compensations: earning three dollars every Saturday was one; being close to the Señorita Cecilia Rosas was the other.

This alluring young woman, the most beautiful I had ever seen, more than made up for my mollycoddle labor and the smock that symbolized it. My chances of looking at her were almost limitless. And like a good Mexican, I made the most of them. But I was only too painfully aware that I wasn't the only one who thought this saleslady gorgeous.

La Feria had water fountains on every one of its eight floors. But men liked best the one on the floor where Miss Rosas worked. So they made special trips to Ladies' Wear all day long to drink water and look at her.

Since I was only fourteen and in love for the first time, I looked at her more chastely than most. The way her romantic lashes fringed her obsidian eyes was especially enthralling to me. Then, too, I never tired of admiring her shining raven hair, her Cupid's-bow lips, the warmth of her gleaming white smile. Her rich olive skin was almost as dark as mine. Sometimes she wore a San Juan rose in her hair. When she did, she looked so very lovely I forgot all about what La Feria was paying me to do and stood gaping at her instead. My admiration was decorous but complete. I admired her hourglass figure as well as her wonderfully radiant face.

Other men admired her too. They inspected her from the water fountain. Some stared at her boldly, watching her trimly rhythmic hips sway. Others, less frank and open, gazed furtively at her swelling bosom or her shapely calves. Their effrontery made me indignant. I, too, looked at these details of Miss Rosas. But I prided myself on doing so more romantically, far more poetically than they did, with much more love than desire.

Then, too, Miss Rosas was the friendliest as well as the most beautiful saleslady in Ladies' Wear. But the other salesladies, Mexican girls all, didn't like her. She was so nice to them all they were hard put to justify their dislike. They couldn't very well admit they disliked her because she was pretty. So they all said she was haughty and imperious. Their claim was partly true. Her beauty was Miss Rosas' only obvious vanity. But she had still another. She prided herself on being more American than Mexican because she was born in El Paso. And she did her best to act, dress, and talk the way Americans do. She hated to speak Spanish, disliked her Mexican name. She called herself Cecile Roses instead of Cecilia Rosas. This made the other salesladies smile derisively. They named her La Americana or the Gringa from Xochimilco every time they mentioned her name.

Looking at this beautiful girl was more important than money to me. It was my greatest compensation for doing work I hated. She was so lovely that a glance at her sweetly expressive face was enough to make me forget my shame at wearing a smock and my dislike for my job with its eternal waiting around.

Miss Rosas was an exemplary saleslady. She could be frivolous, serious or demure, primly efficient too, molding herself to each customer's personality. Her voice matched her exotically mysterious eyes. It was the richest, the softest I had ever heard. Her husky whisper, gentle as a rain breeze, was like a tender caress. Hearing it made me want to dream and I did. Romantic thoughts burgeoned up in my work so that the floor manager, Joe Apple, warned me to show some enthusiasm for it or else suffer the consequences.

But my dreams sapped my will to struggle, making me oblivious to admonitions. I had neither the desire nor the energy to respond to Joe Apple's warnings. Looking at Miss Rosas used up so much of my energy that I had little left for my work. Miss Rosas was twenty, much too old for me, everyone said, but what everyone said didn't matter. So I soldiered on the job and watched her, entranced by her beauty, her grace. While I watched I dreamed of being a hero. It hurt me to have her see me doing menial work. But there was no escape from it. I needed that job to stay in school. So more and more I took refuge in dreams.

When I had watched her as much, if not more, than I safely could do without attracting the attention of other alert Mexican salesladies, I slipped out of Ladies' Wear and walked up the stairs to the top floor. There I sat on a window ledge smoking Faro cigarettes, looking down at the city's canyons and best of all, thinking about Miss Rosas and myself.

They say Chihuahua Mexicans are good at dreaming because the mountains are so gigantic and the horizons so vast in Mexico's biggest state that men don't think pygmy thoughts there. I was no exception.

Lolling on the ledge, I became what I wanted to be. And what I wanted to be was a handsome American Miss Rosas could love and marry. The dreams I dreamed were imaginative masterpieces, or so I thought. They transcended the insipid realities of a casual relationship making it vibrantly thrilling and infinitely more romantic. They transformed me from a colorless Mexican boy who put women's coats away into the debonair American, handsome, dashing and worldly, that I longed to be for her sake. For the first time in my life I revelled in the magic of fantasy. It brought happiness. Reality didn't.

But my window ledge reveries left me bewildered and shaken. They had a narcotic quality. The more thrillingly romantic fantasies I created, the more I needed to create. It got so I couldn't get enough dreaming time in Ladies' Wear. My kind of dreaming demanded disciplined concentration. And there was just too much hubbub, too much gossiping, too many coats to be put away there.

So I spent less time in Ladies' Wear. My flights to the window ledge became more recklessly frequent. Sometimes I got tired sitting there. When I did, I took the freight elevator down to the street floor and brazenly walked out of the store without so much as punching a time clock. Walking the streets quickened my imagination, gave form and color to my thoughts. It made my brain glow with impossible hopes that seemed incredibly easy to realize. So absorbed was I in thoughts of Miss Rosas and myself that I bumped into Americans, apologizing mechanically in Spanish instead of English, and wandered down South El Paso Street like a somnambulist, without really seeing its street vendors, cafes and arcades, tattoo shops, and shooting galleries at all.

But if there was confusion in these walks there was some serenity too. Something good did come from the dreams that prompted them. I found I could tramp the streets with a newly won tranquillity, no longer troubled by, or even aware of, girls in tight skirts, overflowing blouses, and drop stitch stockings. My love for Miss Rosas was my shield against the furtive thoughts and indiscriminate desires that had made me so uneasy for a year or more before I met her.

Then, too, because of her, I no longer looked at the pictures of voluptuous women in the *Vea* and *Vodevil* magazines at Zamora's newsstand. The piquant thoughts Mexicans call *malos deseos* were gone from my mind. I no longer thought about women as I did before I fell in love with Miss Rosas. Instead, I thought about a woman, only one. This clear-cut objective and the serenity that went with it made me understand something of one of the nicest things about love.

I treasured the walks, the window-ledge sittings, and the dreams that I had then. I clung to them just as long as I could. Drab realities closed in on me chokingly just as soon as I gave them up. My future was a time clock with an American Mister telling me what to do and this I knew only too well. A career as an ice-dock laborer stretched ahead of me. Better said, it dangled over me like a Veracruz machete. My uncle Rodolfo Avitia, a straw boss on the ice docks, was already training me for it. Every night he took me to the mile-long docks overhanging the Southern Pacific freight yards. There he handed me tongs and made me practice tripping three-hundred-pound ice blocks so I could learn how to unload an entire boxcar of ice blocks myself.

Thinking of this bleak future drove me back into my fantasies, made me want to prolong them forever. My imagination was taxed to the breaking point by the heavy strain I put on it.

I thought about every word Miss Rosas had ever said to me, making myself believe she looked at me with unmistakable tenderness when she said them. When she said: "Amado, please hang up this fur coat," I found special meaning in her tone. It was as though she had said: "Amadito, I love you."

When she gave these orders, I pushed into action like a man blazing with a desire to perform epically heroic feats. At such times I felt capable of putting away not one but a thousand fur coats, and would have done so joyously.

Sometimes on the street I caught myself murmuring: "Cecilia, *linda amorcita,* I love you." When these surges swept over me, I walked down empty streets so I could whisper: *"Cecilia, te quiero con toda mi alma"* as much as I wanted to and mumble everything else that I felt. And so I emptied my heart on the streets and window ledge while women's coats piled up in Ladies' Wear.

But my absences didn't go unnoticed. Once an executive looking man, portly, gray, and efficiently brusque, confronted me while I sat on the window ledge with a Faro cigarette pasted to my lips, a cloud of tobacco smoke hanging over my head, and many perfumed dreams inside it. He had a no-nonsense approach that jibed with his austere mien. He asked me what my name was, jotted down my work number, and went off to make a report on what he called "sordid malingering."

Other reports followed this. Gruff warnings, stern admonitions, and blustery tirades developed from them. They came from both major and minor executives. These I was already inured to. They didn't matter anyway. My condition was far too advanced, already much too complex to be cleared up by mere lectures, fatherly or otherwise. All the threats and rebukes in the world couldn't have made me give up my window-ledge reveries or kept me from roaming city streets with Cecilia Rosas' name on my lips like a prayer.

The reports merely made me more cunning, more doggedly determined to city-slick La Feria out of work hours I owed it. The net result was that I timed my absences more precisely and contrived better lies to explain them. Sometimes I went to the men's room and looked at myself in the mirror for as long as ten minutes at a time. Such self-studies filled me with gloom. The mirror reflected an ordinary Mexican face, more homely than comely. Only my hair gave me hope. It was thick and wavy, deserving a better face to go with it. So I did the best I could with what I had, and combed it over my temples in ringlets just like the poets back in my hometown of Parral, Chihuahua, used to do.

My inefficiency, my dreams, my general lassitude could have gone on indefinitely, it seemed. My life at the store wavered between bright hope and leaden despair, unrelieved by Miss Rosas' acceptance or rejection of me. Then one day something happened that almost made my overstrained heart stop beating.

It happened on the day Miss Rosas stood behind me while I put a fur coat away. Her heady perfume, the fragrance of her warm healthy body, made me feel faint. She was so close to me I thought about putting my hands around her lissome waist and hugging her as hard as I could. But thoughts of subsequent disgrace deterred me, so instead of hugging her I smiled wanly and asked her in Spanish how she was feeling.

"Amado, speak English," she told me. "And pronounce the words slowly and carefully so you won't sound like a country Mexican."

Then she looked at me in a way that made me the happiest employee who ever punched La Feria's time clock.

"Amadito," she whispered the way I had always dreamed she would.

"Yes, Señorita Cecilia," I said expectantly.

Her smile was warmly intimate. "Amadito, when are you going to take me to the movies?" she asked.

Other salesladies watched us, all smiling. They made me so nervous I couldn't answer.

"Amadito, You haven't answered me," Miss Rosas said teasingly. "Either you're bashful as a village sweetheart or else you don't like me at all."

In voluble Spanish, I quickly assured her the latter wasn't the case. I was just getting ready to say "Señorita Cecilia, I more than like you, I love you" when she frowned and told me to speak English. So I slowed down and tried to smooth out my ruffled thoughts.

"Señorita Cecilia," I said. "I'd love to take you to the movies any time."

Miss Rosas smiled and patted my cheek, "Will you buy me popcorn?" she said.

I nodded, putting my hand against the imprint her warm palm had left on my face.

"And hold my hand?"

I said "yes" so enthusiastically it made her laugh. Other salesladies laughed too. Dazed and numb with happiness, I watched Miss Rosas walk away. How proud and confident she was, how wholesomely clean and feminine. Other salesladies were looking at me and laughing.

Miss Sandoval came over to me. *"Ay papacito,"* she said. "With women you're the divine tortilla."

Miss de la Rosa came over too. "When you take the Americana to the movies, remember not to speak Christian," she said. "And be sure you wear the pants that don't have any patches on them."

What they said made me blush and wonder how they knew what we had been talking about. Miss Arroyo came over to join them. So did Miss Torres.

"Amado, remember women are weak and men aren't made of sweet bread," Miss Arroyo said.

This embarrassed me but it wasn't altogether unpleasant. Miss Sandoval winked at Miss de la Rosa, then looked back at me.

"Don't go too fast with the Americana, Amado," she said. "Remember the procession is long and the candles are small."

They laughed and slapped me on the back. They all wanted to know when I was going to take Miss Rosas to the movies. "She didn't say," I blurted out without thinking.

This brought another burst of laughter. It drove me back up to the window ledge where I got out my package of Faros and thought about the wonderful thing that had happened. But I was too nervous to stay there. So I went to the men's room and looked at myself in the mirror again, wondering why Miss Rosas liked me so well. The mirror made it brutally clear that my looks hadn't influenced her. So it must have been something else, perhaps character. But that didn't seem likely either. Joe Apple had told me I didn't have much of that. And other store officials had bulwarked his opinion. Still, I had seen homely men walking the streets of El Paso's Little Chihuahua quarter with beautiful Mexican women and no one could explain that either. Anyway it was time for another walk. So I took one.

This time I trudged through Little Chihuahua, where both Miss Rosas and I lived. Little Chihuahua looked different to me that day. It was a broken-down Mexican quarter honeycombed with tenements, Mom and Pop groceries, herb shops, cafes, and spindly salt-cedar trees; with howling children running its streets and old Mexican revolutionaries sunning themselves on its curbs like iguanas. But on that clear frosty day it was the world's most romantic place because Cecilia Rosas lived there.

While walking, I reasoned that Miss Rosas might want to go dancing after the movies. So I went to Professor Toribio Ortega's dance studio and made arrangements to take my first lesson. Some neighborhood boys saw me when I came out. They bawled "*Mariquita*" and made flutteringly effeminate motions, all vulgar if not obscene. It didn't matter. On my lunch hour I went back and took my first lesson anyway. Professor Ortega danced with me. Softened by weeks of dreaming, I went limp in his arms imagining he was Miss Rosas.

The rest of the day was the same as many others before it. As usual I spent most of it stealing glances at Miss Rosas and slipping up to the window ledge. She looked busy, efficient, not like a woman in love. Her many other admirers trooped to the water fountain to look at the way her black silk dress fitted her curves. Their profane admiration made me scowl even more than I did usually at such times.

When the day's work was done, I plodded home from the store just as dreamily as I had gone to it. Since I had no one else to confide in, I invited my oldest sister, Dulce Nombre de Maria, to go to the movies with me. They were showing Jorge Negrete and Maria Felix in *El Rapto* at the Colon Theater. It was a romantic movie, just the kind I wanted to see.

After it was over, I bought Dulce Nombre *churros* and hot *champurrado* at the Golden Taco Cafe. And I told my sister all about what had happened to me. She looked at me thoughtfully, then combed my hair with her fingertips as though trying to soothe me. "Manito," she said, softly. "I wouldn't . . ." Then she looked away and shrugged her shoulders.

On Monday I borrowed three dollars from my Uncle Rodolfo without telling him what it was for. Miss Rosas hadn't told me what night she wanted me to take her to the movies. But the way she had looked at me made me think that almost any night would do. So I decided on Friday. Waiting for it to come was hard. But I had to keep my mind occupied. So I went to Zamora's newsstand to get the Alma Nortena songbook. Poring through it for the most romantic song I could find, I decided on *La Cecilia*.

All week long I practiced singing it on my way to school and in the shower after basketball practice with the Little Chihuahua Tigers at the Sagrado Corazon gym. But, except for singing this song, I tried not to speak Spanish at all. At home I made my mother mad by saying in English, "Please pass the sugar."

My mother looked at me as though she couldn't believe what she had heard. Since my Uncle Rodolfo couldn't say anything more than "Hello" and "goodbye" in English, he couldn't tell what I had said. So my sister Consuelo did.

"May the Dark Virgin with the benign look make this boy well enough to speak Christian again," my mother whispered.

This I refused to do. I went on speaking English even though my mother and uncle didn't understand it. This shocked my sisters as well.

When they asked me to explain my behavior, I parroted Miss Rosas, saying, "We're living in the United States now."

My rebellion against being a Mexican created an uproar. Such conduct was unorthodox, if not scandalous, in a neighborhood where names like Burgiaga, Rodriguez, and Castillo predominated. But it wasn't only the Spanish language that I lashed out against.

"Mother, why do we always have to eat *sopa, frijoles, refritos, mondongo,* and *pozole?*" I complained. "Can't we ever eat roast beef or ham and eggs like Americans do?"

My mother didn't speak to me for two days after that. My Uncle Rodolfo grimaced and mumbled something about renegade Mexicans who want to eat ham and eggs even though the Montes Packing Company turned out the best *chorizo* this side of Toluca. My sister Consuelo giggled and called me a Rio Grande Irishman, an American Mister, a gringo, and a *bolillo.* Dulce Nombre looked at me worriedly.

Life at home was almost intolerable. Cruel jokes and mocking laughter made it so. I moped around looking sad as a day without bread. My sister Consuelo suggested I go to the courthouse and change my name to Beloved Wall which is English for Amado Moro. My mother didn't agree. "If *Nuestro Señor* had meant for Amadito to be an American he would have given him a name like Smeeth or Jonesy," she said. My family was unsympathetic. With a family like mine how could I ever hope to become an American and win Miss Rosas?

Friday came at last. I put on my only suit, slicked my hair down with liquid vaseline, and doused myself with Dulce Nombre's perfume.

"Amado's going to serenade that pretty girl everyone calls La Americana," my sister Consuelo told my mother and uncle when I sat down to eat. "Then he's going to take her to the movies."

This made my uncle laugh and my mother scowl.

"*Que pantalones tiene* (what nerve that boy's got)," my uncle said, "to serenade a twenty-year old woman."

"La Americana," my mother said derisively. "That one's Mexican as *pulque* cured with celery."

They made me so nervous I forgot to take off my cap when I sat down to eat.

"Amado, take off your cap," my mother said. You're not in La Lagunilla Market."

My uncle frowned. "All this boy thinks about is kissing girls," he said gruffly.

"But my boy's never kissed one," my mother said proudly.

My sister Consuelo laughed. "That's because they won't let him," she said.

This wasn't true. But I couldn't say so in front of my mother. I had already kissed Emalina Uribe from Porfirio Díaz Street not once but twice. Both times I'd kissed her in a darkened doorway less than a block from her home. But the kisses were over so soon we hardly had time to enjoy them. This was because Ema was afraid her big brother, the husky one nicknamed Toro, would see us. But if we'd had more time it would have been better, I knew.

Along about six o'clock the three musicians who called themselves the Mariachis of Tecalitlán came by and whistled for me, just as they had said the would. They never looked better than they did on that night. They had on black and silver charro uniforms and big, black Zapata sombreros.

My mother shook her head when she saw them. "Son, who ever heard of serenading a girl at six o'clock in the evening," she said. "When your father had the mariachis sing for me it was always two o'clock in the morning—the only proper time for a six-song *gallo*."

But I got out my Ramirez guitar anyway. I put on my cap and rushed out to give the mariachis the money without even kissing my mother's hand or waiting for her to bless me. Then we headed for Miss Rosas' home. Some boys and girls I knew were out in the street. This made me uncomfortable. They looked at me wonderingly as I led the mariachi band to Miss Rosas' home.

A block away from Miss Rosas' home I could see her father, a grizzled veteran who fought for Pancho Villa, sitting on the curb reading the Juarez newspaper, *El Fronterizo*.

The sight of him made me slow down for a moment. But I got back in stride when I saw Miss Rosas herself.

She smiled and waved at me. "Hello, Amadito," she said.

"Hello, Señorita Cecilia," I said.

She looked at the mariachis, then back at me.

"Ay, Amado, you're going to serenade your girl," she said. I didn't reply right away. Then when I was getting ready to say "Señorita

Cecilia, I came to serenade you," I saw the American man sitting in the sports roadster at the curb.

Miss Rosas turned to him. "I'll be right there, Johnny," she said.

She patted my cheek. "I've got to run now, Amado," she said "Have a real nice time, darling."

I looked at her silken legs as she got into the car. Everything had happened so fast I was dazed. Broken dreams made my head spin. The contrast between myself and the poised American in the sports roadster was so cruel it made me wince.

She was happy with him. That was obvious. She was smiling and laughing, looking forward to a good time. Why had she asked me to take her to the movies if she already had a boyfriend? Then I remembered how the other salesladies had laughed, how I had wondered why they were laughing when they couldn't even hear what we were saying. And I realized it had all been a joke; everyone had known it but me. Neither Miss Rosas nor the other salesladies had ever dreamed I would think she was serious about wanting me to take her to the movies.

The American and Miss Rosas drove off. Gloomy thoughts oppressed me. They made me want to cry. To get rid of them I thought of going to one of the "bad death" cantinas in Juarez where tequila starts fights and knives finish them—to one of the cantinas where the panders, whom Mexicans call *burros,* stand outside shouting "It's just like Paris, only not so many people" was where I wanted to go. There I could forget her in Jalisco-state style with mariachis, tequila, and night-life women. Then I remembered I was so young that night-life women would shun me and *cantineros* wouldn't serve me tequila.

So I thought some more. Emalina Uribe was the only other alternative. If we went over to Porfirio Díaz Street and serenaded her I could go back to being a Mexican again. She was just as Mexican as I was, Mexican as *chicharrones.* I thought about smiling, freckle-faced Ema.

Ema wasn't like the Americana at all. She wore wash dresses that fitted loosely and even ate the *melcocha* candies Mexicans liked so well on the street. On Sundays she wore a Zamora shawl to church and her mother wouldn't let her use lipstick or let her put on high heels.

But with a brother like Toro who didn't like me anyway, such a serenade might be more dangerous than romantic. Besides that, my faith in my looks, my character, or whatever it was that made women fall in love with men, was so undermined I could already picture her getting into a car with a handsome American just like Miss Rosas had done.

The Mariachis of Tecalitlán were getting impatient. They had been paid to sing six songs and they wanted to sing them. But they were all sympathetic. None of them laughed at me.

"Amado, don't look sad as I did the day I learned I'd never be a millionaire," the mariachi captain said, putting his arm around me. "If not that girl, then another."

But without Miss Rosas there was no one we could sing *La Cecilia* to. The street seemed bleak and empty now that she was gone. And I didn't want to serenade Ema Uribe even though she hadn't been faith-less as Miss Rosas had been, but only lack of opportunity would keep her from getting into a car with an American, I reasoned cynically.

Just about then Miss Rosas' father looked up from his newspaper. He asked the mariachis if they knew how to sing *Cananea Jail*. They told him they did. Then they looked at me. I thought it over for a moment. Then I nodded and started strumming the bass strings of my guitar. What had happened made it only too plain I could never trust Miss Rosas again. So we serenaded her father instead.

Politics and Politicians

For Lloyd E. Price's "Hanging Was Good Enough For My Father"

It may be something in the air or in the water, but Texas has always been a fertile field for growing politicians—local, state, and national. Alex Sweet paid his respects to them a hundred years ago and columnists, commentators, and novelists have been doing it ever since. Where would you find better subjects for fiction than John Garner, Pa Ferguson, or LBJ? Where would the humorist find anything more bizarre than the antics of the Texas legislature? Serious consideration of Texas politics in fiction took a long step forward with the publication of Robert Rylee's *The Ring and the Cross* in 1947 and reached a plateau with Al Dewlen's *The Session* in 1981. The man who got most of the attention between these dates was, naturally, Lyndon Johnson. He was bitterly attacked by such good haters as J. Evetts Haley (*A Texan Looks at Lyndon,* 1964) and Francis Rosenwald (*A Big Man in Saludas,* 1962) but other writers were more kind. William Brammer in *The Gay Place* (1961) and Larry L. King in *The One-Eyed Man* (1966), while admitting LBJ's crudeness and double dealing, give him credit for real political wisdom and the ability to get things done. Everybody has memories of Johnson. Cactus Pryor used to plan entertainment for him, with comical results, and Larry L. King has bitter-sweet memories of service as an LBJ factotum in Washington. What all this teaches us is that Texas is not about to run out of politicians, and Texas political humorists will not run out of material.

Lloyd E. Price

Hanging Was Good Enough for My Father

And It's Good Enough for Me

FORT WORTH LAWYER LLOYD E. PRICE served in the Texas legislature
and made a hobby of collecting stories about lawyers and lawmakers. In
the following anecdote he is doubly fortunate in his subject—a lawyer
in the legislature.

From "Anecdotes about Lawyers," in *Backwoods to Border*. Dallas:
University Press [Southern Methodist University], 1943. Publications
of the Texas Folklore Society no. 21, pp. 214–215.

W hen Pat Neff was governor of Texas and when the Nation, under
President Harding, was doing its best to return to normalcy, there was
introduced in the Texas Legislature by a member from Dallas a bill to
abolish hanging at the various county seats and to centralize capital
punishment at the penitentiary at Huntsville.

The author of the bill, an intelligent and progressive lawmaker,
had done a great deal of work on it. He had, prior to his election, made
the abolition of hanging a campaign issue and after election, in keeping
with his promise, he made an exhaustive study of capital punishment in
all modern countries, wrote his bill and on reaching Austin promptly
introduced it and had it set down as a special order so that it might
receive prompt and careful consideration.

Before the bill was reached for action, all members had been furnished copies and since the membership had determined that the mea-

sure was a step in the right direction, it was not anticipated that there would be any debate on it, and it was assumed that it would be enacted without much ado. In the nature of things hanging is a disagreeable topic at best, and it was plain that the members wanted to pass the act as quickly as possible and go on to more pleasant subjects.

When the time for consideration arrived and the author from Dallas arose to explain his bill there was a profound and solemn stillness in the House of Representatives. The author was dressed in white and wore a cluster of white carnations in his coat lapel. At first he spoke in low tones, while a sort of funeral atmosphere pervaded the House; as he progressed his voice trembled with emotion, and at times it rose to a passionate appeal. He explained that humane and civilized places like Switzerland and Kansas had abolished hanging and had substituted electrocution. He insisted that hanging was a barbarous and obsolete custom and should no longer be tolerated in a great State like Texas. He recounted some ghastly hanging incidents like the one in Fort Worth when the head of the man being hanged was actually pulled loose from his body before the bulging eyes of the horrified spectators. By now most of the members leaned forward in gloomy silence, anxious for the speaker to quit so they could enact the law and get away from such a sad and dismal subject. As the author sat down, the lawmakers reached for their voting machine buttons.

But at this point a large, deep-voiced member from South Texas gained the floor. He was a conservative lawyer of good ability who by nature and training opposed most all legislative innovations, fads, and fashions, and he opposed on principle every measure that might bring about more concentration of governmental power. He frequently asserted that the principles and laws of the Founding Fathers should be preserved. Before the surprised representatives he then spoke against the electrocution bill and argued for the retention of old-fashioned hanging. The lone opponent of the pending bill was dressed in a black broadcloth suit; he wore a standing collar with white lawn tie—the sort that is worn once or twice and then thrown away like a used picnic paper plate. His resonant voice rose and fell in undulating rhythm, while at intervals he ran his fingers through his black hair that fell in ringlets over his ears. It must not be understood that the Judge was merely staging a show—far from it. He was sincere and spoke with genuine feeling. His speech was substantially as follows:

"Mr. Speaker and Gentlemen of the House:

"I had not thought that I would say anything with reference to this bill, but I feel that I would not be true to my own sentiments or to the wishes of the constituency whom I have the honor to represent, if I did not raise my voice against this iniquitous measure."

At this point a witty young lawyer and ex-aviator from Cooke County, who was always looking for fun, sat down just in front of the Judge and cupped both his ears so as not to miss a word.

The orator continued, "Mr. Speaker, and gentlemen of the House, one of the great evils of this country today is that all the attractions in the country are gradually being moved and centralized in the cities, so that with nothing left to entertain them the country boys and girls are flocking in droves to the attractive cities, where, like moths, they are singeing their wings on the gay white lights. My friends, this measure is not progressive; on the contrary, it is unnatural and abnormal. I, for one, still believe that the people in this country have rights which ought not to be snatched from them by legislative enactment. Why, Mr. Speaker, one of the few attractions now left in the country is for the people to gather together at their own county seat and witness an occasional hanging, and now you want to take even that away from them. Mr. Speaker, I don't know what you think about it, but as for me, hanging was good enough for my father and it's good enough for me."

When the impassioned, booming voice of the orator ceased, the young member who had cupped his ears cried out in a shrill voice, "Amen, the Lord grant it; we all think so." And then he started singing, "The Old Time Religion is Good Enough for Me."

After the hubbub had subsided the bill was enacted with the opposing member from South Texas casting one of the few dissenting votes; and thus passed the hangman's noose and the time-honored gallows from the county seats of Texas.

John Henry Faulk

Cowboy Dick's Last Ride

JOHN HENRY FAULK never became the Texas preacher his mother
wanted him to be but he made a career of preaching lay sermons on
social issues. He became a crusader for justice and humanity and a sharp
critic of unsavory people and practices in his native state. His interest in
the little people began with the collection and preservation of the sermons of black preachers in East Texas—sermons so original and unusual that he considered them a special art form. In his public appearances and in his writing he assumed the pose of a country philosopher,
with varying names and identities, who preached his homely humorous
gospel. His talents took him to the East Coast, where he was blacklisted
during the McCarthy era and had to struggle to clear his name. Eventually he returned to Austin, Texas, and settled near his place of origin.
His droll account of the decline and fall of Richard Nixon is Faulk at his
best.

From *The Uncensored John Henry Faulk*. Austin: Texas Monthly
Press, 1985, pp. 77–78.

Here we are, ladies and gentlemen! Broadcasting to you live, directly
from the arena at the Grand National Championship All-American
Rodeo. The main event has just started! The event that has rodeo fans
all over America on the edges of their seats. We are watching the
Champ of Champions, that wild and woolly cowboy, the Amazing,
Fantastic, Daring Dick Nixon come out of Chute Number One on the
back of the orneryest, buckingest outlaw bronc in rodeo history—
Watergate. It's a spectacular event—a duel between man and beast.

Daring Dick climbed into the saddle a moment ago with that
self-assurance and calm confidence that have made him a champion

rider. Daring Dick, as you know, long ago took the prize as the All-Time Champion trick rider. That's how he got his nickname, Tricky. Today, this isn't a trick ride; it's the real thing. The saddle-bronc ride. The big question is, will those many tricks Dick knows so well keep him in the saddle? Will he be able to stay on during this, the wildest, hardest ride of his career?

To catch you up, when they flung open the chute gate Watergate stood stock still and quivered. Daring Dick, sitting firmly in the saddle like he was riveted there, cut the bronc with his National Interest quirt. That did it! Ol' Watergate came out of the chute like a bolt of lightning, squalling, bucking, and headed straight up. Daring Dick dug his hand-forged National Security spurs in the bronc's shoulders and then in his flanks. Watergate hit the ground, hunched, then shot straight up again into the stars, pawing the air, snorting and sunfishing. Fans swore they could see daylight between Daring Dick and the saddle. But Dick didn't come off. Ol' Watergate came pounding down, stiff-legged, and you could hear Daring Dick's grunt from the jolt.

Right now, Watergate's settled down to some of the roughest, meanest bucking ever seen in rodeo history. Daring Dick's lost his hat! If his head wasn't fastened on tight, it would come off, too. It's snapping backwards and forwards like a drum major's baton. Dick's hanging on for dear life! He's grasping that National Emergency saddle horn, with his teeth clenched and his eyes closed. He's making the ride of his life. Showing his fans that he's no quitter.

Ol' Watergate's no quitter, either. Daring Dick thought Watergate would be winded by now. But Watergate's proving his true breeding. His dam was Secrecy and his sire, Deceit. He's half-brother to Sabotage and full brother to Lying: all bad buckers and mean outlaws. Daring Dick wanted to bar Watergate from rodeo as too dangerous, but the fans would not allow it. Watching this ride, you can see why the champ would try to bar Watergate. That's the worst-bucking, bone-jolting bronco on the rodeo circuit! Ol' Watergate has already thrown a half-dozen of the best riders in the business. To keep down the dust and to make the ride even more spectacular, the judges have spread impeachment all over the arena. When a rider is bucked off and hits that impeachment pavement, they have to carry him out. He can't get up and walk away.

Daring Dick must know that! Just look at that buckaroo hang on! Now his eyes are rolling wildly toward his pick-up men, Rebozo and Alplanalp. But they can't come to his aid. They are staying clear of Ol' Watergate's heels and teeth.

It's a mighty match between the champ rider and champ bronco! How long can the jolting, wrenching ride last? We'll have to watch and see. Right now, we'll pause for a commercial, with this reminder:

> There never was a bronco that couldn't be rode.
> There never was a cowboy that couldn't be throwed.

Larry L. King

My Hero, LBJ

LARRY L. KING was a country boy who got his initiation into politics
when he served as assistant to a West Texas congressman. His gifts and
his opportunities eventually took him to Washington, and he functioned for a while as go-fer for Senator Lyndon Johnson, an experience
which he describes with acerbic humor in the pages below. His play,
"The Best Little Whorehouse in Texas," made King nationally famous,
but his ability for finding and hitting the weak spots was his gift and
was part of his original equipment.

From *Warning: Writer at Work*. Fort Worth: Texas Christian University Press, 1985, pp. 115–121.

Sometime in 1958 I began to see Senator Johnson a bit more frequently. At one meeting in his office, representatives of a half-dozen
executive agencies spent an hour enumerating to several of us the reasons why a new international bridge between the U.S. and Mexico
could not be built at El Paso. Johnson crossed his long legs, feet
propped up on his desk, and drawled, "Now, boys, you all spent the last
hour tellin' me why we *can't* open up another international bridge.
Now I want every one of you to give me one reason why we *can*. Then
I want you to get the hell out of here and *open it!*" (They did—and LBJ
cut the dedication ribbon.)

I had drinks a couple of times in the Majority Leader's suite at the
Capitol along with Texas Congressmen, other administrative assistants,
and favored Johnson staffers. In these sessions LBJ's conversation
ranged broadly: a current political problem in Texas, chances of passing
a Reciprocal Trade bill, an anecdote about Franklin D. Roosevelt, a

stinging parody of Dwight D. Eisenhower. (He would screw his face
into a frown, mimic Eisenhower's flat clipped speech, and give us his
version of the Eisenhower syntax: "Now, I may not know everything
there is about this bill, Senator, and I might make what you might call
a *mistake* now and then, but I am what you might call *sincere* about
this. . . .") Suddenly he would bark a question at an aide about tomorrow's schedule, turn his head abruptly to ask a Congressman "what
you're gonna do to help me and the Speaker when the Education bill
comes to the Floor?" or grab a telephone to dial another Senator.
Sitting under a life-sized portrait of himself that was illuminated by
indirect lights, his in-the-flesh person looking down on us from his
subtly elevated executive's chair, Senator Johnson was invariably jovial
and full of hope. I enjoyed these performances hugely.

I saw the famed Johnson temper for the first time in 1959, during
a three-day tour of duty that seemed no longer than a century.

Senator Johnson came to my home district as part of a state-wide
tour designed to solidify the political base in Texas from which he
would seek the Presidential nomination the following year. It fell to my
lot to act as "advance man"—the nearest thing the Western World has
to a Chinese coolie. The advance man arranges for halls, podiums,
luncheons, or dinners, keys to the city, press conferences, hotel accom-
modations, rendezvous between the visiting pooh-bah and his local
political underlings, or a pitcher of water for the dignitary's bedside
table. He referees disputes over who will sit where at ceremonial func-
tions, and tries to discourage bores or potential troublemakers who
might embarrass the Official Presence. Johnson's own staff attended to
many of these details, but as resident coolie I was responsible for being
on hand to guide everyone through the proper jig-steps.

At his first appearance, on the mezzanine floor of a downtown
hotel where he spoke to about a hundred local leaders and their wives,
Senator Johnson's performance could have served as a blueprint for the
Compleat Cornpone Politician. He was charming, relaxed, and lean.
He slouched on the podium, grinning boyishly, pulling at his ear,
saying how grand it was for "me and Lady Bird to get out of the steel
and stone of the cities and come back here to feel the soil of home under
our feet, and draw close to all the things we hold dear while we gaze on
the Texas moon." He invited all hands to "drop by and see us when

you're in Washington." He reported that the coffeepot was always on, and added that "sometimes Bird bakes a buncha little cookies in the shape of the State of Texas to go with the coffee." (This earned a standing ovation and Rebel yells.) He confessed to vast stores of humility, giving credit for "whatever I may amount to" in equal measure to Celestial Beings, his mother, and everybody present. When he had finished he ambled off to mingle with the crowd, pressing flesh, cooing low, kissing old ladies on the cheek as if he had flushed a covey of favored maiden aunts. Then the party broke up and the Senator's official group retired toward his suite for a brief rest before the evening's scheduled dinner.

With the closing of the elevator door LBJ's sunny smile gave way to thunderstorm expressions. "Goddammit," he said by way of openers, "nobody told me I was supposed to make a *speech!* Didn't know it until I saw the damned podium. Up till then I thought it was just gonna be coffee, doughnuts, and bullshit!" He stared at me down to the blood. "Why in the hell didn't you *tell* me they expected a speech out there? You think I'm a mind reader? Hah?" I didn't think "Yes" was the proper answer, but I was mortally afraid to say "No." So I said nothing.

Within the next twenty-four hours Senator Johnson had berated me and his staffers because (1) his hotel bed was too short and "I have to scrootch my legs up until I fold up like a goddamn accordion"; (2) nobody could locate Senator Dick Russell of Georgia on the telephone at the snap of a finger; (3) we were late for three consecutive appointments because "half of you are crawlin', half of you are walkin', and *none* of you are runnin'," and (4) he couldn't immediately find his reading spectacles. In another town where a press conference had been scheduled (and to which I had clearly heard Johnson agree the day before in a rare cheerful moment) the Senator claimed knowledge of it only as he entered the hotel where local reporters waited. He blew up in the lobby and threatened not to appear. He was finally steered into the hotel ballroom, but not before his histrionics caused passersby to congregate and investigate the commotion. One reporter repeatedly baited Johnson with hostile questions. Finally, ignoring him completely, Johnson silently pointed to somebody else. When the heckler persisted the Senator snapped, "That's it. Thank you, boys." He plunged out of the ballroom, the rest of us chasing along, though handicapped by not having heard the starter's gun.

In the elevator the Senator's first words were: "Which one of you do I thank for *this* little lynching?" No one stepped forward to claim the medal. Those were Johnson's last words for the next fifteen minutes as he brooded silently, staring at the television set in his room. The rest of us stared and brooded with him. I was terrified that I might have to sneeze.

Maybe there is something about Lyndon B. Johnson and elevators not apparent to the eye. Some of his greatest conniptions have been thrown there. Likely, however, this is true because elevators happen to be the first place he is able to drop the necessary public poses and give vent to human frustrations. At any rate, my one head-to-head battle with Johnson started in an elevator the night before he would mercifully leave our district. Following a dinner where he had flashed his usual mixture of country charm and worldly knowledge, the Senator barked directly at me: "Who was that redheaded son-of-a-bitch set two chairs down from me?" I groped for the red-headed SOB's identity, but at that moment I could not have read my own name off a billboard. "Who-*ever* he was," Johnson said, "I don't want that goofy SOB sittin' in the same room with me again. Ruined mah whole night . . ." He trailed off into mumbles, glaring.

The hour was late. I was tired, and just about one more harsh word away from tears or running off from home. In his room the Senator was unhappy because a delegation of local citizens required entertainment. I would have gladly done the job. It required nothing more strenuous than pouring a little whiskey, laughing at the punch lines of old jokes, and massaging shriveled egos. Senator Johnson, however, assigned this choice duty to his own permanent staff people. He thrust a slip of paper in my hand. Just before plunging into the bathroom he said, "I want these people in that *exact* order." The note required two telephone calls to Washington, one to New York, one to Austin, and two or three more to small Texas towns. There wasn't a telephone number on the slip. I sat on my hands and let my juices boil. When the Senator entered the room he gave me one quick glance. Then he asked the room-at-large to whom he had given the note. Eventually all eyes turned my way. It was like standing in front of a firing squad.

I'm sure my voice trembled as I said, "I'm tired of being your lackey while your staff people sit on their rumps and drink whiskey. I've got *my own* man to lackey for." (The last sentence was spoken with some strange, hot pride—which shows what being a second-banana politician will do for your sense of values.) I have the vague recollection that somebody dropped an ashtray. One of Johnson's staffers suddenly snatched the note from my hand and whisked it away, presumably to the nearest telephone.

I am unable to recall the Senator's immediate reaction to the mutiny. Everyone seemed frozen in place. My ears throbbed blood as I plunged from the room. A friend stumbled out behind me, eyes wide and face pale. I would hesitate to quote him exactly, but I think he called on his Lord in a hoarse voice and asked if I had lost my goddamned mind. While I raved about holding Senator Johnson's hat, carrying his bags, and being treated like a stepchild, my friend made frantic shushing sounds and waved his hands as if he might be flagging the Greyhound. He desperately begged that I go someplace to "get a beer, cool off, and for God's sake stay out of Lyndon's sight."

I cooled off enough to worry about whether I'd lose my $16,000 a year job, then returned to a night of feverish sleep. About daylight the next morning the telephone in my room rang.

"You had your coffee yet?"

I said no.

"Come on up and have some," Lyndon Johnson said.

The Senator was in a figured robe. The morning newspaper was scattered about the floor and on the coffee table. He greeted me with a grunt that sounded half-friendly, then poured some coffee and handed it over. Just as I took the cup he said, "You can get kinda salty, can't you?" Then he grinned. My mumbled response consisted of mere sounds without any form resembling known words. The Senator took my arm and stood nose-to-nose, breathing on my eyeglasses. He talked about how "young fellas" like me make big politicians tick. He himself had been secretary to a Congressman, he said, in 19–and–32.

Then he settled on the couch and for perhaps the next half-hour entertained me with memories of New Deal days, and of his Texas boyhood, and praise of my boss. He spoke of how dedicated his staff was to him, and of how very much he loved his staff. He offered free advice ("You oughta get a law degree, young man like you. Come in handy no matter *what* profession you follow."), asked my opinion on whether a local politician had Congressional ambitions "enough that it won't let him sleep nights." Then he so adroitly maneuvered me out of the room with a darling little series of back-pats, soothing clucks, and handclasps that I was in the elevator before I fully realized the audience was over.

I soon came back, though. For when the Senator departed for the airport, I found myself struggling with the bellhop for the honor of carrying his bags.

Cactus Pryor

The Law South of the Belt

RICHARD "CACTUS" PRYOR'S talents as a humorist are displayed in the first section of this book. In the following essay he tells how he developed skills as a survivalist in the South Texas county controlled by George Parr, the political Pharaoh who is said to have had a hand in starting Lyndon Johnson on his career. For the details see J. Evetts Haley's *A Texan Looks at Lyndon* (1964).

From *Inside Texas*. Bryan, Texas: Shoal Creek Publishers, 1982, pp. 35–37.

I don't know who Alice was, but had she known the town when I was living there she would have changed her name.

Alice, Texas, is located about 35 miles south of Corpus Christi, 15 miles from Kingsville, and, back in the '40's, a light-year or two from law and order.

Jim Wells County is where they put her, snuggled up to Duval County just as comfortably as Bonnie to Clyde. The Duke of Duval, George Parr, was the "papacito" of this area occupied predominantly by Mexican-Americans. He ran things in the good old democratic way—poverty was evenly distributed among the have-nots and wealth was evenly distributed among the Parr family and their political cronies.

Papa Parr controlled the area like Willie Nelson controls audiences. He could get it done if he liked you, and he could get you done if he didn't. The fact that he controlled the votes of Jim Wells and Duval counties is legend—from cradle to the grave (and there were tabulated voters from both sources).

I hit Alice, Texas, in 1946 as program director of radio station

KBKI so blissfully ignorant that I thought a Parr was something that eluded you on the golf course. I later learned that you weren't safe from Parr's reach even on the golf course.

Our station was not the ordinary radio station operation. For two things, we had two managers in enthusiastic opposition to each other. The host of our mid-afternoon Mexican-language broadcast was paid just $400 a month. Yet somehow he managed a new Cadillac for himself and one for his wife, plus expensive clothes, diamond rings, and other luxuries unknown to those of our profession.

Once I opened one of his hundreds of daily letters by mistake. A dollar bill fell out. Another letter contained a five-dollar bill. We checked and discovered that Juan Dinero was charging $1 for musical requests, $2 for wedding announcements, and $5 for funeral announcements. The John D. Rockefeller of Tortilla Flat!

Management reacted by demanding half the loot and hiring a Spanish-speaking person to monitor our Latin friend's broadcasts.

Another oddity of our radio station was our involvement with local news. You ever tune in the six o'clock news and hear the newsman say, "Hey! Guess what? Our local deputy sheriff is condoning prostitution and importing professional softball pitchers and boarding them in the county jail so they can pitch for the sheriff's team in the city tournament"? Our news editor Mike Holberg laid that one on our audiences one day. It was the hottest news to hit Alice since they lost Box #13, which contained the eighty-seven votes that put Lyndon Johnson in the U.S. Senate and Coke Stevenson back by the campfire.

The following day Holberg and I were playing golf on Alice's scenic seven-hole version of St. Andrews. Following the slicing ball with my eyes, I saw a battleship approaching us from the Gulf of Mexico thirty-two miles away. No, it wasn't a battleship. Battleships don't wear Stetsons and carry pearl-handled six-shooters on their hips.

Could it be? Yes it was. Deputy Sheriff Sam Smithwick and his entire 275 pounds and six feet four inches all fettled with MAD.

"Are you those two radio guys who put that story about me on the air?"

"Mike Holberg here is our news editor," I volunteered, never one to take credit away from a colleague.

"You guys have got 'til sundown to get out of town."

Republic Pictures surely had a copyright on that line, used in every single one of the western movies they ever produced.

We checked in with the "owner" of the radio station, Alice attorney Ed Lloyd, and laughingly told him of our encounter with the sheriff in the rough.

"Boys," he said (and we were), "let me give you a few facts of life. Who do you think put Smithwick in office? And who do you think really controls this radio station?"

Magically the name Parr came into our minds, and we weren't thinking Jack.

"Take my advice, and don't wait until sundown to leave."

Mike was gone by two P.M., and my wife and I were setting up housekeeping in Corpus Christi by 3:30 that afternoon. The man who succeeded me as program director at KBKI was Bill Mason. He too broadcast some tacky remarks about Deputy Sheriff Smithwick. Mason was sitting in his automobile one lazy afternoon on the main street of Alice. Smithwick walked up to him and shot him to death.

Smithwick later committed suicide in a Bell County jail. And I became devotedly committed to a life of cowardice.

William Brammer

Arthur Fenstemaker in Action

WILLIAM (ACTUALLY BILLY LEE) BRAMMER was an immensely talented Texas writer who produced only one novel, *The Gay Place*. Governor Arthur Fenstemaker, his central character, bears a striking resemblance to Lyndon Johnson, for whom Brammer worked for four years. Brammer plays up the governor's peculiarities, as a humorist should do, but treats him with respect. The novel was a critical success and Brammer was hailed as a Texas F. Scott Fitzgerald. Unfortunately he was not able to complete another novel, and when he died in 1978, his promise remained unfulfilled.

Roy, the governor's Man Friday, takes his friend Willie, editor of a struggling liberal news sheet, to Fenstemaker's office on command.

From *The Gay Place*. Boston: Houghton Mifflin, 1961, pp. 86–87, 91–102.

Fenstemaker roused him at eight with awful exhortations, a compound of biblical wisdom and Hill Country homily. Roy groaned and looked out through the window at the quiet surface of the lake, wondering about the hour. There were no fishermen in sight, nor had the water-skiing contingent from the college arrived.

"Jesus . . ." Roy said. "What's the time?"

"How long, America, O how long," Fenstemaker was babbling.

Roy turned round the face of his clock, blinked in the harsh morning light and groaned again. Fenstemaker badgered him mercilessly. Roy protested: "I'm a sick man, Governor . . . I had three hours sleep last night . . . this morning . . . I'm getting a nervous tic . . ."

"You get over here in an hour?" Fenstemaker said. "I got somethin' important . . . How soon you get over here?"

Roy said he would come as soon as he had strength enough to shave and dress. "I'm sick, Governor," he said. "I got the neurosis."

"You tie your shoelaces?" Fenstemaker said.

Roy said maybe he could.

"You're all right, then," Fenstemaker said. "Psychiatrist friend of mine says man's not really disabled emotionally till he gets up in the mornin' and can't decide which shoe to pull on first . . ."

Roy gave assurances he would get to the Capitol sometime before noon.

"Bring your friend," the Governor said.

"Who's that?" Roy said. For a terrible moment he thought the Governor was going to start in on the business with Ouida.

"That Willie," Fenstemaker said. "Bring that Willie person. I got somethin' for the both of you."

Then the Governor rang off with characteristic abruptness. Roy got slowly to his feet, washed, shaved, fed his cat, and ate a bowl of cereal. He tore off the cereal boxtop for the Fielding boy and listened unhappily for a moment to the sounds of fun and games commencing on the lake.

☆ ☆ ☆ ☆

They climbed the great stone steps and headed down the main corridor of the Capitol building, taking a back elevator that let them off at a third-floor passageway near the Executive Offices. They sat waiting for a few minutes, watching the nice-legged secretaries moving back and forth. Occasionally, the Governor's voice could be heard through the thick wall, a little like Grand Opera from a great distance. Jay McGown passed through the reception room, looking gloomy and efficient. He stopped and talked with them.

"He ought to be ready for you," Jay said, looking back toward the Governor's conference room. His attitude was not so much one of anxiety; Jay had more the quality, characteristic of those constantly exposed to Arthur Fenstemaker, of having peered steadily at the scene of an accident, experienced a revelation, seen death and redemption, God and Lucifer staring back, and somehow, incredibly, survived.

Jay started off toward the pressrooms down the hall. Almost immediately the Governor came banging out of his office, one arm draped round the shoulder of a state senator. The senator grinned at everyone, eyes glazed, the Governor leading him as a blind man toward the door. Then Fenstemaker turned, a great happy smile on his face. "Come on in, you two," he said.

They got to their feet to follow him inside. Fenstemaker had already collapsed in his chair, stretching out, neck and spine resting against the leather cushions. They sat across from him and stared. Fenstemaker pinched his nose, moved a big hand over his face as if probing for minute flaws in a piece of pottery. He rubbed his eyes, sucked his teeth, punched holes in a sheet of bond paper with a gold toothpick. He stood and paced about the room and stared out the windows and scratched himself. "Well goddam and hell . . ." he said. It was like a high mass, a benediction.

"Let me do you a favor, Willie," he said.

"What kind of favor?"

"I don't know. Anything you ask. I just want to get you obligated," the Governor said, grinning and winking at Roy.

"Don't know of anything I want offhand," Willie said.

"Think of something."

"How 'bout some more of that Scotch whiskey then—the smoky twenty-five-year-old stuff you served me last month."

Fenstemaker smiled, showing his shark's teeth. "Hell and damn," he said. "That's no favor." He swung around in the big chair and opened a side panel of the desk. There was the sound of ice clacking in metal tumblers, and he pushed drinks across to them. "Look at this," the Governor said, setting a seltzer bottle on the desk top. "Damndest things . . . Used to see 'em in the movies when I was growin' up. When I could afford a movin' picture show." He held the bottle in one hand and pressed the lever, sending a spray of water across the room. For a moment there was a fine mist suspended in the air between Roy and Willie and the sunlit windows. A lovely rainbow appeared.

"You're a mean sonafabitch," the Governor said, staring at the seltzer bottle. Roy wondered if he was talking about the bottle or his guests, until he repeated himself. "You're a mean sonofabitch, Willie," he said, still smiling.

"I'm lazy and no-account," Willie said. "But not mean, especially."

"You ever think about old Phillips?" He referred to a minor state official now serving a term in the penitentiary who was convicted on several counts of theft and conspiracy from evidence developed in Willie's news columns.

"I think of him," Willie said. "I keep thinking how I wish he'd come back and do it all over again. I'm running out of people to expose."

The Governor spun round in his swivel chair, grinning. "Well you keep tryin' Willie," he said. "What's your circulation now?"

"About the same as it was. About ten thousand. But only about six of it paid. We give away a hell of a lot of copies."

"That's not much," the Governor said. "Ten thousand's not much."

"No."

"How much money you losin'?"

"Lots."

"I imagine so," the Governor said.

"I try not to think about it," Willie said. He looked unhappy for a moment, thinking about it.

"Where's the money come from?"

"I'm not supposed to say."

"You got to say now," Fenstemaker said. "I give you that Scotch whiskey."

"Various sources," Willie said, raising his glass as in a toast. "I don't know who-all. Rinemiller helped raise the original amount. Got it from people like Earle Fielding . . . Some others . . . Hell! You probably know who they all are."

The Governor laughed and leaned toward them. "But it's not your circulation, Willie—it's the *quality* of your goddam readership."

"Suppose they can all read," Willie said.

"Now goddam I mean it," Fenstemaker said. "Anybody who really cares about politics subscribes to your little paper, even if they don't necessarily subscribe to your point of view. People who shape thinkin'—policy makers, lobbyists, lawyers, judges, small-time politicians."

"There's been no one else printing a lot of this stuff," Willie said. "I suppose something's better than nothin'."

Fenstemaker looked delighted. "Exactly!" he said. "Whole basis of my philosophy!"

"What's that?"

"Somethin's better than nothin."

"Half a loaf?"

"Slice of goddam bread, even," Fenstemaker said. He changed moods suddenly. "Now about these hospitals . . ."

"*What* . . . ?" Roy and Willie leaned forward, trying to follow the course of Fenstemaker's conversation.

"Hospitals," the Governor said. "You care about the hospitals?"

"Sure."

"They're a God-awful mess."

"Worse than that," Willie said.

"I got this little bill . . ."

"I know," Willie said.

"I got the votes," Fenstemaker said. "At least I *think* I got them. It's not much of a bill—not half enough of an appropriation—but it'll close up some of the worst places and build some new ones and bring in a few head doctors. And this little bill can *pass* is the main thing. I'll put it through next week if I don't get everyone all stirred up and worried about taxes and socialism and creepin' statesmanship. You gonna help me, Willie?"

"How can I help?"

Fenstemaker slapped his desk and showed his teeth. "Oppose the goddam bill!" His face beamed. "But just a little bit, understand?" he said. "Don't get real ugly about it."

"I don't understand," Willie said.

"Those fellows in the Senate—they think this is all I want, they'll give it to me. But if somebody's runnin' round whoopin' about how good this is, settin' precedents and havin' a foot in the door braggin' on how much more we'll get next year, then all my support'll get skittish and vanish overnight."

"I see."

"Only don't oppose it too much, either. You raise hell and your bunch won't go along. They'll introduce their own bill askin' for the goddam aurora borealis. I need their votes, too. Just oppose it a little bit—oppose it on *principle!*"

The Governor paused a moment and considered the problem. "I want," he said, beginning to laugh quietly, his sad eyes blinking. "I want unanimous consent and dead silence!" He roared his laughter at them.

Willie stirred and looked at Roy. Then he looked at Fenstemaker and said: "That all you wanted? We taking up too much of your time?"

"Oh, *no!*" Fenstemaker said. "Hell no. I got you two here for somethin' else altogether. Just a minute." He leaned across his desk and punched a button. A girl's voice came on the speaker.

"Yes sir?"

"Hah Yew, Honey?"

"Just fine . . ."

"Jay in there?"

"Yes, sir."

"Tell him to get that machine of his and bring it in. Tell him I'm ready for a little transcribed soap opera."

He leaned back in the chair, resting on his spine, looking as if he were in great pain. "How you get to be one of those goddam elder statesmen?" he said.

☆ ☆ ☆ ☆

It was such an improbable story it had to be true. If it were simply some hoked up yarn designed to discredit an enemy, old Fenstemaker's inventiveness would have served him better; there would have been some style, some magic, a sense of possibilities. Fenstemaker didn't insult a man's intelligence—you could nearly always count on that—and this story here was so coarse and bumptious there *had* to be something to it. Otherwise, the Governor would have devised a folktale with source material for his own amusement. Fenstemaker would have invented a better story.

Willie sat listening, trying to set bits and pieces to memory, wondering if he should take notes. The Governor was sprawled in his big chair, looking out the window, beyond the granite ledge where two bizarrely plumed pigeons clucked and strutted, flapping their wings for balance in the careless wind. Roy sat like a bronze figure, cigarette ash spilled down the front of his dark jacket, and Jay McGown stood next to the machine with his hands on the switches. They played the record-ing all the way through, listening in silence, and then once again, stopping and backing up the tape and commenting on the undecipher-able sections before proceeding.

"Once again, Jay," the Governor said, and Jay MCGown spun the reels like a scientist at the controls. There was scarcely any doubt—the voice, one of the voices, was Alfred Rinemiller's; the other Fenstemaker identified as a lobbyist for a group of loan companies. They sat and listened all the way through one more time . . .

—Who'd you say?

—Huggins. He's chairman of the committee and a good friend.

—And you think you could change his mind . . . ?

—I think so. I could work on him. I've done him favors and he knows it.

—Well listen . . . We got to be damn sure. There's a lot ridin' on this. We got to be absolutely certain about it—that's why I'm down here. Our future's at stake—there's a whole pot of money we could lose with just a change of a few percentage points on the usury limitation . . .

—Then you understand it's going to cost you money to save money.

—We know that. We've done business down here before. It's just we want to be dead sure. We can't afford to go throwin' it around. We can't afford it. We've been burned before.

—I'm just telling you you've got my word. Ask anybody. You can depend on it. I can keep the bill in committee, but—hell—you under-stand—you got consideration.

—How many?

—There's a lot of sentiment this year for some kind of legislation in the field.

—How many considerations?

—I don't know. There's Huggins . . .

—He's a rich boy. What the hell's he need—

—Rich family. He only gets a limited amount from them, and he spends most all of it. And he likes women . . .

—We've all got our weaknesses . . .

—That's his. Women. And he's known only the inexpensive ones. I can get a couple who . . .

—Hell! You do, hah? Whyn't you get' em up here, then. We'll have a little party.

—You pay?

—Only kidding. Listen—how much now? You got yours. I thought that would be enough. You realize how much you got there?

—Yes.

—How much? Count it.

—I believe you.

—Go ahead . . . count it . . .

—It's all here.

—How much.

—Seven-fifty. Just like you said.

—Now you goin' to deliver the goods just like you said?

—You've got my vote. I have a good deal of influence on the committee. Enough to stop the thing from being reported out. But it's going to take some work. I expect more for that work. And it'll cost me some hard cash to bring it off.

—How much, goddammit?

—Five thousand.

—You're crazy.

—Take it or leave it.

—You're out of your mind.

—You want your money back? Here . . .

—No dammit, I want your *vote*. But you bring up this subject yourself of what you can do for us in workin' on the others. And then you say five thousand for Chrissake. I could buy up control of the Senate for that much.

—Fat chance . . . All right then. What's your offer?

—Half.

—Half? Half of what?

—Half of five . . . That's twenty-five hundred. And I tell you, mister, we've never thrown money around like that in the history of this organization.

—It's not enough.

—The hell it isn't!

—All right.

—And we want to be damn sure.

—You can count on it.

—I mean damn sure. You're gettin' only a thousand of it now.

—*What?*

—And the balance when we're certain the bill's dead for this session.

—Well now how can I be sure I'll get the rest of it?

—You can count on it, my friend.

—There's no assurance.

—What assurance you give us? And besides—I haven't got that kind of money. Not that much. I'll have to go tap our directors, and that'll be a touchy business. They'll think *I'm* gettin' to *them.* Puttin' the money in my own pocket.

—All right. But they'd better come across. Otherwise, they're liable to find this legislation looking right at 'em again next session. And I'm the boy who can make sure it passes. Think that one over . . .

—Well now it seems you have a good point there.

—Yes.

—So we're all protected.

—That's right.

—How 'bout a drink?

—Fine.

—Bourbon?

—Anything else?

—No. Just bourbon. Like I said, we're a small outfit. *Five thousand!* Why godalmighty, man, that's half my salary for a year.

—Bourbon's fine.

—Seven-Up?

—No . . . Soda.

—We don't have any . . .

—Jesus . . .

—There's a cold-water tap in the bathroom . . .

The tape came to the end of the reel and continued to spin noiselessly in the big padded room. "That's enough, Jay," the Governor said. Jay McGown packed the recorder and left the room. For a few moments they were silent. The Governor stared at his spotted pigeons on the window ledge.

Willie said: "Why'd this fellow bring it to you?"

"I don't know. He's a kind of screwball—doesn't really have much idea what's going on down here. He said he didn't know what to do with the evidence, as he called it, so he brought it to me."

"Just like that?"

"Yes. And I wish to God he hadn't"

"Sounds like something for the grand jury," Roy said. "What the hell's wrong with people? Rinemiller gone out of his mind?"

"Well now this fellow's put it on my back. Listening to what he said in that conversation, he wouldn't look so good in the courts himself. Even if he was just stringin' Rinemiller along . . ."

"He did a pretty convincing job of it," Willie said.

"Yes. So he brings this tape in—just this morning—and puts it all on me. I almost suspect he's trying to make a deal. Seemed to think Rinemiller was one of my boys and maybe if I'd just take care of that bill for him personally he wouldn't be out any money and would be willing to forget everything."

"He say all this?" Willie said.

"No. Just a feeling I had. He's supposed to come back to discuss it after I've had time to think it over."

"He mention calling in the law?" Roy said.

"No. He just kept saying it was a very serious matter. Very serious."

"He has a gift for understatement," Willie said.

"Well," the Governor said. "What do you think?"

"For God's sakes don't get me in on it. You know Rinemiller's an officer in the corporation of the newspaper?"

"I knew he was connected," the Governor said. "Otherwise, I wouldn't have let you know about it."

"How do you know I still won't print it?" Willie said.

"I'd be pleased if you would as a matter of fact. Make the decision for me."

"I just might," Willie said. "It would probably ruin me, but I might if I could get that lobbyist to talk. Who's to say definitely beyond doubt it's Rinemiller?"

"It would bitch up a great many things," Fenstemaker said. "It would put you out of business, and probably take away all those great gains you people made this year in the elections. You know Rinemiller campaigned strictly on the issue of being a liberal? He kept calling himself that. Capital *L*."

"Why'd you want me in here?" Roy said.

"Well, you're a friend of Rinemiller's . . ."

"Rinemiller's a sewer."

"All right, then. I called you because you're about the only one of the bunch I'd put any faith in. You've got good sense. You're always honest with me. I respect you. I want your advice."

"On what?"

"I dunno. How to deal with this thing, I suppose. Tell me what you think? I don't know whether to lay it all out in the open or call Rinemiller in and let him squirm a little or let that fellow have it back and see what he's planning. If he's got a plan."

"What's that?"

"He mentioned the possibility of paying off Rinemiller in marked bills and having some state police there to grab him when he takes it."

"That would be interesting."

"I really don't think he wants any of that, though."

"You think he's bluffing?"

"He might be. Just to see what *I'll* offer *him*. Goddam. He would have me opposin' that legislation for the next four years. And I happen to believe it's needed. Had it in my campaign platform."

"Why you letting him pull you in?" Roy said.

Fenstemaker poured a glass of water, used it to wash down a pill. He got to his feet and paced around the room, pausing in front of a mirror to look at himself. He smiled, baring teeth and pink gums, tapping the enamel with his blunt finger. He turned round and said: "We haven't heard Rinemiller's side of it, you know. That recording might be faked."

"I hope so," Willie said.

"And whether anybody believes it or not, I care about those people downstairs. I care about your bunch, Roy. We got the same objectives—we just disagree on methods. Something like this here, it'll set us all back, disgrace the whole bunch of us, and blow the session all to hell. I got a program to worry about."

"Well," Willie said, "most of our people got elected on the corruption issue, and I suppose it would be only fair to go right back out again for the same reasons . . ."

They were silent for a time. Finally, the Governor suggested they think about it for a few days. They all agreed to think about it. Arthur Fenstemaker's collapsed features came together; he smiled and put an arm around each of the two young men.

In the reception room they stood and talked about seeing each other again in several days. Jay McGown was bending over one of the secretary's desks, making corrections in a television script. The Governor suddenly reached across, took several of the sheets of paper, and began to read aloud. Then he looked up at the ceiling for a moment.

"This is too prissy, Jay," he said. "Can't you brag on me some without it soundin' like I'm diggin' my toe in the ground?"

"It's a problem," Jay said, "bragging on you when you're making the speech yourself . . ."

The Governor looked resigned to another defeat. "Well forget it then—take that stuff out about receiving honorary degrees. I never even got a B. A., anyhow . . ." He turned to Roy and Willie and said: "Everybody's tryin' to blur my public image."

Then he stalked back inside the office.

Lone Star Lamas

For Max Evans' "Booger Boggs Pitches for the Lord"

We expect our men of God to practice the virtues they preach, and presumably most of them do, but we are fascinated by the great exceptions. Sinclair Lewis' Elmer Gantry was an early example, and the ecclesiastical woods have been full of such characters from Aimee Semple McPherson to Jim Bakker and Jimmy Swaggart. Books about such Lone Star Lamas would fill a sizable shelf. Near the top of the list would be Don Imus' *God's Other Son* (1984) starring the Reverend Billy

Sol Hargus. His mother was a waitress in a Texas roadside diner, but his father was a traveling man who never appeared in daylight, so Billy Sol deduces that he is the product of an immaculate conception. He calls Jesus "Brother" and addresses God as "Dad." He becomes a powerful radio preacher who shows great piety in public, but in private he talks profane Texan and pursues the delights of the flesh. Corinda Cassy in Edward Swift's *Principia Martindale,* excerpted here, is cut from the same cloth—an example of the hollowness of holiness.

Good ones as well as bad ones have their humorous aspects. Frank X. Tolbert enjoyed Father John F. Casey, a "rough tongued priest" of Dell City in far West Texas, and Max Evans' Booger Boggs, preacher and pitcher, won a baseball game with the aid of the Lord.

J. Mason Brewer

The Palacios Rancher and the Preacher

J. MASON BREWER, teacher and folklorist, was presented in an earlier chapter. It remains to be said here that black preachers are his favorite subject and his book *Dog Ghosts and Other Negro Tales* is largely devoted to them. Brewer recognizes that they have chinks in their armor, like other men, but he credits them with dedication and effectiveness as fishers of men.

From *Dog Ghosts and Other Negro Tales*. Austin: University of Texas Press, 1958, pp. 60–61.

Oncet dey was a cullud cowboy that done go up de trail for a rich rancher 'roun' 'bout Cuero. Of a consequence, he come to be a knowledge man 'bout cattle, an' dey raisin', an' de prices dey brung. So, li'l' by li'l', he buy a bunch of cattle of his own 'till he done rech de place whar he hab a putty good herd.

He ain't yit ma'ied, tho', but he meckin' eyes at de daughter of a fawmuh, what had a li'l' ranch and fawm rat 'roun' Palacios, so he ast de girl to ma'ie 'im one Saddy night, an' dey gits latched an' buy 'em a li'l' spot of lan' rat close to de girl's pappy's fawm, an' staa'ts to raisin' cattle. Dis cowboy a haa'd wuckuh, so dey comes up fas' in de worl', an' in 'bout six years he done come to be one of de bigges' cattle owners in dem paa'ts.

De girl rail proud of de cowboy, but dey's one thing dat she ain't lack 'bout de way he ca'ie hisse'f, an' dat am dat he ain't evuh traced his steps in de chu'ch house. So one night, 'roun' de turn of week, she tell 'im dat she think he oughta go to chu'ch wid her, since de Lawd done blessed 'im wid a lots of money an' lan'. So de cowboy say dat's awright wid him—he don' hab nothin' 'gainst de Lawd, he jes' ain't hab time to go to chu'ch, he been so busy trawna meck a libin' for 'im an' her.

Howbevuh, de nex' comin' Sunday, de cowboy puts on his gamblin' stripe pants an' dress coat an' goes to chu'ch up to Edna, Texas, wid his wife. De chu'ch dat dey' cides to go to am de Mefdis' Chu'ch, what was raisin' money to buil' 'em a new chu'ch house. When de preachuh gits thoo wid de servus an' de las' Amen done been said, de cowboy walks up to de preachuh an' say, "Revun, you preached a damn good sermon.

"Now, looka here, brothuh," 'low de preachuh; "Ah don' know who you is, o' whar you comed from, but Ah wants to tell you rat now, we don' 'low no cussin' in dis chu'ch house."

"Ah! dat's awright; Ah still says you preached a damn good sermon, Revun," 'low de cowboy; "Ah put a hunnuhd dolluh bill in de colleckshun plate jes' now."

"De hell you did!" yell de preachuh, an' den he look in de colleckshun plate, an' see de hunnuhd dolluh bill what de ranchuh done dropped in hit, an' he say, "Damn if you didn'!"

Max Evans

Booger Boggs Pitches for the Lord

MAX EVANS left the Lone Star State at the age of eleven and has shifted
from New Mexico to Hollywood ever since, but he considers himself a
Texan. He has had an unusually varied career as cowboy, ranchman,
painter, script writer and novelist. His first big success came in 1960
with the publication of *The Rounders,* which was made into a successful
movie and laid the foundation for a television series. A steady stream of
novels followed, set mostly in New Mexico. *My Pardner* returns to
Texas during the depression—the Texas Max knew as a boy. Twelve-
year-old Dan, aided by a remarkable character named Booger Boggs,
drives a small herd of horses across Texas to Oklahoma, where his father
expects to sell them. Boggs is resourceful and unscrupulous enough to
get them there. He has done everything and been everywhere, loves
booze and the Bible with equal enthusiasm, and even proves to be a
first-class pitcher. He disappears when their mission is accomplished,
and Dan is still missing him twenty years later.

From *My Pardner*. Boston: Houghton, Mifflin, 1963, and Albuquerque: University of New Mexico Press, 1984, pp. 85–93.

I had a numb feeling as we rode along. We were getting into the last
stages of our drive, and we were two horses short. It was just plain
awful to let Papa down. I was sick thinking about it.

We reached the edge of Dumas, Texas, on a Sunday. We knew that
was the day, for the churches were filled with singing and shouting. I
watched Boggs up ahead. I could almost see him quiver, he wanted to
get in there and go to preaching so bad. He raised his hand and stopped
the horses. They milled about and started grazing on somebody's lawn.

He rode back to me. "Boy," he said, "it's takin' all my will power
to stay out of that church. I'd like to go in and talk that Reverend into

ten minutes with Boggs. There's a lot of sinners in there and they think they're saved, but ten minutes later I'd have 'em lined up and headin' for a baptizin'."

It sounded like he wanted me to say "Go ahead." So I said, "I'll watch the horses, Boggs, if you want to go in."

"That's a magnanimous gesture, boy, but I reckon we've got to do somethin' about replenishin' this herd of horses. We just cain't let your papa down. And besides, your ma is staying back there worrying herself sick about the mortgages and all that. Now the way I got it figgered is this: these little west Texas towns all have baseball teams. Today is bound to be Sunday. There'll be a ball game around here somewhere."

Well, he was right. We found the baseball grounds out on the edge of town in a big opening. We turned our horses loose on the grass and rode over where a man was dragging the field down with a tractor and scraper.

"Yes, sir, there's going to be a ball game," he said, taking a chew of the tobacco Boggs offered him. "Spearman, Texas, will be here in just a little while. They've got a good team but we've got a better one."

"Is that so?" Boggs said. "What kind of pitchers you got?"

"One good'un, and one bad'un."

"Sounds about right."

I was sure puzzled about Boggs' interest in baseball, but since we were going to graze the horses awhile we might as well have a little fun watching a baseball game.

The crowd began to gather early. They came by truck, car, wagon and horseback. The teams began to warm up their pitchers and everybody was getting excited. Seems like this was an old rivalry.

I followed Boggs around till he found the manager of the Spearman team. This man also chewed tobacco, but when Boggs offered him a chew he reared back and looked out over his monstrous cornfed belly and said, "That ain't my brand."

Boggs said, "How much would it be worth to you to win this game?"

"Well in money, not much. I only got five dollars bet on it. But in personal satisfaction, my friend, it would be a strain for a millionaire to pay off."

I could tell the way he talked they were going to get along.

"Did you ever hear of Booger Boggs who played for the East Texas League?" Boggs asked.

"Sure. Everybody's heard of Booger Boggs. Why?"

"That's me."

"Ahhhh," and he started laughing and laughing. "You're jist a farmhand. Maybe a bronc rider, by the looks of them legs."

Boggs was quiet for once. He let the manager finish out his laugh then he said, "Can you catch a ball?"

"Sure. I *am* the Spearman catcher."

"Well, go get your mitt and get me a glove and ball, my dear associate."

While the unbelieving fat man went after the equipment, Boggs started warming up his arm, swinging it around and around.

"Now, son," he said to me, and I knew he was really going to get serious because of the "son" bit, "this old arm ain't in much shape and it'll never be any good after today, but I just want you to know I'm going to give'er all I got."

"You goin' to pitch?"

"You just wait and see."

He threw a few soft ones at the manager and then he let one fly that purty nearly tore the catcher's arm off. I knew he was going to get his chance. He went around and started a few conversations.

"You folks from Dumas don't know when you're beat. I'm goin' to sack you boys out today." As usual when they looked at Boggs everybody just laughed and laughed. That's what he wanted them to do.

One of the sporting boys said, "If you're goin' to pitch I'd like to lay a little money on the line. Now, if you ain't just a blowhard, why don't you put your money where your mouth is?"

"Well now, I ain't got no money, my dear compatriots, but I've got something better," and he swept a long arm at our horses grazing off a ways. "I'll bet any four of that fine bunch against any two of yours."

One man got so carried away he said, "I'll bet my good wagon and team with the grain and laying mash that's in it and a box of groceries to boot."

That was the only bet Boggs called. They shook hands and had plenty of witnesses.

The game started. I watched Boggs fan three Dumas men in a row.

Then Spearman got a man on base. The next two up for our side struck out and the Dumas catcher threw our man out trying to steal second. Then Boggs fanned another and two grounded out to shortstop. And right on into the sixth inning scoreless. Then I could tell Boggs' arm was weakening. A Dumas batter swatted a long, high fly that should have been an easy out in left field. The fielder just plain dropped it. The man scored standing up.

Well, Boggs took off his glasses, pulled out his shirttail, and went to cleaning that lens. He took his time about it. Everybody was wondering what difference it could make if he cleaned a glass that fit over a blind eye. So did I.

The Dumas fans were naturally rawhiding him quite a bit and the Spearman team was getting uneasy. I watched him closely. He was up to something. I knew that no matter what Boggs was, I'd never see another anywhere like him. Come to think of it, that's a whole bunch to say about any man. He was at *least* three different men and maybe a dozen.

When he got through cleaning his glasses he slowly put them back on. Then he took off his hat and his glove and held the ball high in the air. And he shouted so that everybody quieted down.

"Lord, up there in the great universe, heed my call. Lord, I'm goin to ask you to put some devil on this ball. Just let me use him a little. I want a devil curve and a devil drop and a devil fast ball and I'll guarantee you that the end of the game will belong to you, Lord. What I want is victory. Now I know you heard me, Your Honor, Lord. So it's up to me. And if I don't win this game bring a bolt of lightning down upon my unworthy head and burn me to a cinder. Amen and thanks."

I looked up in the cloudless sky and thought that even the Lord would have to strain to get lightning out of that blue sky.

He pulled his hat back on tight, picked up the glove and ball, squinted out that glassless rim, took a big spit of tobacco, and let fly. No matter what happened to this game it was quite a sight to see him pitch. Those runover high-heeled boots, bib overalls, and that old floppy hat sure were different to say just a little.

That ball whistled in there so solid and fast the batter fell down hitting at it. Boggs didn't waste any time now just wound up once and let it fly. The ball broke in a curve and the batter nearly broke his neck fishing for it. The next one was a drop—breaking sharp and clean. The umpire yelled, "Strike!" and thumbed him out. A great roar went up from the Spearman rooters.

After that it was a walk-in. Boggs had shot his wad on those three pitches. He was faking his way now. The spirit of the home team was broken. The Spearman players started a seventh-inning rally and the way they batted I could have been pitching for them and they would have won.

The game wound up nine to one and we had us a team of horses, one of which was a mare with a colt by her side, a wagon, a lot of feed, plus a big box of groceries.

Boggs was carrying his arm at his side. It was obvious he'd never pitch again, not even for fun.

Edward Swift

Cowgirls for Christ

EDWARD SWIFT'S second novel follows the fortunes of Principia Martindale, a small-town Texas girl obsessed by religion. Her fate is sealed, though she does not suspect it, when she falls into the hands of the owner and operator of Miss Corinda Cassy's Invincible Traveling Vacation Bible School, featuring among other things a marching organization of homeless girls who wear ranch costumes and are called Cowgirls for Christ.

At the almost-deserted village of Hudson in the South Texas brush country, Corinda discovers that Principia is a genuine and authentic healer. With the help of her business manager and secret lover Larry Wayne Johnson, she razes the village and builds a City of God where Principia and her powers bring in huge crowds and huge sums of money. The book has many humorous pages, but the end is tragic, for Principia's gift destroys her.

From *Principia Martindale*. New York: Harper & Row, 1983, pp. 264–277.

E arly one morning, Corinda Cassy flipped a tape into her cassette. "Faith of Our Fathers," as sung by the Armstrong Family, filled the entire trailer home. Then she burst into Principia's bedroom. "We're going to call it a tabernacle, not a church," said the Cowgirl for Christ. "This just came to me in a flash. In fact, we're going to call it The Tabernacle in the Sky. It's going to be all glass and steel, just like The Residence, and it's supposed to look like it's floating up to heaven."

"I feel as though I'm hearing a prophecy," said Principia, closing her Bible and sitting up in bed.

"You are," said Corinda. "Our hotel is well into construction, so it's time to start thinking about our next project. You can't preach in a tent all your life. It wouldn't look right. Groundbreaking will take place in the next few weeks, and in the meantime, I've got to get my precious girls settled in their new home. The Lucky L Ranch is now vacant. Rosita and Sergio are over there cleaning it up, and I intend to march my cowgirls over there as soon as they're out of class. Then later on this afternoon we're going to start rehearsing our groundbreaking routine."

"Lord, how good you are to give us this opportunity to serve," said Principia. "I woke up this morning and didn't know where I was or what I was doing. I felt lost and unworthy, but now I feel as though I've received a thousand blessings and haven't even gotten out of bed."

"I have known such mornings myself," said Corinda, thinking of Larry Wayne. "After we break ground for the tabernacle, we'll have two buildings under construction at once. Judson's going to be so noisy no one will be able to sleep past six-thirty, but some of are awake much earlier than that anyway."

The groundbreaking ceremony took place as scheduled and was reported in major newspapers throughout the state. In the Sunday edition of the *Fort Worth Star-Telegram,* there was a color photograph of Corinda and Larry Wayne with the cowgirls standing around them and the new hotel going up in the background. Principia was shown standing in front of the small tent. She was holding the architectural renderings for The Tabernacle in the Sky and staring into the clouds.

Other newspapers ran similar picture stories on the hotel and tabernacle under construction. In the *Christian Reporter* Principia was shown lying on her day bed and receiving a man from Longview who had growths on both sides of his face. The newspaper credited her with five healings in the past two months. "But I can't remember any of them," she said after reading the article. "I'm going to have to start writing everything down. I want to know who these people are and why they think I healed them."

She began receiving letters from all over Texas and nearly half the population of New Bethel. All her friends back home promised to visit her and bring Principal and Wilma Lee with them.

"I don't want my parents visiting me until we've got more to show them," she said to Rosita, who was sweeping out the bedroom. "It would disturb them to see that I'm living in a trailer home. They always told me: 'Nice people don't live on wheels.'"

"Children should listen to their parents," said Rosita, pointing the broomstick at Principia. "Then they might learn something. But it's impossible to tell you this. My daughter, Rubendella, she has always listened to the wrong people."

A few days later Rubendella was in the news again. She had given a talk at Baylor University and had presented slides of the way Judson had been, the way it was and the way it would be. She used architectural renderings to depict the Judson of the future. From Baylor she drove to Southwestern Baptist Theological Seminary in Fort Worth, where she was scheduled to give the same presentation.

Applebee's eye caught the notice in the paper. He was sitting on the curb in front of the Golden Rule Pawn shop where he worked and lived. It was Sunday morning. Downtown Fort Worth was quiet. There were few cars on the streets. Saint George was scratching in the vacant lot not far away, and Applebee was keeping one eye on him. "Rubendella's in town," Applebee shouted. Saint George stopped scratching and lifted his head. "I got just enough time to get there and hear what's on her mind."

At the assembly hall, Applebee sat in the back row and waited impatiently for the first glimpse of Rubendella. When she walked across the stage, he almost didn't recognize her. She was dressed in a black tailored suit, wore no make-up and her hair was fashioned into a bun at the nape of her neck. "She looks a good fifteen years older than she really is," Applebee said to the man on his right, who was wearing an Odd Fellow Lodge tie tack.

"You better not tell her that," the man answered.

"I don't even intend for her to see me," said Applebee. "Wouldn't know what to say to her anymore. That's why I'm sitting way back here in the back."

Applebee stayed for only half the presentation. When he saw the slides of the buildings under construction he got up and left the hall. "A little bit of mediocrity goes a long way," he said when he was on the street again. It was a cold February Sunday, but sweat was pouring from his brow. "She's really got her act down is all I can say, but, then, that's Rubendella."

In the next few weeks Rubendella gave her slide show at the First Baptist Church of Dallas, Hardin Simmons University in Abilene and several Hispanic Baptist congregations in El Paso. She gave herself three days off each week and on those days she put on her high heels and tight pants, a nylon blouse and Indian jewelry and drove to the nearest city to see all the movies. She would sometimes see the same picture over and over until she had memorized the lines and could act out all the parts while driving from one place to the next.

She sent Rosita postcards from every city she visited and clipped out her newspaper interviews and sent them home as well.

"There is too much happening too fast," Rosita said after she read the clippings about her daughter addressing the Southern Baptist Convention in Houston. "I never know where my Rubendella is going to turn up next." She was sitting in front of her parents' graves and glancing at the article in her hand. "I never know where Sergio and I will turn up either. Now we are living in the Lucky L Ranch because our house is going to be a parking lot, but where we are is not home. The little cowgirls we live with are too silly, and the big one is worse. They will grow up to be just like her too."

Every day Rosita visited her parents' graves, sat there a few minutes and talked to them about all the changes she was witnessing. During the construction of the tabernacle, the graves were almost covered over, but Rosita threw herself between the wooden crosses and refused to get up. "I'm going to be buried right here anyway," she said. "You might as well cover me up right now and get it over with."

Corinda Cassy was marching her cowgirls up and down the dusty road when out of the corner of her eye she caught a glimpse of Rosita lying between the graves. "Stand up before you're covered up!" Corinda shouted. The drill team dispersed in all directions, but Rosita did not move. Corinda rushed over to the construction site. She stopped the workers and told Rosita it was all a mistake.

"This is only one of many mistakes," said Rosita, still lying on her back. "I will stay here until I have proof in writing that these graves will not be covered up."

Corinda dismissed the workers for the day. She left Rosita lying between the graves and went to the ranch to telephone the architect.

Together they decided to incorporate the graves into a rock garden adjacent to the tabernacle.

"Let's get started on the garden right away," she said. "I want a bubbling fountain in the very center of it, and a few trees, whatever kind will grow here, with lots of twinkling lights in them. If we're going to have to do this, we might as well do it up good."

After hanging up the phone, she wrote a letter stating that the graves would not be destroyed. Rosita, still lying on the ground, read the letter three times before she was satisfied. Then she got up and went about her work.

"It's going to cost me a great deal of money to make this slight change," Corinda said to Larry Wayne that afternoon during their "hour of prayer." "But I can see no way of getting around it without bad press."

"If there was a way of getting around it," he said, unbuttoning her blouse, "I'm sure you would have thought of it."

When the garden was completed, Sergio made a wooden bench and Rosita placed it in front of the graves, but Corinda Cassy replaced it with a bench of her choice, one made of stone, which she said was more in keeping with the total environment she was trying to create.

"What does it matter" said Rosita, "just as long as there's something to sit on? What does it matter?"

There were days when she was so busy caring for Principia and the cowgirls she was only able to sit on the bench for a few seconds, but according to Rosita a few seconds were better than none at all. She often passed her time there looking back, retracing everything that had happened from the time Applebee arrived in Judson to the present. While reflecting over the years that had passed all too rapidly, she sometimes took refuge in a strange, almost comforting sadness that obliterated the once constant smile on her face.

Sergio didn't think it made his wife any happier to linger over the past. "Her eyes get sadder by the day," he told Corinda, who said Rosita would get used to the changes in time.

"A few changes are good, but not so many," said Rosita when Corinda suggested naming the town Jericho. "I will dig up my parents and leave with their bones if you change the name. I'll never stop cursing you either."

After some thought, Corinda decided Rosita was right, the town was known as Judson and should go on being known as Judson, but the main street leading to the yet unfinished tabernacle should be called the Avenue of the Redeemed. In order to have the avenue widened into a glistening thoroughfare, she had the date palms cut, then the cottonwood, and after that she started wondering what she could do to improve the smaller street. Finally she decided to have it paved as well, and on the north side of the intersection she called it the Pathway to Eternity. On the south side it was known as the Road to Righteousness. Miss Cassy told a reporter from the *Baptist Standard* that the Lord had spoken to her in a dream and instructed her to make these changes. "And if He's willing," she was quoted, " I will make even more."

"How could she make any more changes than what she already has?" said Applebee. "There's nothing left of the place as it is." He folded up the *Baptist Standard* and stuffed it into one of Johnnie Chapman's shopping bags. They were sitting at the Water Gardens. It was Sunday, and there was a wind blowing through the business district. "The only one who's getting the good end of the bargain is Rubendella," Applebee said. "She covered Texas last year, and now they've got her traveling around the south. Newspapers says she's going to launch a campaign in California next, and if I know Rubendella she won't come back after that."

"She'll just keep on a'going," said Johnnie Chapman, lifting her feet out of the water. They were just beginning to wrinkle from being under so long. "Best not to think about all this. Try not to anyway."

She had told him this before, dozens of times, but it had never done any good. He didn't enjoy reflecting on his years in Judson, but there were times when he could not help doing so. "Too much reflection on some things is poison," Johnnie had told him, and for that reason he stopped playing the fiddle because the old jealous tune brought the past too close to the present. Yet without any effort at all there were moments, sometimes whole days, usually in the summer when there was sand in the air, when his thoughts would go rolling like a ball of twine unraveling down a hill. Then he would usually sit on the curb just outside the entrance to the pawnshop or walk down to the Water Gardens to soak his feet and think of Judson.

During those times, he would also think of Principia, but it would only be a painful half thought, a thought that registered without completely making itself known, for the truth was he did not enjoy thinking about her at all, but there were times when Judson would come back on him all at once and he would search for a way to make the past crumble from his memory and drop to the hot sidewalk like beads of sweat pouring from his face.

The Golden Rule Pawnshop, owned by Applebee's ex-brother-in-law, didn't always provide the necessary distraction because it was located on the north side of downtown Fort Worth, a district that was under reconstruction most of the time. The shop was in a corner red brick building of three stories. In the back behind the display cases was an archway covered by a chintz curtain and behind the curtain was a large room where Applebee lived. All around him old buildings were coming down and new ones were going up. Sometimes during the night he would be awakened by an explosion of dynamite, and the next day the hull of a building that had been standing the day before would be nothing but a pile of bricks. With each building that was ripped to the ground he would think of Judson and wonder if he were destined to live within the sound of demolition for the rest of his life.

From time to time he would consider moving to a quiet section of town, but he was never able to make that move because there were a few good things about living in the pawnshop, and he reminded himself of them everyday: he was close to F. W. Woolworth's, his favorite place to have lunch or a cup of coffee, and he wasn't too far from the bus station where he knew he could find Johnnie Chapman, when she wasn't in the pawnshop that is, or down at the Water Gardens washing out her rags and waiting for him to show up.

But most of the time he endured long, unavoidable afternoons in the shop. He dreaded those days most of all because invariably he would have a difficult customer, something would be stolen or someone's voice would remind him of Corinda Cassy, Principia or Rosita, and then either a quiet internal rage or a long brooding sadness would sweep over him. When that happened he would often leave the customer to browse, or from time to time he would attempt to tell the story of Judson, but less than midway through he would usually stop himself, finish the business at hand and go out front with his coloring book and sit on the curb.

Applebee was never far removed from Judson, and before long he realized he never would be, not only because it occupied a large part of his mind but because the *new* town was too often in the news. When The Residence was completed there was a grand opening. Newspaper reporters and television anchormen arrived from all over Texas to inspect the new seven-story hotel: a stair-stepped pyramid of mirrored glass, the top floor of which was a penthouse occupied by Larry Wayne and Corinda.

In a press conference held in the lobby of mirrors Larry Wayne, dressed in white silk, told reporters the hotel was run by a staff of thirty devoted Christians and every room was booked for six months in advance. Corinda said she was certain they would need to expand their facilities in due time. "I have," she added, "purposely designed the Tabernacle in the Sky bigger than what is now necessary, for midway through the construction of the hotel the Lord gave me the vision of growth and I want to allow much room for expansion."

"Speaking of expansion," said Larry Wayne, "our station, The Radio Church of God, will begin broadcasting in about a month."

"Oh, yes," said Corinda, wrapping herself in her cowgirl cape, "we will be on the air waves with music, interviews and, of course, Principia's healing services. She's now living in a modest apartment on the ground floor of the hotel. There's a tape recorder by her bed, and when she feels the spirit leading her into communication with her followers she will simply record herself for future broadcast. None of her talks will be edited very much, but some of them will be spliced together so we can create one long program, which will be like a medley of beautiful songs."

After the press conference, Corinda and Larry Wayne relaxed on the terrace of their penthouse. "The Radio Church of God will become known in religious circles throughout the world," Corinda said, "but this is not enough. We've got to televise Principia during her healing services. We've got to televise my precious cowgirls prancing across the stage too. Sooo many many lost souls can be won this way."

"And yours might be one of them," said Larry Wayne.

"One day you'll ask me to forgive you for saying that," said Corinda. "You never take me seriously on anything that has to do with my inner strength. I want this to be the most inspirational program on television. I want it to speak to the minds and hearts of *everyone*. Even you will be moved by it."

When The Tabernacle in the Sky was completed, Corinda delayed the opening ceremony until television cameras could be installed and checked out. The tabernacle, connected to The Residence by an underground passage, was a dome-shaped structure with three spires of varying heights and three steps leading to three front doors. The main auditorium could seat three thousand, three hundred and thirty-three people, and the proscenium arch, shaped like a heart, was draped with a silver curtain.

A few days before the grand opening, Corinda invited the press to tour the building. "I just want our holy city to be uplifting," she told the reporters, but a writer from the San Antonio *Sun* said it was anything but. "The Residence," he wrote, "is a modern-day pyramid, which, unlike the ancient structures of its shape, does not appear to be in relationship to the guiding forces of the universe, and as for the much-talked-about Tabernacle in the Sky, all I can say is that it can be seen for miles around. The mirrored glass is constantly doing battle with the blazing sun. If visit you must, a cloudy day is recommended."

"That happens to be the silliest, most stupid journalist I've ever read," said Corinda, stomping through the penthouse in her purple boots. It was the day of the grand opening. She was wearing a red cotton dress with a ruffle around the hem and a concho belt slung low around her hips. "This man obviously suffers from cleverness," she said to Larry Wayne, who was sitting on the couch with a towel wrapped around his waist and his feet on the coffee table. "Principia is not allowed to read the newspapers today. She is not allowed to answer the telephone or turn on the radio or the television. She is not to have visitors, unless I approve of them. She's nervous enough about the first service in our beautiful tabernacle, and I don't want anything or anybody to upset her."

Principia spent the morning and afternoon in her apartment. She read Edgar Young Mullins, listened to tapes of the Armstrong Family and lunched with Rosita and Sergio, who had been instructed to keep the conversation light.

When it came time to leave for the opening services, Rosita combed Principia's hair, which had grown to her waist, and pinned it out of her eyes with silver barrettes shaped like musical notes. She had chosen to wear a gown with cathedral sleeves and silk slippers that clung to her feet as though they had grown there. "I feel so unsure of myself tonight," she said when they left the apartment. Sergio gave her an arm to lean on as they walked through the tunnel to The Tabernacle in the Sky, and along the way Principia's thoughts kept turning back in time. "I wonder what Aunt Wilda is doing right now," she said as they approached the double doors leading into the tabernacle.

"Your aunt is no longer living," said Rosita.

"Oh, that's right," said Principia. "I must have been thinking about someone else. Sometimes it's hard to remember who isn't living anymore."

When they arrived backstage, Larry Wayne said the tabernacle was only a third full, but no one was expecting a full house on the first night anyway. Still, he delayed the opening until he was sure everyone had arrived and was seated.

Principia stood in the wings and swayed back and forth, finding her balance first on Sergio and then on Rosita. "I feel weak all over," she said, peering through the curtain at the congregation. "Why do I keep looking up and expecting to see the stars instead of a ceiling? It looks like they could have left the roof off this church, doesn't it?"

Rosita turned to Sergio and whispered in Spanish, "All things resemble their owner." It had been one of her mother's favorite proverbs.

"In this case it's true," said Sergio.

"New Bethel Church was nothing like this," Principia continued, still looking through the curtain. "There you could look up and see the clouds and stars."

"Now you are the star," said Sergio, trying to make pleasant conversation. "And all these people have come here to see you."

"If only I knew what to expect I'd feel better," said Principia. "I don't like all this waiting around."

At eight o'clock the curtain went up and the cowgirls, each carrying a Christian flag and singing:

> "Do Lord, Oh Do Lord,
> Oh, do remember me,
> Hallelujah!
> "Do Lord, Oh Do Lord,
> Oh, do remember me,
> Forever . . ."

pranced across the stage with Corinda Cassy in the lead. On command and still singing, the cowgirls executed countermarches and gate turns, pinwheels and left flanks, right flanks and a series of diagonals before returning to rank and file formation. The congregation broke into applause as the drill team left the stage. Corinda returned to take a bow for the entire group, and then waving the Christian flag, she marched off with her head held high and her cowgirl cape flapping behind her.

For several minutes after that, the stage was empty. Principia was still standing in the wings, but she didn't feel led by the Spirit to make her entrance. "I don't think I can do this tonight," she said.

"Oh yes you can," said Larry Wayne. "You can't let us down now." He gave her the slightest push—that was all it took—and suddenly she was standing on the stage. The audience broke into thunderous applause as she walked to the microphone, which was surrounded by white lilies. She stood there and for a long time did not speak. She stared at the paying audience, but she couldn't see beyond the first row. The spotlights were blinding, yet she continued to stare directly into them.

"I don't know what to say," she finally said. Her voice was weak. "So I'm going to stand here for a few minutes. I hope you won't mind."

The congregation was silent. Principia didn't move. She stood there and allowed her mind to drift far away. She had no idea what she was thinking. The spotlight seemed to burn away her thoughts before she was aware of them. Then, when she had lost track of where she was, something happened. It was as though an electrical current had shocked her into life, for she began speaking with an authority that the *Christian Reporter* said could only issue from the mouth of a saint.

"If you came here to see Principia Martindale you came here for the wrong reason," she said. Her voice was angry. "If you came here to see this building, you came here for the wrong reason too. This building is nothing but a shell, and so is Principia Martindale, but the Lord God who created life is all . . ."

While she preached members of the congregation walked down the aisle and up on the stage to touch her. People kissed the hem of her garment, touched her arms, her hands, her hair. But she was so absorbed in her sermon and the blinding light that she wasn't aware of their presence until she felt someone tugging hard at her sleeve. Then she realized she was surrounded by people. They were sitting at her feet, or standing, straining to get a better look, or to touch her, any part of her. Some were on crutches, one was in a wheelchair and others appeared to be perfectly healthy. "What have I been saying?" she asked.

"It's not what you say that's so important," someone said. Principia started twisting her hair with both hands. The people began closing in. They touched her, kissed her, stroked her hair and ripped off pieces of her dress. Corinda and Larry Wayne tried to form the mob into a single file, but it didn't work. Finally Principia broke away and ran. Before she made it to the wings, she fainted. Sergio and Larry Wayne carried her offstage, and when she was revived she said she felt as if she were living inside a nightmare. "Suddenly everything was so scary," she said. "I wish I was still in the tent. It was so old-fashioned and comfortable."

"But you weren't comfortable there at first either," said Corinda. "In time you will find comfort with this new place."

Two days later the newspapers were filled with accounts of Principia's first service in the tabernacle. One reporter called her "hypersensitive" and "neurotically religious." Another said that her power, if she had any, was located in her little finger, and that she possessed an insane stare which convinced some people she was a mystic when in reality she was anything but.

"Hide the newspapers quick," Corinda Cassy screamed over the telephone. She was talking to Rosita, who was about to serve Principia breakfast. "We simply can't have her reading these idiotic articles about herself."

Then she hung up and called Larry Wayne in the ground floor office. "We're going to publish our own inspirational magazine each month, and we're going to call it *The New Heaven*," she instructed. "Right now you've got to find me some able editors and some writers who can communicate our true worth and intentions."

Within two months the first issue of the magazine was printed. By then Principia was more comfortable with her Sunday evening services and *The New Heaven* announced that very soon she would be giving two healing services each week. The first issue also contained an article about the wheelchairs, crutches and eyeglasses left behind as proof of a healing. These objects were hung on the back wall of the tabernacle. Corinda Cassy had written the article herself, but she did not mention that some of the wheelchairs had been retrieved, some of the crutches had been taken back and that a lady from Kerrville had come looking for her eyeglasses but could not find them.

"We want our magazine to emphasize the positive and forget about the negative," said Corinda to the editor-in-chief, Bill Collins, who had been hired straight out of Baylor's graduate school and was eager to succeed. "The magazine is going to be one of our most successful projects."

In the second issue, Corinda interviewed Principia, who said: "Sometimes it scares me to stand before all those people because I forget where I am, and then suddenly I wake up, and don't always know what I've done or said."

☆ ☆ ☆ ☆

The reporter had quoted Corinda Cassy:

"I'm not through yet. I've only just begun. The Lord has now asked me to build a prayer tower. It will be a single shaft of reinforced concrete with an enclosed elevator, and on the very top will be a flying-saucer-shaped structure inside which rows and rows of telephones will ring twenty-four hours a day and be answered by devoted Christians with prayers on their lips. The tower will go into construction immediately and within a year it too will be finished. At first I thought I would call it The Pillar of Prayer, but the Heavenly Father instructed me otherwise. He told me that I was completely off base and then brought me back down to earth again. Now, with both feet firmly planted on the ground, I am sooo happy to announce that we will call it The Prayer Tower and nothing but. Simplicity is always best. I have lived my life with this in mind."

Frank X. Tolbert

Father Casey Speaks His Mind

COLUMNIST, NOVELIST, AND FRIEND OF MAN, Frank X. Tolbert
(making his second appearance in this volume) traveled widely in Texas
and knew practically everybody in the state. He published his findings
for many years in the *Dallas Morning News* and in a few good novels.
Tolbert's interest in characters led him to a "rough-tongued priest,"
Father John F. Casey, of Dell City in far West Texas. Tolbert describes
Casey with a humorist's twinkle in his eye.

From *Tolbert's Texas*. Garden City: Doubleday, 1983, pp. 47–49.

H e was known as San Isidro, the Farmer or the Laborer. He died in
A.D. 1130. And he was canonized, or so goes the legend, after an angel
was seen operating his plow. He is the patron saint of farmers and
others who work with their hands.

San Isidro lives again in 1983 in Dell City, Texas, in the brawny
person of Father John F. Casey, aged seventy-four.

Dell City (pop. 383) is in Hudspeth County in heavily mineralized
earth just west of some salt lakes and the nine-thousand-foot-high
Guadalupe Mountains. Dell City is the center for a lush farming community which blossomed out of the desert about a quarter of a century
ago when it was found to be over an underground lake.

Father Casey is a rough-tongued Boston Irishman, his brogue
somewhat softened from many years spent with Spanish-speaking
parishioners.

"I took four years of Spanish in high school and one year of it in
college. Yet, Castilian Spanish is a waste in my parish. You gotta speak

Juarez Spanish. They don't know what the hell you're saying in Castilian," said the padre.

He played football at Boston College and four other colleges. Then he became a carpenter. And he was thirty-two when he entered the priesthood.

The muscular, 190-pound, former football center did all the carpentry work, all the plumbing, all the electrical wiring and the plastering on the two large buildings that comprise San Isidro Catholic Mission.

The original 1955 model church is now a recreation hall and the old priest's living quarters.

His latest triumph is the new church with an auditorium which seats more than five hundred. It would probably cost at least two hundred thousand dollars, maybe more, to construct if you didn't have San Isidro's 1983 disciple on the job.

"I built that church with fifty thousand dollars and twenty pounds off my butt," said Father Casey.

He only had help on the concrete block walls and the roof.

The front of the new church is graced with pictures of the angel at San Isidro's plow, these artworks in brilliant Mexican tiles.

Father Casey once applied for an on-the-premises beer license for San Isidro. "He said he needed a beer license to keep his congregation together," said Judge Tom Neely of Sierra Blanca, the capital of Hudspeth County. Judge Neely told me he didn't know how Father Casey came out on his application.

"Actually I sold beer at church dances and suppers until someone turned me in and the liquor control people stopped me," said the padre. "Now my parishioners have to bring their beer. Hell of a note! I never got a beer license."

The feast of San Isidro, around May 10, is always a big day at Father Casey's church. On that date he also blesses the crops.

Several years ago I was in Dell City when Father Casey got a complaint from one of the farmers, Joe Díaz.

"Padre, you bless my crops in May and in June I got some hail damage. What kind of a deal is that?" said Mr. Díaz.

"Hell, Joe, you never go to church. What do you expect?" was Father Casey's reply.

Dell City is rather isolated. It's about seventy miles to the nearest real town, the county seat Sierra Blanca, and one hundred miles to El Paso.

About a decade ago or more the Dell City citizens petitioned the state to let them form their own political division, called Sam Rayburn County, in honor of the late speaker of the House of Representatives from Texas.

The Dell City citizens' main gripe was that it is seventy lonely miles to the Hudspeth county courthouse.

Nothing came of the petition though. Hudspeth County is almost as big as the state of Connecticut in area but has less than three thousand inhabitants, most of these in and around Sierra Blanca and Dell City.

Sam Rayburn County if it had been organized, wouldn't have had enough human types to afford a courthouse—unless Father Casey would build it.

Picaros and Vagabonds

For George Sessions Perry's "Under the Bridge"

A vagabond is a drifter. A picaro is a drifter with a purpose. He is looking for somebody to cheat. The type has been interesting to humorists since Lazarillo de Tormes appeared in Spain. Specimens—from medicine-show operators to tin-horn gamblers—joined the westward movement in the New World and in literary form appeared in John Steinbeck's *Cannery Row* (1945), and, in modified form, in Jack Kerouac's *On the Road* (1957). Once they were called bums or hoboes.

Now they are lost in the tide of "homeless" people who spend the winter in the Sunbelt, demanding food, shelter, and showers. George Sessions Perry found three of them under a bridge over the Brazos River, Dillon Anderson followed a pair of them across Texas in *I and Claudie,* and Ben K. Green depicts himself as a skillful young horse trader. We laugh at them, but in our hearts we envy them their freedom and irresponsibility.

George Sessions Perry

Under the Bridge

GEORGE SESSIONS PERRY was a native of Rockdale, Texas, and his best stories deal with his family (*My Granny Van,* 1949), the sandy-land farmers near his town (*Hold Autumn in Your Hand,* 1941), and the happy hunters and fishermen in the river bottoms farther out (*Hackberry Cavalier,* 1944). *Hold Autumn in Your Hand* won the National Book Award and Perry was well known on the East Coast when he died tragically in 1956.

Walls Rise Up, his first novel, is a humorous confection following the predatory activities of three vagabonds who take possession of a deserted fishing camp under a bridge over the Brazos River near Rockdale. Jimmy, the leader, thinks they are being directed by the Higher Powers. They victimize everybody in sight and have incredible adventures, amorous and otherwise, until a flood washes out the camp and brings the interlude to a close.

From *Walls Rise Up.* New York: Doubleday, Doran, 1939, pp. 26–36.

This camp was really nice. The bridge that it was under was old but the floor had been covered with tarvia, so naturally it wouldn't leak. There were two wooden boxes hanging on a wire with tin plates and cups and knives and forks in them. In one there was two loaves of stale bread and some onions and potatoes and a bucket of grease and some salt and pepper and coffee and molasses. And since it was hung on wire like that, there weren't any ants at all. There was also an extra-good butcher knife made out of an old saw blade, and a single-shot twelve-gauge shotgun and three shells in the grub box.

The bridge ran east and west high up over the river so that the camp was better than fifteen feet above the water. Besides, there was plenty of room for the south breeze to sweep through. But before I forget, there was also an oil lantern with a dirty chimney and nearly a gallon of kerosene and an old ax with a wired-up handle.

I guess the river must have been about two hundred feet wide at the camp. There was a long, broad sand bar on our side and rock cliffs on the other side running straight up about twenty feet. Up the river a little way it forked, one fork running north and one east. And down at the first bend below us there was an island. I'd say about a quarter of a mile below us. It was long and sort of curving, about the shape of a raw weenie, a hundred yards long by about thirty yards wide.

"If we ever get in any trouble," I said, "we can hide on that island."

"Naturally," Jimmy says, "the Higher Powers wouldn't send us to a place that didn't provide for emergencies. I guess they know better than anybody that the flesh is weak and the best resolves sometimes crumble."

Mike dished out three plates of stew and some of that stale bread. Then we sat down on the cot and started eating. Jimmy kept standing up.

"What's the matter, Jimmy?" I said. "You got a boil on your hind end?"

"No," Jimmy said. "That old canvas on the cot looks pretty rotten. I don't see how it's holding you two up as it is."

"All right," Mike said, "let's get up. We don't want to bust Jimmy's bed."

Jimmy just grinned and sat down in the sand. "You boys are sure nice to me," he said.

Mike went over and got him some more stew.

While we were eating, Mike said, "Ain't that water I see in the bottom of that old skiff?"

I said it was.

Then Mike began to cuss Eric and said a leaky skiff was an abomination before God and he never liked anybody that owned one and now he knew how Eric came to sit down on the tracks.

But Jimmy said that was no way to speak about our late lamented benefactor and let's take a look at the neighborhood. Besides, he said, the water in the bottom of that old skiff would be a wonderful place for me and Mike to wash dishes.

Not far up the sand bar we found a spring of pretty good water. It ran about a four-inch stream of clear cool bubbly water down a little channel of clean gravel. Also there was water cress growing in the spring which the running water rippled like a woman's hair in the breeze.

Over on the high bank we saw a woman herding what looked like a hundred turkeys.

At the sight of these turkeys Jimmy grinned big and broad and of course that made us feel good. Then he says the first time we go to the store we'd better get a nickel's worth of garlic. Without garlic, he says, the dressing tastes flat.

When we walked up onto the bridge we saw a truck farm on one side of the road where somebody was raising tomatoes and cabbage and okra and onions and black-eyed peas and sweet potatoes. On the other side of the road there was a corn and cotton field.

"That truck farm's so perfect," Jimmy says, "that I suspect it of being a mirage."

We argued it wasn't but Jimmy was so certain it was that Mike and me had to go over and pick a bucket of mixed vegetables and bring to him before he'd admit it was real.

When we got back from picking he pointed down the road. At the first bend there was a filling station with a sign on it that said: "Gasoline. Groceries. Beer. Ice. Catfish."

For a little while we all just stood there looking.

"I wish you hadn't said what you did about Eric," Jimmy says to Mike. "He has left us many good things."

"I guess so," Mike said, "but he could just as well patched that old skiff as not."

It was late afternoon but the sun was still beating down strong and hot.

"I don't claim to be any smarter than the next man," I said, "but there's one thing I've always noticed."

"What's that?" Mike said.

"Well," I said, "it's just this: it looks like a man can get thirstier under a bridge than nearly anywhere on earth."

"I never give it no thought," Mike said, "but it does seem to be true."

"And what's more," I said, "it don't make me especially thirsty for spring water."

"I've been thinking," Jimmy says, "about the time that Mr. Mattocks, the hardware man in our town, shot his best customer by accident showing him a gun . . . . We're all happy now and good friends but there may come a time when we will lose patience with each other. That old shotgun just ought not to be down there."

"You mean swap it for beer?" I said.

"That's one way of getting rid of a menace," Jimmy says. "Would you like to run get the shotgun, Mike?"

"Sure," Mike says.

"And bring those three shells," Jimmy said. "They might make the difference of a bottle."

We walked on down the road till we came to the store. When we went in the proprietor was down behind the back counter rolling something that rattled with three Negroes and a Mexican.

When he stuck his head up over the counter he saw the shotgun and raised both hands. The Negroes and the Mexican crawled on out the back door.

The storekeeper was about five and a half feet tall. He had one eye that didn't work and was the kind of man that's always sweating.

Jimmy just grinned at him.

"Friend," he said, "if you think we've come in here to burgle your store, you're all wrong. All we intend to do is be neighbors and customers."

"Oh," the storekeeper said, grinning in a way that made me glad he didn't owe us any money.

"We're living down under the bridge," Jimmy said, "and mean to carry on my brother's fishing business."

"Is ole Sam Rutherford your brother?"

"Poor Sam," Jimmy said. "He was up until about three o'clock this afternoon when he contested that fast freight for the right of way."

"Too bad," old Gotch-Eye said. "I got my fish from him."

"Oh, me and my friends here, Eddie and Mike, will carry on the fish business just the same."

"You catch 'em and I'll sell 'em," Gotch said.

"By the way," Jimmy said, "Sam and I was talking this morning and we went over the account book together."

"Book?"

"Didn't you know Sam put those things down in a book?"

"No, I didn't."

"Well anyway, we'll be willing to take it out in trade."

"Take what out in trade?"

"That little amount you owed Sam for those fish."

"How much was it?"

"I'd have to step down to the bridge," Jimmy says, "and get the book."

"Well, I'll make you a proposition," the storekeeper said. "I'll settle with you boys for what baloney and cheese and crackers you care to eat and what beer you'd like to drink between now and closing time."

"Uncap three cold ones," Jimmy says. "My throat is caked with this Brazos Bottom dust . . . . And by the way, I guess you're still closing at the regular time."

"Sure. Eight o'clock."

"That ain't what Sam said."

"All right then. Ten."

You could write your name in the frost on those brown bottles.

I know it must have made Jimmy's teeth ache because he just tilted that first bottle up to his mouth and let every bit of the beer run out.

We had had three apiece when Mike said, "What about the shotgun, Jimmy?"

"We must grease it and cherish it," Jimmy says. "As long as we keep it, it will protect us from harm. A shotgun is good against burglars and intruders. It will sweeten the nature of the surliest husbands. And finally," he said, "it will always swap for this fluid amber delight."

"By God," Mike says, "it's wonderful how that man can talk and how good that talk can make you feel."

"What our lives would have been without him," I said, "I shudder to think about."

"Here," Jimmy said, modest, trying to turn it off like nothing had happened, "eat some cheese."

Dillon Anderson

The Windmill Fixers

IN THE 1950s Dillon Anderson was a Houston lawyer involved in so many civic and organizational matters that he might have been called Mr. Houston. His ability and usefulness earned him an invitation from President Dwight D. Eisenhower to come to Washington as the president's Assistant for National Security. In the same decade he produced his two special contributions to Texas humor: *I and Claudie* (1951) and *Claudie's Kinfolks* (1954). Anderson once remarked that these books "were in no sense autobiographical," but that he envied his two picaros "their liberty, free from committees, protocol, and taxes." Clint Hightower, the brains of the duo, picks up Claudie (the muscle) in New Orleans. Fearing the police, they head for Texas, where they find themselves continually in hot water as one scam after another collapses. "The Windmill Fixers" is a fair sample.

From *I and Claudie*. Boston: Little, Brown, 1951, pp. 124–141.

I am a man that can move fast when I'm on the trail of something really good, and this will show you what I mean: It was on a Saturday that the Widow Wiley and Emma gave our trailer house a tow to Dallas and left us in the park; on Sunday I met Angus Pratt at a band concert in Dallas, and by Monday I and Claudie were on our way again. Then, while the trailer swung and swayed along behind the big green cattle truck, was the first real chance I'd had to explain to Claudie about our new specialty.

"Claudie," I said, "there is more of nearly everything in Texas than any other state in the Union, and this goes for windmills too. Also, you will find more wind in Texas to turn these windmills, more trouble in locating water for them to lift, and more space that needs watering."

Up ahead in the cattle truck, Backlash, the fat little colored driver, sloped for Waco. He had our dollar and the nearly full bottle of vanilla extract we had given him for the lift. He was driving so fast that the wind screamed and whined about the eaves of the trailer house like she-panthers at midnight. Backlash was due in Waco before dark, and the sun wasn't over three quarters of an hour high.

"Another thing to bear in mind Claudie," I went on—"even the best windmill is apt to get out of whack now and then."

"Windmills or no windmills, I don't like the way that boy is driving up there." Claudie was sitting on the trailer floor holding the coal-oil stove, the lantern and the coffee-pot in his lap so they wouldn't jostle about.

"Well," I told him, as I braced my folding chair against the rear door, "it's hard to be choosy when you've got to hitchhike for a trailer house. Now don't get me off my subject again, please."

"What's that?" he wanted to know.

"Our specialty," I said. "We're going to be windmill fixers."

"But we don't know nothing about windmills," he argued.

"Not yet," I admitted, "but listen to me, Claudie: we've wandered all over Texas, we've dabbled in this and we've dabbled in that; we've been specializing in other people's business, but so far I've been finding better jobs for us than we can hold."

"We've sure been fired from some nice jobs," Claudie admitted.

"That's what I'm trying to tell you," I went on. "We need a specialty, and I've got it all planned."

"Uh-huh," was all I got from Claudie.

"Now I'm going to tell you about it," I said. "While you were wasting your time yesterday in Dallas at that pin ball arcade, I talked to a man who is a real windmill expert—fellow by the name of Angus Pratt. Look what he gave me: a picture folder put out by a Waco concern. It shows all the parts of a windmill and exactly how they work."

I let Claudie see the folder; then I explained it to him as best I could, and as he seemed to understand it fairly well, I went on: "They can teach you there in Waco how to fix windmills. A two weeks' course. That's where Angus Pratt learned about windmills. I and you will sign up there for a little higher education tomorrow."

Claudie nodded his head, but the look on his face was vacant, like that of a man playing music by ear. I told him I was afraid he was never meant to be anything but a hewer of wood and a drawer of water.

About this time two police officers came roaring alongside us on motorcycles, and Claudie started swallowing and running his hand around under his collar. He actually looked at me like he figured I must have planned to get us arrested. With the Louisiana law after us anyway, and here we were getting arrested, I suppose I must have given Claudie about the same kind of a look as Backlash slammed on the brakes and brought us to a very rough stop.

The biggest officer—the big one with two guns on his hips and a forked scar on his cheek—said to us in a very harsh way: "What the hell kind of contraption is this? Where is your permit?"

Backlash dug out his permit, but of course it did not cover our trailer house or any part of it. The officer looked us up and down; then he said, "You will all have to come with me to the Justice of the Peace."

"Officer," I said, and I knew this had to be good, "you look like a fair-minded man to me. This truck and these cattle belong to a nice man in Waco, Texas. He is a very honest man; he is very prominent in the cattle business; also he is without malice aforethought." The officer listened.

The other officer came up and said, "I think he is about to outtalk you, Elmo."

Elmo gave the other officer a very bilious look and said, "Just who the hell is making this arrest?"

"So far, nobody is," the other officer said, and he said it in a very haughty way.

Then I made my move. "Elmo," I said, "I think you are a fine type of officer. Tell you what: If you'll let Backlash pull us off this road, nobody will be violating the law anymore. Let's all let Backlash take this truck of cattle on to Waco."

Elmo then said in a loud voice that we'd better get that damn trailer off the highways of the State of Texas before somebody got into trouble. He spat on the side of the road and looked hard at the other officer. As Backlash pulled us into a green pasture by the side of the road, I noticed that the sign on the mailbox said E. C. Wigginbotham.

We unhooked the trailer under the shade of some pecan trees, while the motorcycles sputtered off toward Dallas. Backlash left, fast, in the other direction; then I and Claudie looked things over. We were about a hundred yards from a big white farmhouse surrounded by some cedar and hackberry trees, a red barn, a silo and a tall windmill. I pointed out to Claudie that the windmill was running at a fast clip in the brisk June breeze. Claudie had no sooner scotched the wheels and leveled up the trailer then we heard dogs barking. Then we saw a whole pack of them spilling out from behind a long lilac hedge by the big house. They came bouncing our way, and along behind them came a big square-shouldered man carrying a double-barreled shotgun over his shoulder.

He walked up to the trailer house, shushed the dogs, and said in a very sarcastic way: "You fellers seem to be making yourselves pretty well at home." He was about nineteen hands high, and he looked even bigger than that, carrying the gun and all. He had a big black bushy mustache. His eyes were bright blue, and he had a way of squinting them like a man who has spent his forty-odd years in a high wind.

I took off my hat and said: "Mr. Wigginbotham, right now we do not exactly have any way to get out of here."

"Well," he told us, "you'd better figger a way to get out. You are trespassers, and I don't want the sun to go down on you here." At that, I looked out toward the west, and there was the sun, not over an hour high.

"Mr. Wigginbotham," I said to him as I looked up toward the house place, "I don't like the way that windmill of yours sounds. Ever have any trouble with it?"

"Some," he said, but he didn't say it like a man who counted on having any more.

"Listen to it," I went on as I cupped my hand over my ear. "Hear that *calung-capluk, calung-capluk?* Sounds to me like there's something loose somewhere."

"What do you know about windmills?" Mr. Wigginbotham asked me. He was drawing a mighty fine bead on me with both eyes, but he'd quit talking about trespassing.

"We're windmill fixers," I told him, and I held his eye to be sure he didn't look at Claudie. "You'd better let us check it over in the morning, first thing. An ounce of prevention is worth a pound of cure."

"There is something to that, all right," Mr. Wigginbotham allowed, then I went on: "My name is Clint Hightower. I and my assistant here, Claudie, will have that machine singing like a new one before noon tomorrow. It won't cost you a penny."

Mr. Wigginbotham agreed to let us take a look at the windmill the next morning.

Even a trespasser has certain rights in Texas if he hasn't been run off by sundown, and a share in the chuck is one of them. We had a nice supper that night with the folks at the big house. Mrs. Wigginbotham was a fine cook; she served us hot biscuits, fried chicken and cream gravy, three or four kinds of garden sass, and wild plum jelly. It all smelled so good and looked so good that Claudie didn't even close his eyes when Mr. Wigginbotham said Grace before we ate.

Mrs. Wigginbotham was not much bigger than a bar of soap, but she ran things around that house. She was the law and the prophets, and she was prompted from time to time by her old-maid sister Lula, who lived with them. Miss Lula and the Missus, as Mr. Wigginbotham called them, had little black snapping buckshot eyes, soft fair skin, and dark straight hair. They both had very small hands, too, but with big knuckles.

The ladies were pretty nice to us; nicer, in fact, than Mr. Wigginbotham was. From something in the air, I had a hunch that if he'd liked us more, they'd have liked us less. As we were eating, I noticed, too, that Miss Lula was putting a right agreeable eye on Claudie from time to time.

After supper the ladies went back into the kitchen to do the dishes. I and Claudie went out on the front veranda, where we sat with Mr. Wigginbotham in some big wicker chairs by the honeysuckle vines. We looked out over the long row of hollyhocks that nodded between us and the low ridge of blue hills in the west, and it was awful quiet, except for the regular *calung-capluk* of the windmill and the homey sound of clean pots and pans being put away in the kitchen.

After a bit I said, "Mr. Wigginbotham, it's nearly dark. I think I and Claudie will go on down to the trailer house and turn in."

"No," he said, "when the Missus and Miss Lula get the dishes done, we'll have the music."

"Music?" Claudie asked, and cleared his throat.

"Yes, Miss Lula has a talent for music," Mr. Wigginbotham answered. He said it in the same way you'd speak of someone having the bots. "We have music every night of the world." In the half-dark I thought Mr. Wigginbotham looked older than he had before.

"You all must like music an awful lot," I said.

"I listen to it an awful lot," he allowed. "Tonight you can help me with that."

"We can do better than that," I told him. "Claudie, here, can sing bass."

"He don't have to," Mr. Wigginbotham answered. "I just wanted some company with the listenin'."

About this time Mrs. Wigginbotham came to the front door and said: "All right, Elbert, we've finished the dishes. You can bring the men on in."

When we started into the parlor, the Missus handed the coal-oil lamp to Mr. Wigginbotham, and he put it in the holder on the wall; then he turned the reflector around to where it put the best light on the organ.

It was a beautiful brown organ, as big as some I've seen in churches. It had a dozen or more stops above the keyboard; and along the top, as well as along the sides, it had frilly carved wood decorations. The name of the company that made it was printed right on the front of the organ, but in such fancy letters a man couldn't even read it. I noticed that there were real sacred pictures on the parlor walls—Jesus and Joseph and some other people with long beards, that must have been prophets or scribes or Pharisees, anyway. There were some good mottoes, too. One, in a silver frame over the organ, said "Music Hath Charms," in sloping gold letters.

While Miss Lula pumped away at the organ and knocked off a few chords to warm it up, Mrs. Wigginbotham sat close by in a big chair that had red plush on it as deep as it is on seats in trains. I and Claudie sat where we were told, on a green sofa with a hard bottom, and Mr. Wigginbotham went over to a rocking chair by a window on the far side of the room from the organ.

Then Miss Lula turned on her talent. She played and sang a number of her old favorite hymns, like "Rock of Ages," "Beulah Land," and "Old Rugged Cross"; next some songs about nice places a long way off, such as "My Old Kentucky Home," "Blue Ridge Mountains of Virginia," and "Little Gray Home in the West." Toward the end, she rang in a few numbers about long-ago love: "Down by the Old Mill Stream," "Silver Threads Among the Gold," and "Moonlight and Roses." She veered her target toward Claudie, I thought, when she sang one called "Comin' Through the Rye."

It was all better than average as such music goes, and I liked it pretty well since I like even ordinary music more than no music at all. Miss Lula had a sweet, silky voice up in the higher notes that women sing, but on the low ones it had a way of bogging down into a blur as a duck call sometimes does when the reed gets wet.

The music had been going on for over an hour when I looked over at Mr. Wigginbotham. His eyes were plumb glassy; he was gazing out of the window, and he looked, for all the world, like a man who had just gone clear across the country in a covered wagon. Then he looked like a man learning he'd have to go all the way back when Claudie asked Miss Lula if she could play "Mother Machree." Claudie said he wanted to sing it.

Now Claudie sings a fine brand of country bass, and after he'd finished with "Mother Machree," he did a duet with Miss Lula. She pulled out the *vox humana* stop, and they sang the one that begins, "Mine eyes have seen the glory of the coming of the Lord," while Claudie stood there by the organ and turned the sheets of the music. Miss Lula must have been ten or twelve years older than Claudie, but the way they looked at each other when they sang together was enough to put a man's teeth on edge. I noticed Mr. Wigginbotham was pulling the left end of his mustache down to his mouth. He seemed to be biting it.

After a while it was over. I could tell that the ladies were pretty much taken with Claudie, and he was more taken with himself than I liked to see. When this happens he is likely to talk himself into such deep water that I have to bail him out, but this time he didn't exactly. He only said, "There's a bad note in that organ."

"The organ does need tuning," Miss Lula said as she smiled at Claudie.

"Claudie, here, can fix it; he was a piano tuner before he started windmill fixing," I stated.

At this Mr. Wigginbotham got up and said it was time to wash his feet and go to bed, so I told them all that Claudie would tune the organ as soon as we got through with the windmill; then we went back to the trailer.

As we walked away from the Wigginbotham house I said, "Claudie, remember—the windmill comes first. I don't want you to touch that organ until we are through with the windmill."

"Wait a minute," he said. "You are the one that wants to fix the windmill."

"I'm only the one that had the idea," I answered. "You shouldn't expect me to do all the thinking and the work too. Now please don't try to start an argument, Claudie."

"No," Claudie went on, "I ain't tryin' to start no argument, but who's gonna go up on that damn windmill tower?"

"Claudie," I said, "you are too trying to start an argument. You know it makes me dizzy to climb up on high places."

The next morning, after breakfast, Mr. Wigginbotham went off early to the cotton field and I and Claudie went out to the windmill. There was a thirty- or-forty-mile gale blowing, and I could tell it was going to take about everything Claudie had to stay on the tower long enough to make any showing at all, even if we got the windmill stopped. We found a lever on one leg of the tower that was very hard to work, but when we finally worked it, the windmill sang to a slow stop.

Claudie was balky as an old mule about going on the tower, even after I found him a monkey wrench and a pair of pliers. It was only when I pointed out that the ladies were watching him from the back porch that he gritted his teeth and started up the ladder. It made me right nervous to see that big lug picking his way along on the little bitty ladder, but as soon as he got to the platform up there, I felt better about things. I stood there looking up at him until I almost got a crick in my neck. I told him to check everything.

When Claudie came down, he said everything looked all right to him, but he had taken a little bolt out of a place where it didn't seem to belong and had put it into a place where it fitted better. We worked the lever, and the windmill started again with a loud whine. I told him I thought it sounded smoother, but he said he didn't notice any difference. "Leave that part to me," I said; "it's still running, ain't it?"

"Yes, it's running all right," he answered, "but it ain't pumping near as much water as it was."

We took a bucket of cold, fresh water up to the house and found that the Missus and Miss Lula were waiting for us on the back porch. They said the windmill had not been so quiet in years. They gave us some gingerbread with hard sauce on it; then Claudie, carried away with things going so good, said he was ready to start work on the organ. But when we went into the parlor, the ladies said we should sit down and rest up a bit from our windmill work. They showed us the family album and a big leather-backed Bible with everything Jesus said printed in red; then they showed us some stereopticon views. Just when we got to the one of Mount Etna in eruption, there was a worse racket outside than a volcano erupting against a tin roof. The noise was so loud that it started the dogs to howling and the guineas to chattering, and as we all ran out of the house, a peacock a mile or so away let out a long, high scream.

It was the windmill, all right. It was in an awful shape, and right there before our eyes it was getting worse. The vane and the blades were all winding themselves up and batting together, until finally all the machinery up there stopped completely. That windmill was tied in knots, and some big, bent pieces kept springing loose up there and falling around the yard, while I and Claudie and the ladies stood off at a safe distance and watched.

Mr. Wigginbotham came from the cotton field in a lope; he swore a little and said some things that really stung our professional pride. "What have you bastards done to my windmill?" was what he kept wanting to know.

"Calm yourself, Mr. Wigginbotham," I said. A soft answer like that is supposed to turn away the flame of wrath, but this only seemed to turn it up. The veins stood out on his forehead like fishing worms on the bottom of a can, and he kept opening and closing his mouth without saying a word.

Then I went on: "I knew it was loose somewhere; I knew something like this was bound to happen from the way that machine sounded last night."

"You've ruined it," he said.

"Oh, no," I told him. "It just broke down before we could locate the trouble."

Just then a big metal brace of some kind sprung loose from the windmill and landed on the smokehouse roof; it bounced twice and fell to the ground, not ten feet away from where we were standing.

"You've ruined it," Mr. Wigginbotham said again, and I decided it was best just to let the matter drop there.

"Elbert—" The Missus started to say something, but Mr. Wigginbotham paid her no mind.

"The stock—" he said as he stood there looking at what was left of the windmill "—how are the stock going to get water?"

I thought he moved into much easier territory for me with this question, so I said: "I and my associate, Claudie, will take care of that. Leave it to us, Mr. Wigginbotham. How many head are there?"

"Thirteen cows, eight mares and a span of mules," he said.

I looked at Claudie, and he looked down toward the silo; then I said, "Claudie, maybe you'd better start drawing water right away. It's a warm, windy day, and the stock will be getting pretty thirsty."

"No you don't," Mr. Wigginbotham said to me, and I could see that, when you got away from the house where the Missus ruled the roost, Mr. Wigginbotham knew how to take charge. "You're the fellow that didn't like the way my windmill sounded last night. Well, I didn't like the way it sounded a few minutes ago. You can draw the water." He had the same look on his face he'd had the day before when he had the shotgun on his shoulder. He stood there looking at me as the stock started coming from the pasture toward the empty water tank beneath the windmill. Finally, he said, "The rope and the bucket are there by the well," and as he turned to walk up toward the house I said, "Yes, sir." He took Claudie with him.

A camel is supposed to be able to drink enough water to last him for several weeks, and I'd always thought no other animal could match a camel in this way, but I'd never before drawn water with a small bucket for thirteen cows, and nine of them fresh. For a man who has no liking for manual labor of any kind, drawing a lot of water is a very aggravating thing. Just when I'd begun to hold my own with the cows, and they had quit bawling, the horses and mules came along. They were hot and thirsty, too. Then along came three big red brood sows with their litters—a part of the job that Mr. Wigginbotham hadn't even mentioned. They weren't any part of my trade, but they were there, and they were thirsty.

Along about noon the cattle grazed off, and I was just getting a little ahead of the other stock when the water bucket sprung a leak. At first it was just a small leak, but it soon got so bad that I wasn't able to get the bucket up more than half full from the well. I didn't see another bucket around anywhere, and since Mr. Wigginbotham was still up there on the back porch watching me, I didn't think it was a good time to quit to go look for a bucket. Then the cattle came back for more water, and I couldn't help thinking what soft jobs those Israelites had in Egypt; they only had to make bricks without straw.

It must have been one or two o'clock when the stock all wandered off again, and I tried to stand up straight for a little rest. I couldn't do it. Long, keen, galloping pains arched up from my hips and looped across my shoulder blades. I found it was almost easier to draw another bucket than to quit and straighten up—but not quite. I just stood there, bent over the well casing, panting like a collie pup in the noonday sun.

After a bit the Missus and Miss Lula came down to the well and brought some cheese and crackers and a mug of cold buttermilk. While I ate, they told me Mr. Wigginbotham was still in a pretty ugly frame of mind. They said he had been trying ever since the windmill went out to get a telephone call through to a man in Dallas. He was trying to reach a fellow named Pratt there who could come out and fix the windmill, they said. He couldn't get Mr. Pratt on the phone, and this had made him a whole lot madder than he had been before.

"Angus Pratt?" I asked.

"Yes, that's his name," the Missus said. "How'd you know?"

"In the windmill business I know the right people," I told them. Then I asked them what had happened to Claudie. They said he was tuning the organ; he had told them he thought he would have it in tune by the time they got back from town.

"You're not leaving?" I asked as I felt a cold sweat pop out on my forehead and between my shoulder blades.

"Yes," Miss Lula said, "we're going to drive in to Midlothian to the meeting of the Missionary Society." They left in the old sedan, and as I stood there by the well I couldn't help thinking I'd like to be one of those missionaries so the ladies could send me off to a cannibal island somewhere.

It must have been an hour later that I saw Mr. Wigginbotham leave the house and go off toward the barn. I figured he must have got his call through to Angus Pratt, and I knew that time was working against us from then on. So I went up to the house to see how Claudie was getting along.

From the back porch I called him, but nobody answered. I looked and saw Mr. Wigginbotham hitching up a team of mules down at the barn, so I went on in the house to find out what had happened to Claudie. The ox was in the ditch, and I couldn't see how anything I might do could make matters any worse. Claudie wasn't there, but when I went into the parlor I could see him through the front window. He was fooling around the trailer house.

I had to try the organ. I tried the low notes first, with the stops in; and when nothing happened, I pulled out all the stops and pumped away for all I was worth. Nothing happened again. I tried the high notes and the middle notes, and I pumped until those pains started arching up into my shoulders again the way they had at the well. All I got was one little guff, like the noise a cow's foot will make when she pulls it out of a boggy place. That organ was deader'n a doornail. "Well, Clint," I said to myself, "there goes the ball game. It serves you right for depending on that big, ugly lug, Claudie, for anything but manual labor and singing bass."

Just then the telephone rang—two longs, a short, and a long. I answered it, and sure enough it was the Dallas call. Mrs. Pratt was on the line, and she said she had a message for Mr. Wigginbotham.

"I'll take it," I stated. "I work here."

"Tell Mr. Wigginbotham that Mr. Pratt is on his way. He'll be there in an hour," she said.

I hung up and ran out the front door and went down to the trailer house. Claudie was there, leaning up against the trailer door, cool as a cucumber. The expression on his face was as simple as a notch on a stick.

"Claudie, you clumsy cluck," I yelled at him. "What the hell have you done to the organ? How are we going to get out of here? What are we going to do when Mr. Wigginbotham learns you've ruined the organ too? What are we going to do when Mr. Pratt gets here? He's a real windmill fixer."

Claudie was so mixed up that he couldn't say a word. The trouble he had caused didn't seem to be dawning on him at all.

"I can't answer all them questions at once," he said. Then I looked back toward the barn, and there came Mr. Wigginbotham in a wagon. Two mules were pulling it, and they came toward the trailer in a fast trot. As they pulled up even with us, Mr. Wigginbotham jumped out, and I asked him in a nice polite way what it was he had in mind doing.

"I'm going to pull your trailer down the road toward old man Nate Pinkney's place. He needs a couple of good field hands. I can't use you here." He had some chains and bailing wire, and with almost no help from Claudie and none at all from me he fastened the trailer house on behind the wagon.

I began to feel a little left out of things so I said: "Mr. Wigginbotham, while you were hitching up those mules, a phone call came for you from Dallas. They said Angus Pratt was on his way. He's a windmill man."

"That's good," he said without looking away from what he was doing. "I need a windmill man."

I said, "Mr. Pratt is a good one," but I don't think Mr. Wigginbotham heard me, since he was back in the wagon by this time. He spoke to the mules, and they went off so fast that I and Claudie had to run to catch the trailer house. We got in just as Mr. Wigginbotham turned south on the highway. He popped the whip at the mules, and they went down the road in a full gallop.

As we jostled along the road behind Mr. Wigginbotham's wagon, the sun was low and dark red in the west. While it slid from behind a lead-colored cloud bank into the gray dusk, I watched a long north-bound freight train pass about a mile away—edging along betwixt us and the sunset. The train whistle sounded lonesome and restless, and it did what a train whistle often does; makes a man wonder if things aren't a lot prettier and easier where the train is going than they are where the train is whistling. I looked at Claudie and thought of all the misery and bother he had caused me since sundown the day before. He looked down at the floor, and, as I sat there, I wondered how much longer a man with my talents could put up with him.

"It's a good thing," I remarked, "that we are getting out of here before the Missus and Miss Lula learn what you did to that organ."

"That's the way Mr. Wigginbotham feels about it, too," Claudie answered.

"Does he know about the organ?" I asked.

"He ought to, Clint," Claudie said. "He told me he wanted me to give it exactly the same treatment I had given the windmill."

Ben K. Green

Maniac Mule

A NATIVE OF CUMBY, TEXAS, Ben K. Green, according to his own story, was practically born in the saddle and spent his life with horses. He became a successful horse trader while still in his teens and went on to study and practice veterinary medicine. The question has arisen: did all the adventures he describes as his own really happen to him? His publishers are convinced that they did. The spokesman concedes, however, that Ben was a combination of "knavery, skill, and salesmanship" and credits him with "pure unadulterated con" in his relations with the public. He may have used considerable artistic license in plying his craft, but the stories themselves are quite wonderful and full of sly and subtle humor. Young Green, as he describes himself, lived by his wits, as a true picaro must, and was lucky to boot, as a true picaro hopes to be.

From *Horse Tradin'*. New York: Alfred A. Knopf, 1967, pp. 66–73.

It was early in the fall, and the horse and mule business had begun to take on new life. Mule buyers were buying young feeder mules, which were mules from three to five years old, broke but not in good condition, that they could put a bloom on in time for the late fall horse and mule market. On this nice brisk Saturday morning, which was a little bit cool, there were a few scattered watermelon wagons around on the public square, and you could see an occasional wagon with a bale of cotton—cotton picking had just started. You could tell we were about to have a real fall Saturday in Weatherford, Texas.

I rode around the square with nothing particular on my mind, stopped and sat on my horse and visited with a few fellows. While I was talking, I noticed a man driving a good team of mules to a wagon and leading a better mule tied to the back of the wagon. The mule he was leading was a four-year-old mare mule with no harness marks. She was real typey, the kind that would sell for a lot of money. I reined my horse up and rode away from that non-profitable conversation to ride over where that man stopped his wagon to find out why he was leading an extra mule. It would be supposed that he had brought her to town to sell. As I came near his wagon horseback, I noticed the mule was standing very quietly on a loose halter rope and showing no signs of fear from the people or other teams around her. She was an exceptionally nice-made mare mule, black with a mealy nose, white underbelly, and no scars or blemishes—strictly fancy so far as mules go. In order to conceal my anxiety at seeing a nice mule, I said to the man in the wagon: "You want to buy a mate for that mule?"

That set up a conversation, and he told me that he was too old to break young mules when he already had a broke team; he had worked this mule some, but she was just green-broke and had just shedded in for a four-year-old. His conversation matched the mule's general condition, and there was no reason to doubt what he said. He had already told me that the mule was for sale "iffen the price was good enuff." After much persuasion, I got him to price the mule—instead of making a bid on her first. He thought she was worth $135, but that if I had a mate to her the span would sure bring $300. We talked on, and I finally bid him $100. He told me that if he didn't have to spend all day in town trying to sell the mule, he would take $125 for her. I finally agreed to give him $115, and he sold her to me and throwed the halter and rope in. I reached in my pocket and paid him in cash—I never had gotten down off my horse. I reached over and untied the mule from the wagon, dallied the rope around my saddle horn, and led her down to Jim Merritt's barn.

Jim Merritt was an old-time horse and mule buyer who had come to Texas from Georgia. He knew the mule business and was always a good buyer for an exceptionally nice mule, since he had a trade that would buy the better kind of mules. There was not a doubt in my mind but what I had just made $25, and maybe even $35, by leading that mule about three city blocks.

Mr. Merritt wasn't at the barn, but I was so sure this mule would suit him that I led her in, unbuckled the halter, and rode on. Mr. Merritt was my good friend and had always been more than fair in all my dealings with him, and I knew all that was left to complete the trade was to wait until Mr. Merritt got to town to pay me a reasonable profit for my thirty minutes work and, of course, my shrewd ability as a young mule man. I thought of something that I wanted to do and rode away from town for three or four hours.

I came back up the street about the middle of the afternoon, and there was a whole bunch of men standing in front of Mr. Merritt's mule barn—but nobody was very close to the gate. That nice, black, mealy-nosed four-year-old mare mule had kicked and torn down a chute, the partition gate between the barn and the back lot, and was backed up with her hindquarters in the corner of the barn, her mouth open, bawling in an unknown mule tongue. Her eyes were popped out like they were on sticks, her ears were stuck forward, and at the least excitement she would rush against the other side of the barn and knock herself down. She had already peeled and skinned her shoulders a little bit.

All the rest of the horses and mules had gotten themselves into the back lot and crowded into one corner away from her. Nobody knew who the mule belonged to—Mr. Merritt was there, and he knew he hadn't bought a mule like that. I sat on my horse and looked over the crowd at my mule that nobody knew was mine. I damn near didn't want to claim her myself.

I choked, tried to act unconcerned and said: "Mr. Jim, have you got a mule with the colic?"

He replied, "Colic, my foot. Somebody has turned a mule in my barn that's a maniac."

That started the conversation, and there were two or three people in the crowd who had seen a crazy mule before. I stood up in my stirrups, looked at that mule, and said: "Mr. Merritt, people are the only things that have got little enough sense to go crazy. She must be loco."

Nobody could remember having seen a mule that was loco act like that. Somebody had called old Dr. Justice, a village horse doctor of the old order who had treated lots of horses and mules. He had no suggestions to make, except that he thought something ought to be done with the mule. The mule stood still in one corner for some time, and the crowd finally got tired of watching and began to drift away. I still hadn't gotten off my horse and thought maybe it best not to, as I rode up close to Mr. Merritt and said: "Mr. Merritt, that's my mule, but she didn't act like that when I put her in there and turned her loose."

He sucked on his pipe a few times, finally took it out of his mouth and said: "Benny, you sure got a booger. If we could get in there and look around on the ground or in that hay or manure, we'd find a ball of cotton that had been saturated with chloroform and stuck up that mule's nose. She was asleep when you bought her."

I looked at her a few minutes and said: "How did they ever get the cotton in her nose?"

Mr. Merritt gave a deep belly laugh and answered: "Benny, that's your problem, but we've sure got to get that mule out of my barn before dark."

I needed help bad. Amateurs and town cowboys weren't going to do me any good. I went on down to the wagonyard, and everybody knew about the mule, but it still hadn't leaked out who she belonged to. I talked to two or three of my advisers, but nobody knew how to put chloroform in a crazy mule's nose without catching her!

After while I found a cowboy friend of mine who was ever bit as crazy as that mule. We took two lariat ropes, and he walked a rafter in the barn, tied the end of the rope to a beam, and dropped the loop down over the mule's neck—which started another mule war. When she choked and fell on the ground, I ran in with another lariat rope, tied her forefeet together, and laced her to the saddle horn on my horse. I had already gone and bought a good supply of chloroform because we figured we'd waste most of it. I had some big wads of cotton already made up in my britches pocket. My wild friend jumped down from the rafters, and I pitched him a wad of cotton. He poured chloroform all over it, grabbed that mule by the ear, and jobbed the cotton up her nose while I drug her enough to keep her feet off the ground. In a few minutes she was lying nice and still. We put a halter with a long rope on her without any trouble. I turned my foot-rope loose while my friend slapped her in the face with his hat and made her get up. She was a nice, quiet mule.

We rubbed all the dirt and hay off her and brushed her while we had her in the dark part of the barn. Needless to say, there was a fair audience at a good safe distance on the other side of the gate. I took several wraps on my saddle horn with the halter rope and asked them to open the gate. My friend Mr. Merritt looked much relieved when he saw we had the mule caught, and he was glad to open the gate and get the people out of the way—which wasn't much trouble when they saw me coming toward them with my mule.

I started across the square for no particular reason except to get the mule out of the way of the people and things before that chloroform cotton came out of her nose. I wasn't sure where I was going or what I was going to do with her. Out on South Main about three blocks from the square, I met a man that I had particular reasons for wanting to become the owner of this nice, quiet mule. He ran a dairy out on the edge of town, and he had a bull tied to the back of his wagon. There were very few trailers or trucks, and it was not uncommon to see gentle cattle being led tied to the back of a wagon. He was bringing this bull to town to be put with some more cattle to be sent for sale to the Fort Worth stockyards.

This good old dairyman was the kind of fellow who starved his mules, scolded and whipped his dogs, bemeaned his family, and made his living by stealing milk from calves. About two years before this, when I was an even younger trader, he had sold me a spoilt-bag milk cow without letting me in on the secret that her bag was spoilt—and since she was a dry cow, I couldn't tell it. After I had sold the cow and took an awful loss on her, he told me that was cheap knowledge—it would keep me from buying another spoilt-bag cow, and he had no remorse for contributing to my education.

As I approached his wagon with my mule and saw that big fat bull tied to the back of his wagon, I wondered if his education was entirely complete. Riding very slow, but without stopping, I said: "What are you going to do with that bull?"

"I would ship him to Fort Worth or I would trade him for that mule," he answered.

The mule was so classy that anybody would like her at a glance, and most anybody in those days could tell she was a young mule without looking in her mouth.

I reined up my horse, and he stopped and began talking. He said the bull was fat and would weigh two thousand pounds and bring five cents a pound, which would be $100—that was all my mule was worth and we would trade even. I knew that bull didn't weigh but fourteen hundred pounds and wouldn't bring more than four cents, but I also knew enough about my mule that I considered it a good trade. I said: "We'll have one more trade," as I stepped down off my horse and tied the mule to the back of the wagon. He went to complaining about having a new lariat rope on the bull and he wouldn't let me have it—but, of course, he wanted the halter that was on the mule. I didn't think it was best to let him get close enough to that mule to smell the chloroform, and I didn't want to be fooling around the mule's head taking the halter off. I didn't want to chum around with Mr. Milkman long enough for me to change and take his rope off the bull and put mine on; so I reached over, untied the bull, and turned him loose.

I said: "I'm a cowboy and horseback. I don't need a rope for just one bull." I stepped on my horse, started driving the bull off toward the shipping pens, and Mr. Milkman turned around and started home with his mule.

This good gentleman had been known to sing awful loud in church and frown disapprovingly at cowboys who didn't attend meetings, but I heard from reliable sources that he almost lost his religion over that mule. I never bothered to ask what actually became of that crazy mule.

Urbs and Suburbs

For Joyce Gibson Roach's "A High Toned Woman"

Western specialists are telling us these days that western history is really urban history. There is much to be said for the idea. Even on the frontier most of the population was concentrated in the settlements, and for the last hundred years the cities have absorbed more and more of the rural population. Owen P. White comments on the transition in El Paso around the turn of the century. As a boy he saw the town change from an honestly sinful border town to a minor metropolis claiming to be clean but actually as wicked as ever.

The best humorists now are city humorists. They may talk about country people, but they publish in city newspapers and magazines. Columnists like George Dolan, Alex Burton, Bill Porterfield, and Molly Ivins were and are eagerly read. Rural folk are easy to poke good-natured fun at. Dan Jenkins does it in *Fast Copy*. Joyce Roach memorializes the village matriarch in "A High Toned Woman," beginning her account in rural Jacksboro and proceeding to the Neiman-Marcus store in Dallas.

City humor also addresses the more ludicrous side of life in urban Texas, attacking the massive egos and feeble intellects of some city dwellers. Bud Shrake deals with oil billionaires and bisexual interior designers, for instance, in his cutting satire *Peter Arbiter*.

Owen P. White

El Paso Moves Out

OWEN WHITE claimed to be the first Anglo child born in El Paso. For a good many years it was his only distinction. He had ambitions to be a writer, however, and when *Out of the Desert* (1924), a whimsical history of El Paso, got favorable reviews in eastern journals, his fortunes improved. He used to tell how a New York magazine offered him a job and wired, "Come at once!" Owen wired back. "Can't come. Don't know where to put in the commas." A second wire said "We can hire college graduates at twenty-five cents an hour to put in the commas. Come at once." Owen came. For the rest of his active career he wrote books and articles, mostly about Texas. His exposés of corruption sometimes endangered his personal safety, but he never backed off. He was always the humorist and loved oddballs—was something of an oddball himself. He was or pretended to be, an enemy of civic progress, preferring the old days when vice was open and honest to later times when the authorities swept it under the municipal rug and pretended it wasn't there.

From *The Autobiography of a Durable Sinner*. New York: G. P. Putnam's Sons, 1942, pp. 41–51.

In 1879, when it was a town without law officers, wherein men could take life straight, as they took their liquor, El Paso was utopian. In 1887 it wasn't. Even I, at the mature age of eight as I stepped from the train, could tell it wasn't. The evidence was before me in the shape of a man with a gold cord on his hat, a badge on his shirt, and a .45 on his hip. He was having a hard time to protect the arriving passengers from the assaults of a riotous mob of hotel runners and hack drivers, who very clearly wanted to sail right in and take us all apart. With the aid of this policeman who had only one arm—his other one having been shot off in a gun-fight—my father managed to get us through the mob and transport us to the home he had secured for us.

During the time I had been away what had happened to the town of my birth?

In the year in which I was born El Paso began to undergo a change of life. In that year four great railroads began laying their tracks in the direction of its barrooms and gaming resorts, the result being that the town at once began to fill up with border parasites coming in to prey upon the railroad pay rolls. For the first six or eight months these men, and the few women who were with them, came in a trickle, but by the end of another six, with the railheads drawing nearer and nearer, they arrived in a flood. They came in buckboards, buggies, wagons, stages, on foot, and on horseback. They ate what they could get, drank anything, slept with anybody; worked feverishly during the day erecting shacks to live in, and caroused vigorously throughout the night. This was a wicked period in the life of El Paso. Everything was under control: under control of gals and gunmen, to the end that in one year more killings took place in El Paso than had ever taken place in the entire careers of any of the so-called really tough towns of the frontier. But what of it? These killings were unimportant. No one, not even the relatives of the deceased, gave a damn about them. No one had time to, because everyone's attention was centered on the race between the Santa Fe and the Southern Pacific, which were, each one, trying to beat the other into the town.

The Southern Pacific won: it brought its first train in on May 13, 1881, and immediately El Paso underwent a series of changes that were quick and startling.

Before that train pulled in there had been but one one-story brick building in El Paso, not a single board floor, and only two panes of window glass, while as for such effeminate luxuries as mahogany bar fixtures and square pianos in the dance halls, they were, of course, unknown. But within just a few months these deficiencies, as well as another of which the innocent old-timers had hitherto been happily ignorant, had been remedied. Brick buildings began to replace adobe ones; ornate bar fixtures and fancy gambling tables ousted the make-shift equipment formerly in use; pine boards took the place of Mother

Earth on the floors in the dance halls. At the same time a new element in the life of El Paso, a blondined hand-decorated, female element, recruited in the East and Middle West and shipped in by the carload, arrived to compete with the brown-skinned, black-eyed señoritas of the earlier day.

From this time on life in El Paso became indeed alluring. A wonderful prosperity, one that the prophets said would endure for many years, was on the way, and so the Sinners, knowing that plucking the Christians would be easy and profitable, garbed themselves becomingly for the harvest. It was a gorgeous display. The calcimined women, both in the humble cribs, and in the big parlor houses which were the pride of the town, donned beautiful gowns—scanty perhaps, but none the less beautiful—the bartenders discarded their flannel shirts in favor of white jackets and thousand dollar diamonds; and the members of the gambling fraternity blossomed out in all the glory of imported, tailor-made suits, fast trotting horses attached to red-wheeled road wagons, and kept women.

Behind all this, of course, was the idea of money. In previous times when El Paso was really heroic no one cared a great deal for cash. They didn't have to because a man's social standing depended far more upon his ability to handle his liquor and shoot straight than upon his financial rating. But now it was different. Whether it wanted to or not El Paso was doomed to become a great metropolis, and so concurrently with blondes, bar fixtures, and red-wheeled road wagons, the trains now began to disgorge men who planned to embark in more or less legitimate enterprises. These new citizens—and among them came six uncles of mine, all on my mother's side—then got busy as rapidly as they could to turn El Paso into as good a place for the sale of the more sedate things of life as the gals and gamblers had already made it for gay and frivolous entertainment.

Thus by 1887 whenever a cattleman, a cowboy, a miner, a prospector, a merchant, a lawyer, or a thief anywhere in Arizona, New Mexico, or West Texas found an extra dollar in his pocket he headed hell-bent to El Paso to get rid of it. The town's Christians, who peddled groceries, hardware, mowers, plows, coffins, and mining machinery took unto themselves much credit for this, but deserved none of it. They knew it: they knew that the thing that brought customers from afar into their stores was El Paso's invitation to step right up to the Sinners' bench, and they took advantage of it. They even encouraged it.

It was about four years before the antics of the Sinners began to affect me in any way. I don't know exactly why that was. Perhaps I was too high morally, or too low mentally, to be contaminated, but in either case it is quite true that until I was twelve years old, I took very little interest in what went on outside my own sphere of activity. Within that sphere I was very busy, busier than I had ever been, as I had more to attend to. I had to ride, shoot, trap, go to school, both day and Sunday; have measles, mumps, whooping cough, and chicken pox; and at the same time try to catch up on my reading. I never could. I never have. I've quit trying because I now realize that it's impossible for me to overcome the three or four thousand years' start that the publishers of this world have on me.

In spite of all this effort and opportunity, so trifling were the achievements of my first four years in El Paso that I hesitate to record them, even as I frequently hesitated, at the time, to mention them to my mother.

The first time that I got drunk, for instance, I tried to conceal it, but how could I? My breath betrayed me, even if my staggering gait did not, and so when she cornered me I had to confess that her youngest son, with whose Sunday school record she was so pleased, had not only had a great deal too much to drink but had even robbed a house in order to get the liquor.

I had jimmied my way into the cellar of an absent neighbor, found there a barrel of wine, and, with the aid of a yard of rubber tubing which was there also, inhaled as much of it as I could hold. For this unparalleled piece of wickedness I was not punished. I knew why. My mother could never wield a switch, a buggy whip, or a paddle when she was convulsed with mirth. But two days later, when I again staggered in after a second trip to the barrel, it was very different. So different that never again did my mother ever see me under the influence of liquor. It was hard to avoid, I admit, but I managed it even though on one disastrous occasion it cost me several hundred dollars to get by with it.

When this happened, to go a bit ahead of my story, I was nineteen. It was Sunday afternoon and in Charles Beiswinger's place I encountered a man for whom I had unbounded admiration. He was Fred

Fenchler. He was the best-loved sport in El Paso. As a gambler who would sit in with any company he was known from El Paso to New York, and from Mexico City to Paris. Naturally, when Fred asked me to have a drink with him, and then followed that up with an invitation to dine with him at his home, I was overcome with gratitude. We dined. It was a wet dinner, very wet, and at its conclusion I was again grateful when my host suggested that I trail along while he went up town and played a little roulette.

He played, in the gambling room back of the Oxford Saloon, buying checks at five hundred dollars a stack. I played also, buying at five, but with far better luck than he did. I won, he lost heavily, and as his was a patronage that was much valued by the house, we were served with all the champagne we wanted. Unfortunately I wanted much more than I could carry, and to relieve myself I retired to the washroom, whither I was followed by two kind strangers who held my head for me and did everything they could to ease my suffering. When I was feeling slightly better these good men suggested that they take me home.

"No," I said, remembering my mother, "take me to the Sheldon Hotel." They did so. They took me to the hotel, got me a room, and put me snugly to bed. I was deeply grateful, but in the morning when I awoke and found that I didn't have even a dime left out of approximately eight hundred dollars, I felt differently. I was mad, but I can see now that I shouldn't have been. I should have remained grateful because from that experience I learned two valuable lessons. One is that whenever any Good Samaritan offers to do me a favor I look him over carefully, search him for the ace up his sleeve, and then (lesson number two) if I don't find the ace I play safe by turning my back on him anyhow.

Having been baptized into the Episcopal Church shortly before we left Tucson (though I so resented being called a Child of God by the preacher that I bit him) I naturally became one of the lambs in that flock after my return to El Paso. In a way I couldn't help it. My father was not at all religious, nor was my mother disagreeably so, but as she was an Episcopalian—probably because that route to Heaven was broader, smoother, and easier to travel than any other then advertised—I also became one. It was not at all painful. On the contrary, I really enjoyed going to Sunday School and cutting loose with the text and the collect for the day. This was easy. It was no trick at all for me, with my spongelike mind, to memorize these short bits of Scripture and I did it gladly, especially as there was a reward at the end of the route. I didn't know what that reward was to be. I only knew that at Easter a grand prize was to be given to the child who had made the best record on texts and collects and so I set out to win it. I had but one real competitor: a gifted lad who in later years made quite a name for himself by becoming a piano player in a honky-tonk theater and marrying one of the joint's giddy-looking beer slingers.

I finally beat this fellow, and at Easter, before a church packed with fathers and mothers, I was called up to the pulpit, patted upon the head by good old Dr. Higgins—who later backslid and became a homeopathic physician and a really sincere drinker—and was presented with a prize that was of no more use to me than a nail in my foot. It was a full-rigged ship! Think of it! A ship in the desert, a ship with no sea to sail it on. I carried it home, put it carefully away in the woodshed, and forever thereafter religiously refrained from texts and collects. Nevertheless I was very proud of the record I had made, and so was my mother. My father was noncommittal.

For the first four years of it I enjoyed going to public school as much as I enjoyed going to Sunday school and for much the same reason. I liked it because, although I was very quarrelsome and, as my father said,

> Felt that day lost whose low descending sun
> Viewed at my hand no bloody battle done.

I enjoyed a competition wherein I was always able to keep myself near the top of the class without having to do enough studying to interfere with my other pursuits. But this was not because I was talented or abnormal. I was neither. I was just an ornery, ordinary kid, who was a great trial to his teachers, largely because my erratic parents had given me a very stiff course in memory training. That was the secret of it, and never, up to the end of his days, did my father relax in his efforts to turn me into an anthology of queer and assorted poetry. For three selfish reasons I never resisted him. I liked him, I liked poetry, and I liked money. Knowing these things my father would proceed in this way: at the breakfast table he would pull from his pocket a poem that he had clipped from a newspaper or a magazine, would hand it to me, and would say: "Son, learn this, recite it to me when I come home tonight and I'll give you a quarter."

No matter how long the offering I never failed to earn the money and have never regretted it. I doubt if there is another man in the United States today who can recite "The Duel in Cowlick Holler." But I can, and I enjoy doing it, because

> You see, 'twas all a case, sir, of liquor and profanity
> That had struck a sorta snag, sir, in muscular Christianity.

My father's interest in my education was not confined solely to filling me to the muzzle with classical learning. He was also practical. For example, prosperity having begun to shower down upon him, he sold his old bay horse and bought for himself a standard-bred trotting mare from Kentucky. She was a beauty. He named her Tom, after a stunning young lady who was a bookkeeper for the Singer Sewing Machine Company, and a good deal of a high-stepper in her own right. Tom—meaning the mare now—was also wicked. Late every afternoon when my father would turn her head in the direction of the feedbox she'd run away with him and he never knew it. I can still see him making the turn into the back lot where the stable was. He was a small man, and there he'd be, with his feet braced against the dashboard, his cigar clenched in his teeth, the lines wrapped twice around his hands, and Tom, traveling at top speed, paying no more attention to him than if he hadn't even been in the buggy. She'd dash up the stable gate, and come to a sliding stop to keep from knocking her own brains out, whereupon my father would unwrap the lines, look down at Ed, the colored man, and at me, and say: "Ed, by God it takes a man to drive a horse like this." Ed would grin and say nothing and neither would I.

In some way my father found out that I was very much afraid of that horse. That settled it. No son of his was ever going to be afraid of any horse on earth, if he could help it, and so one morning at breakfast, without giving me the slightest hint as to his criminal intent, he told me to come to his office that afternoon at half past four. I went, walked in, and he looked up and said: "Go back downstairs, son, unhitch Tom, and drive her home." I did, or rather I went down and unhitched Tom, but I didn't drive her home. She went there herself. She did it every day for weeks. It got monotonous. It got so that the merchants, saloon-keepers, and gamblers on San Antonio Street used to line up on the sidewalks to make bets on whether or not I'd survive the trip. They could set their watches by my regular afternoon runaway. Tom never failed to make it a good one. We took all corners on two wheels and why I was not killed is still a mystery. But I wasn't. I even got over being afraid of Tom, but never of being afraid of the ridicule my father would heap upon me if I had an accident. Finally I had one, but he never heard of it. One afternoon Tom miscalculated her speed, skidded too far when she came to her sliding stop, and tore the shafts off against a gatepost. This was terrible, or might have been if I hadn't gotten the blacksmith to work far into the night putting in a new pair of shafts which were exact duplicates of the old ones. For all of which I paid out of my own pocket.

Having thus cured me, as he thought (and he was partially right about it) of my fear of wild horses, my father took up the matter of wild women. His procedure was about the same as before. Without giving me any advance warning he again told me to come to his office after school, and of course, I went . . . .

But before telling of that afternoon I'll go back to an afternoon some months before. It was a cold day and when I went into the house I found my father sitting hunched up in front of an open fire. He was crying, real tears glistening on his beard, and when I walked over and stood beside him he looked up at me and said, fiercely and as if he was filled with rage about something:

"Son, Alice Abbott's dead, and by God, even if she wasn't respectable, if she doesn't go to Heaven I don't want to go there. And you don't either. It'll be no place for us."

I knew what he meant. Alice Abbott, a large, fat woman, and madam of the swankiest and highest-priced bordello in El Paso was known, by sight, to every man, woman, and child in the town. No one could miss her, as it was her habit every afternoon, accompanied by four of her beautiful girls to drive through the streets in a high stanhope rig drawn by a pair of beautiful white horses. Miss Abbott's reason for doing this was obvious; as obvious as if she had had a sign, THIS FLESH FOR SALE, hung on her rig. Consequently the pious minority in the town looked upon her as such a vile, wicked old woman that they were all glad to hear about it when Miss Kitty Freeman, who ran quite a large bawdy house of her own, shot several holes through her with a .45.

But my father, who knew Alice Abbott better than anyone in El Paso, was not glad to hear of it. He knew her as the most charitable woman in the town; as the only person in it, in fact, to whom he could go without hesitation and ask for help for poor, sick people, either white or Mexican, who were unable to pay for food and medicine. He always got it, and there was never but one stipulation: "Here, Doc, take it and spend it wherever you want to. The only thing is: don't ever tell anybody where it came from."

And that was why my father was sitting in front of the fire that afternoon crying real tears that he was not ashamed of.

On the afternoon in question, though, he was not crying. Instead his eye twinkled as he handed me a bunch of about twenty bills and told me to go out and collect them. I looked at the address and I gasped. Every one bore a number somewhere on Utah Street. "Why, Dad," I said, "you don't mean it. You don't mean that I'm to go down there, and go in those houses, and get this money from those women?"

But he did mean it. He knew what he was doing. He knew that in common with almost every other normal twelve-year-old kid in El Paso my feeling regarding the girls on Utah Street was one of overwhelming curiosity mixed up with some kind of a mysterious fear. It was true. Many times, sneaking out at night, I had walked down Utah Street to take in the sights but had always kept strictly to the middle of the road. I didn't dare tackle the sidewalks for fear that some of the semi-naked women, standing in the doorways, or leaning out of the windows, and reaching for the men who went by, would grab me, drag me inside, and ravish me. But, "to be or not to be, that was the question." Did I want to be ravished? I didn't yet know; that was a thing I was beginning to get very curious about and that was why my father, who knew I was curious about it, wanted me to go down and collect those bills from those women. He didn't explain it to me very fully but I got his idea when he said in reply to my protest:

"Of course, son, I want you to go to those places and collect those bills. Why not? Those women won't hurt you. They're not nearly as bad as most people say they are; in fact many of them are very good, and the sooner you find that out, and get acquainted with them, the easier it will be for you to get along with them a few years from now when you'll be calling on them for something other than to collect money."

I'll never cease to be grateful to my father for sending me out with those bills. It cured me of curiosity, because by calling on the Utah Street ladies between three and four in the afternoon, when they were just getting up, many of them nursing hangovers, and all with their warpaint off and their face grease on, and their hair in curlers and their rooms reeking with the odor of liquor and cigarette smoke, I unavoidably came to the conclusion that the beauty of sin, as they peddled it, was entirely mythical. As far as their treatment of me was concerned, sin didn't even exist. In the many months that I collected accounts from them not one of those women, although they were, as I noticed with detached interest, a bit careless in the matter of clothes, ever said a wicked or a suggestive word to me. Instead, because I was Doctor White's kid and they had a great respect for him, they all were very nice to me; they all paid me, and so in time, I really learned to like many of them. But I was not so deluded as not to know that when they were really practicing their profession they were tough sisters. They had to be, because they had tough men to deal with. Generally those dealings were carried on at night. Sometimes they were not. Sometimes, due to the early arrival in town of men who couldn't wait, hell would begin to heave in the red-light district in the middle of the afternoon. Whenever this happened my job became very interesting. I'll never forget, for instance, the afternoon when Bass Outlaw, a Deputy U.S. Marshal, Kid McKittrick, and an unknown, who was promptly buried and forgotten, started to shoot up Miss Tillie Howard's very high-class establishment. I was not two hundred feet from Tillie's place, whither I was headed to present bills to a couple of her girls, when the bombardment began. I heard a fusillade of shots, a police whistle, a few more shots, and then, running from Tillie's front door and dashing across the street into an Italian saloon, came the unknown. Behind him, with a gun in his hand, limping badly but making good time nevertheless, came Uncle John Selman. Uncle John crossed the street, pushed open the swinging door of the Italian's saloon, fired one shot, turned, and seeing me, asked if my Dad was in his office. "I reckon so," I said. "What's the matter?"

"Bass Outlaw shot me in the leg," replied Uncle John, and as he hobbled away I went on into Tillie's place to see what had happened. It was easy to assemble the particulars. Early in the day, Outlaw, Mc-Kittrick, and the stranger started to lay the foundation for a spree. By three o'clock that preliminary had been completed, and as the ethics of the enterprise demanded that after a certain amount of liquor had been consumed a sporting house had to be visited and shot up, the trio chose Tillie's place as the one in which they would put on their show. But no sooner had they arrived and gotten inside and yanked out their guns and cracked loose at the bric-a-brac and the chandeliers than Miss Howard, foreseeing a rough time ahead for everybody, ran out on her back porch and began blowing a police whistle.

Hearing that whistle Constable John Selman, who was playing seven-up in the Monte Carlo near by, responded by running into the alley and starting to climb over Tillie's back fence. That move brought on disaster. As Selman threw his leg over the fence, Bass Outlaw, who had come out on the porch to take Tillie's whistle away from her, saw it and just for the hell of the thing put a bullet in it. No one bullet had ever yet stopped John Selman and this one didn't. On the contrary it gave him a personal interest in what was going on inside Tillie's place that he hadn't had before, and so, limping across the yard, he went into the back hall, where he was instantly shot at, and unanimously missed, by the three celebrators. When Selman returned the fire he didn't miss. With his first shot he got Outlaw, who dropped in the hall, with his second he destroyed McKittrick in one of the parlors, while with his third, as we have already seen, he demolished the stranger, in the saloon across the street.

Obviously this was fine shooting, but when I got inside where the atmosphere was full of smoke, women, and profanity and the floor was littered up with a couple of dying citizens, it was very clear that neither Miss Howard nor any of the denizens of her joint gave a damn about that part of it. They were just plain mad. Mad because the two dying citizens were bleeding all over some very costly Oriental rugs.

H. Allen Smith

The Silent Treatment

THE MOST PROLIFIC, and perhaps the best, of the Texas humorists is
the late H. Allen Smith, whose thirty-three books have amused two
generations of Texans and spread cheer far beyond the boundaries of
the state. After a long and distinguished career as a journalist, Smith
retreated from the world and settled almost out of it in the West Texas
town of Alpine, where he churned out a steady stream of books and
articles until he covered his typewriter for the last time. The antics of his
zany characters (one of them is a gifted pig who witches water wells)
delighted his fans, and his articles, like "The Silent Treatment," commented, with insight and humor, on the peculiar behavior of mankind.

From *The Best of H. Allen Smith*. New York: Trident Press, 1972,
pp. 239–247.

Up to now this book has been concerned, in large part, with the
usage and misusage of language. As a concluding exercise, let us consider the negative side of things—the *non*usage of language. I am inspired by the fact that my neighbors, Bob and Liz Gaffney, are not
speaking to each other again, which means that all's right with the
world.

This last time they went for seven straight weeks speaking to each
other, saying, "Yes, dear" and "May I help you to some more potatoes,
love?" and "Listen, you louse, quit acting like you were the All-Wise."
Somehow, life is much duller in our neighborhood when Bob and Liz
are on speaking terms. We thought it would never end, and then a day
or so ago they resumed giving each other the silent treatment.

This is the way it came about: Bob has a habit of wiggling his foot
whenever he's reading the newspaper. He crosses his right leg over his

left knee, and as he reads, he moves his right foot back and forth in a sort of continuing twitch. When he came home from the office the other night he and Liz were on excellent terms. They chatted about the day's events all through dinner, and then Bob sat down to read.

"Quit wiggling your foot," Liz suddenly said.

Bob looked up from his paper momentarily confused. "What's that?" he asked.

"I said," Liz told him, "quit wiggling your damfool foot."

"I didn't know I was wiggling it," said Bob, "but if I was, I can't see that it's any concern of yours. It's my foot and I'll wiggle it to suit myself."

"If you only knew," said Liz, "just how maddening it is. You sit there and wiggle that foot until I could scream. Why don't you get control of yourself?"

"I'm in perfect control of everything, including my foot," said Bob. "It so happens that I get a certain amount of pleasure out of wiggling my feet. It relaxes my shins. I like it."

Liz stood up, her eyes narrowed. "A typical excuse," she said. "Who ever heard of anybody having tense shins! Well, you can wiggle your foot off at the hinges for all I care. But you'll wiggle it without me!"

She marched out of the house, got into the car, and drove over to spend the evening with us.

I didn't attempt to lecture her. I didn't tell her that she should be more tolerant of Bob's wiggling foot, because I get a certain amount of enjoyment out of people who are Not Speaking to Each Other.

I have been interested in this aspect of human relationships for a long time. A dozen years ago I worked on the staff of a New York newspaper and one of my good friends was the paper's drama critic. One afternoon I was walking down the hallway that led to the locker room. My friend, the drama critic, was coming toward me. As we neared each other, I said, "Hi, Doug." He stared straight ahead and hurried past me. At first I thought he was merely in the grip of a horrifying hangover. A few minutes later I walked over to his desk in the city room. He didn't look up from his typewriter, and I asked him if he wanted to sneak out and have a couple at Nick's. He still didn't look up. "What's eating you?" I wanted to know. He continued typing, so I went back to my desk and thought about it awhile, and then wrote him a note, asking for an explanation. A copy boy handed the note to him, and without reading it, he tore it into bits.

He never spoke to me again. In the beginning I spent hours trying to figure it out. I had not done a single thing I could think of that would cause him to quit speaking. I had a mutual friend approach him, to ask what was troubling him. He said, "Don't mention that scum's name in my presence."

I left the paper, still unspoken to, and not long after that he died suddenly, and now I'll never know. Or maybe I shall know. If my evil life transports me to his place of residence in the hereafter, the first thing I'm going to say to him on arrival is, "Hey, why did you quit speaking to me?" The chances are he won't even look up from his shoveling.

A few years later I became acquainted with Bob and Liz Gaffney. In this couple I found the art of Not Speaking brought to its finest flower. I didn't realize just how expert Bob and Liz were until the trip to New England. The four of us decided to take a vacation together driving through New England. I did the driving and Bob usually sat alongside me while the two women occupied the back seat. We were in various hotels and motor courts and restaurants; we visited historical sites; we played some tennis, and stopped once to bowl, and did some swimming. We were together almost constantly for eight days, and I thought we had a fine, congenial time. It wasn't until after our return home that my wife and I found out that Bob and Liz had not spoken to each other throughout that trip.

We sat down, after we found it out, and retraced our journey, remembering every detail, and the more we thought about it, the more astonishing it became. We knew, of course, that the Gaffneys some-times went for two or three weeks without speaking at home. But that involved, as a general rule, only the evening hours and weekends. On the trip they were in each other's presence twenty-four hours a day, for eight days, without speaking a word to each other, and the important thing was that they didn't speak with such finesse we know it. That's art.

The technique of Not Speaking has never, to my knowledge, been adequately investigated by sociologists or psychologists. Being inter-ested in the subject, I have for several years been conducting quiet observations, with special reference to the rules of the game. I've found out that there are few husbands and wives who don't quit speaking now and then. And the number of people who live in the same neighborhood and don't speak is beyond calculation. In my own bailiwick I know of two businesses where the partners carry on from day to day, month after month, without speaking to each other. In a nearby village there are two brothers who are business competitors and whose stores are directly across the street from each other. They have not spoken for thirty years. I have tried to find out what started it, but I get conflicting stories. The most sensible version is as follows:

Thirty years ago, when the brothers were boys, their mother forbade them to enter a certain poolroom. One day the younger of the two crept into the forbidden resort and found his brother already there, playing pool with a town character. The younger brother said, "Shoot me a game when you get through, will you?" The older brother said, "You get the dickens out of here; you're too young." So the younger brother went home and said, "Mamma, Joe he's down in the poolroom." And when Joe came home his mother gave him what-for. After the yelling had died down, Joe turned on his younger brother and said, "You little tattletale twerp, I'll never speak to you again as long as I live!" It's beginning to look as if he'll make it.

I have read about a man named George Smith who works in box offices at various sporting events around New York and who quits speaking to people wholesale. Each Christmas he sends out calendars to all his acquaintances. Across the top of the calendar is printed: "I am not speaking to the following persons—"

Underneath is a list of the proscribed, perhaps two dozen altogether. The names on the list change from year to year, although I've noticed that there are a few individuals who seem to have permanent listing.

This George Smith sits in his box office and people line up in front of him for the purpose of buying tickets. Some of the individuals whose names appear on his calendar must surely show up before his wicket from time to time. He has to deal with them. I have no direct knowledge about it, but I can imagine how he manages it. His adversary stands face to face with him and asks for certain seat locations.

"Two in Section C, down front," says the adversary.

If George Smith has the requested seats, he can simply shove the tickets over the counter. His adversary either knows the price already or can look on the ticket for it. He lays down his money, George Smith gives him his change, and George has never uttered a word. His honor is intact.

Let us suppose, however, that the requested tickets are not available. How should George handle it? Could he scribble a note? He could not. Note writing is as flagrant a violation of the rules as is actual talking. Could he simply shake his head from side to side? He could not. Head shaking is out. George can do one of two things: He can sit there like a bump on a log, saying nothing, acting as if he didn't hear, hoping that his adversary will be smart enough to ask for seats in another location. Barring that, George can direct his gaze past his adversary and speak to the person next in line, saying, "Hey, you in the checkered shirt. If you're looking for seats in Section C, down front, there ain't any more. Might fix you up with good seats in Section F." This may be confusing to the man in the checkered shirt, but it gets George Smith off the hook. His adversary takes the seats in Section F.

There are many stories about people in the theatrical world who quit speaking to each other privately, but who are required to talk each other half to death onstage. I have heard of vaudeville teams whose two members carry on hilarious conversations on the stage every day, but once they walk through the wings they wouldn't speak to each other if their toenails were pulled out with chilled pincers. The same thing is true in the legitimate theater, where a man and a woman will go through a torrid love scene before the audience while giving each other the silent treatment elsewhere. It even happens in the world of sports. It is recorded that the late John McGraw as manager of the New York Giants, was not on speaking terms with Charlie Herzog, his third baseman. If Mr. McGraw had some message to convey to Mr. Herzog, he did it through a third person, and Mr. Herzog conveyed his answer, if any, via the intermediary. Once during a tight and exciting game Mr. McGraw forgot himself when Mr. Herzog was at bat and yelled a single word straight at him. "Bunt." Mr. Herzog promptly swung hard and hit a homerun.

Mr. Herzog said later that he had chosen to be insubordinate because Mr. McGraw had no moral right to address a direct remark to him.

Bob and Liz Gaffney, however, remain the chief source of my information on the art of Not Speaking. One Saturday afternoon a few months back, I went over to the Gaffneys' and found Bob sitting on his terrace smoking a cigar and glaring at the grass.

"Where's Liz?" I asked him.

"Don't know," he said. "She drove off an hour ago. I imagine she's gone to get her hair done. We're going to dinner at the Mangans' tonight. We're Not Speaking."

"You people sure do a lot of Not Speaking," I ventured.

"Sure," he agreed. "Why not?"

"It's not quite civilized," I said. "It's not mature."

"Don't be silly," Bob said. "Not Speaking is the greatest weapon the human race has ever devised for itself. I think maybe you confuse Not Speaking with sulking. That's a mean, moody sort of thing—sulking. Not Speaking is a coldly calculated business. It can drive people out of their minds if it's not handled properly."

"How long have you two been Not Speaking this time?"

"Started day before yesterday," he said, and then, almost to himself, he added admiringly, "Lord, how that woman can Not Speak!"

I told him I didn't see how they could carry on their day-by-day affairs without speaking. He said it's like everything else—all a matter of practice. He verified my notion that there are certain hard-and-fast rules that must be observed—such as the interdiction against writing notes and head nodding or head shaking.

"It's the same as in international law," he said. "You've got to have rules and mutual agreements in conducting a war. In Not Talking, it's no problem at all when there's a third party present. You simply make your feelings known with declarative sentences, addressed to the third party. But where the two of you are alone together, the thing would be most difficult if there weren't certain rules. Neither Liz nor I would ever stoop to note writing. Yet there's a way of communicating by writing that's perfectly legitimate."

He said that Liz had given a demonstration of it a couple of hours earlier. She had brought some stationery and a fountain pen out to the terrace where Bob was sitting. She sat down and began writing, murmuring the lines to herself, as follows:

"Dearest Mother: We are all well physically, but I think Bob is mentally sick. He acts like a beast at times. But don't worry—this is my cross and I will bear it. Do you remember the Mangans? They are *so* nice. They have invited us to dinner tonight and I think it should be fun. I may have told you once about the Mangans and how peculiar they are about people being on time for dinner. They are serving to-night at seven-thirty and that means we should be there on the dot. I'm going to wear my new evening gown, the chartreuse I wrote you about. Well, I'll have to cut this short, as I'm expecting the man to repair the TV any minute, and I think Bob wants to talk to him about it. Your devoted daughter, Elizabeth.

"You see how much she accomplished?" said Bob. "She didn't say a word to me—just sat there talking out the letter to her mother—and she managed to let me know that we're supposed to go to the Mangans' for dinner, that we're supposed to be there at seven-thirty, and that we're supposed to dress up a bit, and that I shouldn't leave the house because the TV repairman was coming."

"Marvelous!" I exclaimed. "But how did you let her know you'd go to the Mangans'? Or did you?"

"If I hadn't intended going," he said "I'd have thrown back my head and laughed diabolically. Diabolical laughter doesn't constitute speaking, yet in a way it is more effective than speaking. However, it happened that I wanted to go to the Mangans'. Now, you see that bush right over there?"

I saw it. Bob said he waited a few minutes after Liz had finished murmuring the letter to her mother. Then he got up and walked over toward the bush and said:

"Well, hello there, little bird. What are you doing frisking around on a hot day like this? You better go on home to your mamma. We're going to leave later on today, going out to dinner about seven-fifteen, and we don't want you fooling around the house while we're away."

That did it. "She knew," said Bob, "that I was willing to go, and she knew what time we'd leave the house. She got right up and went inside, and I heard her on the telephone. It happens I don't know who she was calling, but I'm almost certain it was the hairdresser. Inciden-tally, the telephone is a great help."

"Yes, I know," I said. I could remember many times when one or the other of them had called us. If it was Bob calling he'd usually speak to me, while Liz would talk to my wife. If we hadn't known about their habits, we'd have thought sometimes that they had gone crazy. I would be summoned to the phone and Bob would say to me, without any preliminaries, "Hey, I just wanted to let you know that if my idiot wife has lamb one more time for dinner this week, I'm going to take a club and part her hair with it."

That sort of thing.

Sitting that afternoon on the terrace, Bob observed that the rules for Not Speaking are pretty well standardized.

"We've learned one important thing recently," he said. "It's permissible to make faces. You can't make a face at the other person. You make it without facing them. The most popular face is the one registering disgust. Like this."

He shrugged up his shoulders a bit and then contorted his face in a most eloquent manner. The expression clearly said, "Such colossal stupidity! To think that I'm saddled with this horrible creature for the rest of my natural life! How I'd love to bust her one!"

"Sometimes," Bob explained, "you have to hold it for quite a while. If I'm making that face, I make it at right angles to Liz, and if she doesn't happen to be looking in my direction, I have to hold it till I feel she does see it. I might add that there are legitimate ways of attracting her attention. Grunts, snorts, and whinnies are allowable sounds, perfectly proper, and most effective at times. Just a couple of evenings ago I was sitting in the—"

We heard a car approaching and Liz drove up, her hair freshly set, as Bob had guessed. She got out of the car and came up on the terrace.

"Hi," she said to me. She didn't look at Bob, and Bob didn't look at her.

"Do you know anything about electricity?" she asked.

"Only that it makes lights turn on."

"Oh that's too bad," she said. "We've got a fuse blown out in the basement; I thought you might be able to fix it."

I started to say I could replace a fuse, and then I realized that she was talking to Bob, through me. He groaned and then whinnied, and went into the house, and I heard him clumping down the basement stairs. He was back in a few moments, and I got up to leave.

"Tell your wife," he said, "if you're on speaking terms with her, that I can't come up tomorrow to get that magazine she told me about. I'm leaving tomorrow morning for Pittsburgh on business. Be back Tuesday night La Guardia Airport, flight 402, arrival 9:12 P.M., Eastern Standard Time. Tell her I'll pick up the magazine later in the week."

So I went home and, in a fairly loud voice gave that information to the dog.

George Dolan

I Gonna Be A Artist

FROM 1957 TO HIS DEATH IN 1988, George Dolan was a much quoted columnist for the *Fort Worth Star-Telegram*. He was a kindly humorist who specialized in the pranks, peculiarities and peccadilloes of people he knew or met in what he called West Texas (people in Fort Worth define anything west of the city limits as West Texas). He made exceptions for visitors like Zsa Zsa Gabor or for outsiders like cartoonist Ace Reid, who occupied the Draggin' S Ranch at far-away Kerrville, but mostly he stayed fairly close to home. His pieces were short, usually ended with a punch line, and were never indignant or critical, even when the good old boys were playing outrageous practical jokes. At times George was puzzled, as he was by the "art" of the metal sculptor treated in the following sketch, but he tried to be understanding.

From *Slightly Left and Right of Center*. Fort Worth: Branch Smith, Inc., 1967, pp. 124–125.

Dr. Sam Jagoda, Jr., a Fort Worth radiologist, sculpts from scrap metal. He culls junk yards for his raw material, tears his car seat covers hauling it home, then welds it into quaint shapes in his basement.

One of his objets d'art started as a mountain range and wound up a bird.

What was meant to be a penguin tipped over and became an iguana.

He titled one of his pieces "We Two Kings of Orient Are." He didn't have enough for three kings.

He began work on what he was calling "War Bird." But, when done, the bird was huddled inside drawn-up wings, peering out timidly. It became "Worry Bird."

Dr. Jagoda fashioned an ostrich with a body made of a Harley-Davidson motorcycle transmission cover turned upside-down.

He put together a beagle, as a salute to Him and Her, with a boiler plate body, railroad spike legs and drooping ears made of automobile fan blades. The beagle is called "It."

The artist started his creative efforts after seeing a picture of junk sculpture in a magazine. It carried a four-figure price tag.

Dr. Jagoda got a welder to show him how to use a torch and, that same afternoon, made a cast-iron owl.

Now his art has been exhibited rather widely. His catalog includes entries like these:

"Sweet Bird of Youth—Note the wide-eyed innocence of this sleek beauty. It has been called to my attention that I put the feet on backwards. This is O.K. because youth has a lot of adjustments to make and this one does not know where it is headed anyway. Art is flexible.

"Tree—This has been useful at Christmas and other times when one needs a fire-proof and indestructible tree. If you brush against the branches, they will wave to and fro rhythmically and you will be cut to pieces."

Dr. Jagoda is the only artist I know who makes good sense.

Edwin Shrake

Billy Roy Eanes's Roman Banquet

TEXAS BORN AND EDUCATED, Edwin Shrake writes best about the Dallas-Fort Worth metroplex, his home territory, and he does not much like what he sees. He is particularly depressed by the antics of offbeat characters and crude oil billionaires. Don R. Swadley, retired University of Texas at Arlington professor, speaking of the protagonist of *Strange Peaches,* remarks: "He rejects all that Texas and Texans stand for" (*Twentieth Century Western Writers,* James Vinson, ed., Detroit: Gale Research Co., 1982, p. 703). Shrake slashes hardest and cuts deepest in *Peter Arbiter,* set in Dallas but harking back to the declining years of the Roman Empire. Peter the narrator, is a bisexual (perhaps omni-sexual would be a better term) interior decorator living with a gay furniture designer called Al. They contend for the favors of a sexually precocious teenager spoken of as Guy-Guy and attend a series of parties given by, or for, the rich people of the area. The excerpts which follow are from a long and often unquotable description of an entertainment given by billionaire Billy Roy Eanes. The event reminds Shrake of the banquet arranged by a freed slave, as described by Roman satirist Petronius Arbiter.

From *Peter Arbiter.* Austin: Encino Press, 1973, pp. 27–34, 52–56.

As it stands on the highest hill east of town, above a lake that is large enough for sailing regattas, we could see Billy Roy Eanes's house while we were yet a mile away turning through the gates onto the main road that winds through his estate.

The uniformed guards at the gates found my name and Albert's on the list and admitted us with no bickering over the presence of Guy-Guy. We motored up the drive between rows of tall oaks that partially screen several hundred acres of clipped green Bermuda grass. As we topped a slight rise the entire house came into view. It is a white colonial mansion with thirty-two columns on the front porch, and behind it in a semicircular compound are guest houses, a gymnasium, stables, hangars, servants' quarters, barracks for the guards and their officers, warehouses, the clubhouse for the golf course, the yacht club and whatnot—each building in the same white colonial architecture but with lesser numbers of columns than the main house. All the houses in the compound are grouped around a parade ground in the center of which is an enormous gold-knobbed American Eagle flagpole surrounded by twenty-one polished brass cannon that are shot off by the estate's honor guard during Billy Roy's favorite ceremonies on Flag Day, George Washington's Birthday, San Jacinto Day, Pearl Harbor Day, and D Day while a famous evangelist recites the Pledge over the loudspeaker system. To the left of the main house in a prominent location is a tower with clocks the size of big Ben facing in the four primary directions. Every hour the clocks chime and a recording of *Nearer My God to Thee* is played—a reminder to the old man, Billy Roy, of how fast his life is passing. Precisely at noon each day a servant dressed in black comes up to Billy Roy, looks him in the eye and says, "Twenty-four more hours have slipped away."

An attendant took our car to park it in a nearby field, leaving us standing and gaping in front of the main house. Although I had been responsible for the decor of Billy Roy's wife's master bedroom, and so had been at the house on several occasions, I had never been able to adjust to the prodigious dimensions of the place. "I don't see the appropriate Peter Arbiter touch anywhere," said Albert, who had designed and built a chair for Mama Eanes and had hand-carved the arms, legs and back but had never been allowed inside the gates before.

We wandered about, looking at one astounding thing after another, feeling like Lilliputians invited to dine with Gulliver—until we saw the master of the estate, Billy Roy himself, playing ball on the lawn with a crowd of boys, and a few girls, whom I guessed to be children of the servants.

Billy Roy was clad in cleated shoes and a football jersey of the sort worn by the professional football team he owns. He was wearing the same number worn by his quarterback. Beside him stood two black servants holding a huge canvas bag filled with footballs bearing the trade name *The Duke*. Both servants wore sweatshirts and baseball caps of the type affected by football coaches, and one had a whistle on a chain around his neck. They would hand Billy Roy a football and he would lob it into the crowd of children fifteen feet way. After each toss, the two servants would shout, "Way to drill it in there, stud!" and "Way to fire, Billy baby!"

If the children, squealing and tussling for every ball thrown, happened to let one drop, the black man with the whistle would blow a shrill tweet and the two servants would shout, "They got hands like boards, baby!" and "Run it til we get it right!" Occasionally Billy Roy would wipe the sweat from his balding head, give his gold-wire spectacles to be cleaned by a boy who was carrying a silver vase, and would mutter, "Got to have some blocking up there . . . can't do it all myself . . . kill the quarterback, that's the name of this game . . . darn it, you guys, give me three and a half seconds and I'll pick em to pieces . . . ."

The servant without the whistle had the duty of counting each ball that came out of the canvas bag. When he reached fifty-four—the limit of the bag—he called the number to Billy Roy, who promptly quit the game. Billy Roy rubbed his bicep and said, "That's enough for today, coach . . . got to take care of the arm . . . lot riding on this baby . . . ."

The two servants in billed caps made certain they were returned all fifty-four balls, which meant they had to chase children around the lawn and become involved in two or three episodes of keep away. Billy Roy beckoned to the boy with the silver vase. Lifting his football jersey, which proved to be all he was wearing other than the cleated shoes and white athletic socks, Billy Roy peed into the vase. The boy then shut the lid on the vase, disclosing a bowl built atop the lid. The boy poured the bowl full of water from a flask at his hip. Billy Roy washed his hands in the bowl, flicked his fingers and dried them in the boy's hair. Recognizing us as guests, Billy Roy waved and smiled in a very friendly fashion.

"Come along to the showers," he said. "Got to take a shower and have a rubdown after every workout, you know, or you stiffen up. We can't have that. Coach would be mighty put out."

We followed him into the gymnasium. First we paused in a locker room to disrobe and were presented with rubber sandals and with white towels marked BRE. All the while Billy Roy was chatting with us: "I don't think we're getting out of there fast enough on the EGO Pop, do you? . . . Next time I see Wanda cheating up I'll hit the X-end and teach him a lesson . . . Tell me the Bears are a mean bunch, eh? Well, we'll be a little meaner, that's a two-headed blade on that sword to cut both ways, eh boys?" We nodded and answered as best we could.

Next we proceeded into a room that contained a large heated pool divided into sections for hot mineral baths, for whirlpool baths, and simply for soaking and splashing. Off that room opened smaller rooms that contained sauna baths, steam baths, sunlamps, massage tables and masseurs, and beds for relaxing. Many of the male dinner guests were frolicking in the pools or sitting in one of the hot rooms. Two nude Mexican boys rubbed Billy Roy with salt, bathed him in a cold shower, bathed him in a hot shower, and escorted him into a sauna. The three of us followed. We sat on wooden shelves in the sauna for ten minutes or so, hardly able to talk for the sweating, while Mexican boys poured water on scalding rocks and placed on the fire herbs and potions that rushed through the body passages and opened up the sinuses. Another servant played the harmonica for our amusement. "If you lose your health you've lost everything," Billy Roy told us.

"Holy shit, is this real?" said Guy-Guy.

"Don't try to make sense out of it," Albert said wisely.

Just as I thought I might fall over from the heat, Billy Roy walked out of the sauna. We went with him into the room with the pools. Not since I played football in college, or at least not since basic training in the army had I seen so many naked men assembled in one room. They were of all shapes, sizes and ages, about seventy or eighty of them ranging from Negro and Mexican servant boys of ten to oligarchs of seventy-five. Billy Roy padded happily among them, his rubber sandals flapping on the tile, his belly hanging down so far as to render his member all but invisible. He ordered glasses of mineral water passed among us. "A toast to my genius!" he cried good-naturedly.

We played water polo and shot basketballs at a hoop mounted at one end of the large pool. At last Billy Roy led us out of the bathing facility and into the locker room, the boy with the harmonica dancing beside him. Those who wished stopped off for massages. Billy Roy weighed himself and wrote his weight on a chart on the wall. He sat on a bench in front of a large locker while his clothes were laid out. A fan blew the clean wet laundry smell through the room.

Billy Roy put on cotton shorts with red hearts on them. He put on a white cotton tee-shirt. Then he put on green socks, a gold shirt with gold cufflinks, a white silk tie, a green suit and brown alligator shoes. He combed his scant gray hair straight back, shot his cuffs and adjusted his spectacles of thin gold wire. He looked at the way we were dressed and frowned as though he had not noticed us before. No doubt we were not outfitted for Billy Roy's taste. Albert was wearing a white linen Edwardian suit with a red silk shirt and wide white tie, white silk hose and white loafers. I had on a rather conservative gray pinch-waisted suit with vest, a canary yellow shirt and a patterned red tie. Little Guy-Guy wore a purple velvet suit that we had found for him that day. He also wore his red, white and blue polkadot necktie and his yellow shades. Billy Roy shrugged, smiled again and we followed him toward the party.

In the vestibule of the gym a porter in white pants, white shirt and white sneakers counted us as we went out. Above the door was a golden cage from which a myna bird shrieked: "Billy Roy Eanes did it the hard way!"

Once outside we smelled the beef and pork being barbecued in the pits and the baby goats turning on the spits. Their rich crackling odors floated across the grass from an area where we saw dozens of white-capped men at work with spoons the size of shovels and forks the size of pitchforks. We came to a wing of the house that was big enough to be an airplane hanger. In the entrance to the enormous air-conditioned banquet hall sat two stewards counting the guests. Just inside was a sign:

ON JUNE 19 BILLY ROY EANES DINES OUT.

The walls of the banquet hall were painted with scenes depicting Billy Roy Eanes arriving as a youth in the city. Billy Roy bartering with bumpkins. Billy Roy as a merchant king. Billy Roy manipulating fleets of trucks and airplanes. Billy Roy operating printing presses and television stations. Billy Roy riding herd on uncountable livestock. Billy Roy striking oil. Billy Roy at the Super Bowl and Billy Roy at the White House. A silver urn on a pedestal in the corner contained, it was rumored, the hair that was clipped off Billy Roy's head the first time he could afford to visit a barber shop. I heard a guest remark that the most spectacular murals were in the gigantic parlor-museum of the main house. Those murals were devoted to space flights (Billy Roy at Moon Base, Billy Roy circling Venus) and various wars. "That's the room that shows how he really got rich," whispered the guest. "This stuff in here is pretty minor by comparison."

My gaze roamed from the murals. I saw there were dozens of stuffed animals ranged about the room or set on platforms on the walls. All looked most lifelike. There were elk, moose, elephants, kudus, tigers, wild mountain rams, panthers, peccaries, water buffalo, a rhino. "Billy Roy never shoots nothing small," another guest said.

The two-hundred or so guests had been seated at long tables covered with red and white checkered cloths according to a chart presided over by a fat black man in a white uniform with tails, gold braid and epaulets, not unlike the summer dress uniform of an admiral or the suit Cab Calloway might wear to an inaugural ball. Albert, Guy-Guy and I were placed near the head of the table where Billy Roy was to sit.

Mexican and Negro boys appeared with bowls of warm water. They washed our hands and cleaned our nails and sang cheery tunes. A black waiter stepped forward with tumblers of scotch and ice.

"I'm a drink toter first class. Won't be no dry moufs here," he said.

A murmur rose from the guests. Six blacks wheeled in a copper casting of Billy Roy's champion Clydesdale horse. Flanking the horse were platters, engraved BRE, bearing barbecued ribs, chicken, cole slaw, barbecue sauce, potato salad, pinto beans, jalapeno peppers, red chilis, sliced onions, scallions, pickles, garlic bread, hot sausages, beef tacos, boiled shrimps, fried quail and oysters on the half shell. The blacks distributed the platters among the tables. The drink toter filled my crystal goblet with rosé wine.

"What's for dessert?" I asked.

"Man, you jokin," said the waiter. "Lots of folks never sees dessert. They sleep by then."

To the music of four guitars, two harmonicas and an accordion—playing some country air that was not familiar to me but prompted us to accompany the other guests in clapping time to the music—Billy Roy marched to his table, nodding and waving, clasping both hands over his head, calling out names of certain friends or acquaintances. He sat in a cane rocking chair piled with cushions and looked out at the faces of his guests.

"My friends," he said, "it was inconvenient for me to come to the table just yet, but I was afraid you would get nervous without me. Now that I'm here, you all can relax. Just set back and enjoy yourselves. As for me, I've got to finish my game. Knowing you are all sportsmen at heart, in the great tradition of this country, I know you will understand that once a game is begun it must be played to its conclusion. A sportsman don't like the word quitter! You always got a winner, and you got a loser. My friends, you are all winners. Needless to say, I'm the biggest winner of all!"

Billy Roy turned to an elderly, wise-looking black man who sat crosslegged beside him with a Chinese Checkers board on his lap.

"I jump you here," said Billy Roy, "and here, here and here."

He smiled again at the crowd and with a forefinger pushed his gold wire spectacles onto the bridge of his nose. While the black was pondering a move, waiters moved about the table carrying baskets that contained wooden hens which sat as if brooding. From beneath the hens the waiters removed eggs and passed them to the guests.

"These are for the stomach," Billy Roy said, holding up an egg. "Suck a egg before ever great meal and you'll never have gas."

I could envision a chick inside, and I began looking for a place to hide my egg. But I heard a guest say, "I bet this here's a treat," and I cracked open the egg to discover a nice fat fig.

By now an orchestra of musicians in dinner jackets had begun to play dinner music on a platform behind Billy Roy. The orchestra had eight violins and six saxophones. Servants weaved around the table clearing empty platters. A silver dish clattered to the floor. "Leave it lay, but box his ears!" shouted Billy Roy. A janitor with a broom swept out the silver dish along with scraps that had fallen from the table. The guests applauded. "I love a fair fight! Fortune took that dish from me, but I'll get more!" Billy Roy cried.

Billy Roy looked at the Chinese Checkers board. Then he took the board in both hands, flipped all the marbles into the air and tossed the board onto the floor. The old black man scrambled out of the room. Billy Roy looked furious while the waiters poured wine from decanters labeled "100 years Old."

"It's sad but true, wine lives longer than men do!" said Billy Roy, sipping the rosé, his expression softening. "Drink it up, my friends. I swear you've never had wine better than this. Did I say better? You never had anywheres near as good. The last dinner party I had my guests were kings, prime ministers, sheiks, potentates, sultans, presidents, dictators—in other words, a classier bunch than you. But the wine I served them was cheaper. That proves who my real friends are!"

A black man with frizzy hair in what is called an Afro brought in a silver skeleton with movable joints. He got up on the stage and began arranging the skeleton in various postures as in a dance that was frozen by steps.

"Bones, Bones, you see, is what we are!" Billy Roy said. "So eat, drink and love life while you can my friends. Life has been good and generous to me, and I'm giving back a measure of what I've got. I have took as I pleased and I give as I will. That's the mark of a man!"

We applauded again. The waiters brought out trays upon which were engraved the signs of the zodiac with appropriate foods on each tray: goat testicles for Capricorn, a jug of water for Aquarius, a trout for Pices, a broiled ram's penis for Aries, a piece of beef for Taurus, kidneys for Gemini, a crab for Cancer, what seemed to be a hairy undigested glob for Leo, a piglet for Virgo, a tart and a sowbelly for Libra, fried vinegarones for Scorpio, the eye of a bull for Sagittarius. A hunk of earth with grass growing from it was in the center of each tray, and atop that was a bee's nest.

"Dig in! Dig in! This is life I'm offering you!" shouted Billy Roy.

Before we could reluctantly lift our forks, the waiter yanked off the trays and showed that beneath were other trays loaded with stuffed capons, Canadian bacon and barbecued chickens decked out with wings and colored to look like The Flying Red Horse. At the corners of each tray were four chocolate cherubs peeing red sauce into bowls in which lay fried butterfly shrimps. After a few bites of capon and another swig of wine I felt I'd had enough to eat. I leaned back, rubbing my stomach, and looked at the fifty other guests who shared our table. Twenty or more were women in their finest plumage. My attention was caught by a woman who laughed loudly as she wandered among the tables chatting with guests. She had blue hair and wore a pair of sequined glasses that she would occasionally allow to rest on her huge bosom. The glasses were held in place by a gold chain but probably would have stayed on her bosom anyhow, it was such a shelf.

The bearded fellow at my right—Guy-Guy was at my left, between Albert and me—nudged me and nodded toward the woman.

"That's Mama Eanes," he said, assuming I didn't know her. He was a local gossip columnist who printed many favorable items about Billy Roy. "She's the old man's wife. I'd hate to tell you what she used to be. But I will say you wouldn't have wanted to take her home to mother unless your mother was very broadminded. Huh! Huh! When she met Billy Roy she was a fry cook and he was a cab driver, two jobs on about the same level if you ask me. Him and his talk about potentates! Thirty years ago a potentate wouldn't of allowed Mama Eanes to cop his joint, though I guess they do now. What the hell is a potentate?"

"A ruler with tremendous power."

"Yeah, then I guess they would. Looking at her makes you wonder how things work. She ain't pretty and never was except for having twenty-seven pounds of tit. But I've got to hand it to her. She takes care of what's her own. She nags like a bluejay, and if she doesn't like you, you're sunk in this town. But if she does like you, consider yourself a wealthy man. Billy Roy owns so much property you couldn't fly over all of it in one day. He's got so many servants and employees that not a tenth of them would recognize him if they saw him. But them or most anybody at this table would fall down and wallow in cat turds if he told them to, he'd tell them to if she told him to.

"One of his secrets is he buys everything for himself," continued my dinner companion. "If he wants a wool sweater, he sends for wool from his champion rams and has the sweater knitted at his own textile mill. He likes good honey, so he brought bees from Greece and Turkey to breed with his own bees, and now he's got the best honey in the world. He wanted granite for the walls of his office, so he had it cut from the mountains of one of his ranches in Mexico and shipped it here on his own barges, trucks and railroad. That makes him feel like he doesn't depend on anybody. He likes to say he's just making do with what the land provides. Some other guys at this table have come up from nothing, too. See that skinny fellow down there with a chicken leg sticking out of his mouth? He's worth about eight million, which makes him pretty ordinary in this crowd. A few years ago he was a cedar chopper. He was pure trash, lived in a tin and tarpaper shack with a fat hairy wife and half a dozen kids and drove around in a twenty year old pickup. He sold enough fence posts to buy a piece of land, built a house on the land and sold that. Since then he's cut down every tree on hundreds of acres and has sold thousands of houses. He was stupid enough to know that people like to live jammed together on flat, cleared ground. They want lots of neighbors around them and no trees for the Indians to hide in. The trick to that business is to make the houses ugly and you'll be a big success. But people get a yearning for trees after a while. Safe trees. So after he's chopped down all the trees to clear the lots, then he goes into the nursery business. He sells little tiny trees to the people who bought the houses. They plant the trees and water them and in thirty years the trees are grown but the people who bought them are dead. And what happened to the original trees? That fellow disguised them as fence posts and sold them back to the people. Nice business, I'd say. Huh! Huh! He's doing real well. The other day he ran an ad in the paper that said:

MY OWN HOME FOR SALE. I AM BUYING A MANSION.

"That guy next to him, the one who looks rich, inherited a pile of money and quadrupled it in the market. He was a big deal in those days. Apartments in Paris, New York and Mexico City. Gigantic house here with indoor tennis courts, swimming pool, skeet range. Ate like an emperor. He's knocked over more martinis than most people ever drank. But he started building some office buildings, the market took a dive, his friends called in some notes on him, and once you start down-hill there's no stopping. He's lost everything now but his big house here. But he doesn't want the whole town to know he's broke. So he took an ad in the paper today that said:

AM WILLING TO AUCTION OFF MY SPARE FURNITURE.

"The only reason he's here is that he was always kind to Mama Eanes and she sees to it he gets invited. His other friends avoid him because he's started to smell poor. But Mama Eanes might take it into her head to pull him out of the ditch, so nobody has completely counted him out yet."

My garrulous companion lit a cigar, giving me the opportunity to turn back toward Billy Roy.

"You don't think we were going to eat that grub on the astrology signs, did you?" Billy Roy said to the table, laughing. "I serve a fancier meal than that! I'd hate to have it in *Who's Who* that Billy Roy Eanes made his guests eat grass and gonads for dinner. I like a little joke, but I do admit I'm interested in this here science of astrology. I'm a cultured man and there's not much I don't know, but astrology has a lot to teach us. Don't ask me how the stars and the planets can affect our lives. Just take my word for it that they do."

☆ ☆ ☆ ☆

He stood up and most of the guests made as if to rise. But Billy Roy spread his hands gracefully and gestured them back down.

"No need to get up friends," he said. "I just got to make peepee. You all go right ahead on with your dinner. A guest in my house is as good as a king. Damn sight better in most cases. What's a king but a damn aristocrat? Hey boys?"

☆ ☆ ☆ ☆

The delicacy that followed in the progression of food stuffs was one of the oddest I have ever observed. It encouraged Billy Roy to abandon the little Mexican boy and return to his chair. Each guest was served a plate upon which was a plump baby possum wearing a baseball cap. "They look dead but they still got hair on," whispered Guy-Guy. Half fearing the surprise this time might be that the possum was real, I plucked warily at mine. The hairs came out and proved to be a confectionery of some sort. The eyes were cherries. The possums were made of chocolate with creamy banana custard innards. While we were breaking off possums' ears, snouts and the like, there was a loud knocking at the door. I imagined it might be the police and tucked my feet under me to be ready to run if Great Luke had set the Law on us. But the bearded gossip columnist identified the new arrival, who lurched through the tall doors and weaved along the enormous length of the room whirling his white felt cowboy hat around his head as if he were Tom Mix leading a rodeo parade.

"That's Calhoun, the undertaker. He's late because he was in charge of Crouper's funeral," the gossip columnist said.

Calhoun wore a black silk western suit with mother of pearl buttons and purple piping. He clomped along in his cowboy boots, grinning at the guests and carrying a handful of lilies, several of which dangled from broken stalks. His wife paced beside him, daintily clutching up the hem of a purple evening gown. Calhoun stumbled against various guests, laughed and whooped as they lifted him back to his feet. By now the musicians in dinner jackets had replaced the country band, and there was a girl singer in a tight red sequined dress that bared her shoulders.

"Sorry I'm late, Billy Roy!" yelled Calhoun as chairs were dragged up and places made for him and his wife at the host's table. "We had to go to the funeral dinner. That was some champion munchfest!" He fell into a chair and pulled his wife down beside him. "Hod damn with the price of that buryin and that dinner, it cost old Crouper's wife meeny meeny a dollar to get dirt throwed on top of him. Worth it though, I suppose. She didn't seem to be having the worst time of her life. You thank so hon? Wheeeoop! I must of drunk a quart of bourbon! But that don't mean I'm through drankin. A spot of that red wine would keep my blood a-pumpin."

"What did you have for dinner?" Billy Roy asked.

"I don't have the best memory in the world," replied Calhoun, putting on his hat. "My name and address are about all I can manage, and sometimes my phone number. But near as I can recall we had ambrosia, salmon salad, mashed potatoes, hot rolls with butter, cranberry sauce, giblet gravy, English peas, roast turkey with dressin, hot raisin pie with ice cream. Sounds like Thanksgivin', don't it? Well, what bothers me is if I can eat a turkey, who's to say turkey won't turn about one of these days and eat me? Anyhow my wife here got sick and threw up, but I put away about two pounds of sliced white meat plus all the side dishes, and I don't care if the drought never lets up! My business is always, Billy Roy, as you well know. I'm thanking of selling franchises in other cities. People are poppin off fastern I can get em out of sight. Thank God for re-frigeration! Hey! Why ain't Mama eatin?"

"You know she won't touch a bite until the silver is put away," Billy Roy said.

"I'm goin home then," said Calhoun.

"Oh Calhoun, sit down," Mama Eanes said. She had been standing beside the kitchen door supervising the waiters, but she came over and embraced Mrs. Calhoun. "My dear how marvelous to see you!" they cried in unison. They exclaimed over the jewelry they were wearing. Mama Eanes pulled off a gold bracelet and gave it to Mrs. Calhoun for examination. "It weighs a pound and a half. Get tired lugging it around," said Mama Eanes.

Mrs. Calhoun removed her diamond earrings and Mama Eanes studied them through rhinestoned glasses.

"My husband is so generous," said Mrs. Calhoun. "No woman has a kinder husband."

"She kept after me to buy them damn thangs until I thought I was gonna be my own customer," Calhoun said. "If we had a daughter, I'd chop her ears off. Why women like to pin glass beans to their lobes is a question for Kang Solomon to answer. Thank how cheap thangs would be if it wasn't for women! Whut a simple life a man could have! I envy a hod damn queer, I really do!"

"It's not the queers I'm worried about!" said Mrs. Calhoun. "Lord knows Calhoun crawls into enough beds, and not into mine more than twice a year, but the beds he visits belong to female tramps. He hasn't laid a hand on me in five months now. Time's coming up, Calhoun, you dreading it already? Tells me he's tired. I bet he's wore out! From screwing his hymn soloist all afternoon or dragging a manicurist away from one of those stiffs and banging her behind the slab! But just let him get the idea that I'm hot for the yard man or the delivery boy, and he'll holler his brains out."

While the two women clung to each other and discussed their problems, Calhoun gathered his arms and legs beneath him like a frog, crept over and tackled Mama Eanes. She flopped onto the floor, her dress slipping up around her mottled thighs. Mrs. Calhoun fell with her. Blushing and giggling, Mama Eanes pulled down her dress.

"Haw! Haw!" laughed Calhoun and Billy Roy.

"I seen beaver!" Calhoun yelled.

"You did not!" said Mama Eanes.

The amplifying system had been squawking and screeching, but suddenly the girl singer's voice could be heard clearly:

> *"Is there any reason why*
> *You'd fall in love with someone*
> *Only half as good as me . . . ."*

"Lay on some food out here! My guests are starving!" Billy Roy shouted.

Immediately a swarm of servants not only cleared off the tables but wiped them clean, swept the floor and sprinkled sawdust. More wine was brought out. Calhoun stood up and began flinging lilies and singing in a voice that obliterated the girl on stage:

> *"I don't care if it rains or freezes*
> *long as I got my plastic Jesus*
> *mounted on the dashboard of my car . . . ."*

He finally ran out of breath and had to quit.

"Never had a sangin lesson in my life," Calhoun said. "Always had a wonderful voice. But when I was a kid I was too busy for studying sangin. I worked in a fried pie factory, as a carpenter, drove a truck, was assistant to a circumcision doctor, sold rural mail boxes, was a meter reader . . . ."

"Where'd you learn to snore?" said Mrs. Calhoun.

"Then I picked up my current trade while I was in the army," Calhoun said. "There's no better place to practice the undertakin trade. Got all the clients you need. My proudest day, the day I knew I'd make it as an undertaker, was the day we stopped for lunch during an embalmin' and ate chili and drank Cokes right there beside a raw stiff who'd been in an airplane crash and fire. How you feel, Billy Roy? Comin to see me pretty soon?"

"My dear old friend, don't joke with me about that," said Billy Roy.

"Now you made him sad," Mama Eanes said to Calhoun.

Platters of coconut cakes, banana layer cakes, raisin pies, sugar cookies and cream tarts were placed on the tables along with wine and cognac and steaming pots of coffee. Vases of flowers were spotted around the room. I heard singing from the kitchen and saw a man in a white chef's hat reeling with a bottle of cognac when the door swung open briefly. The guests were quite festive again, and some were even dancing, but the host sank into melancholy at being reminded of his own impermanence.

Seeing his master thus disturbed, old Hamhock crept up, made his eyeballs flop about like fishes, sputtered and spat and said, "Mist Bill Roy I gots ten dollah says we doan win no championship."

"Kindly, faithful Hamhock," said Billy Roy, patting the aged black man on the head. Billy Roy smiled, wiped his spectacles and looked at the other servants busy at their tasks. "Hamhock cares about me. Don't matter that I'm the boss and he's just a poot on the scale of things. Servants are men, you see. Niggers, wops, spics, chinks, they all sucked tits when they were babies, just same as me. But hard luck has kept them down. When I die, I'll see to it that my servants are took care of. Mama Eanes, that's your chore. I'm announcing now so they'll love me as much while I'm alive as when I'm dead."

The servants paused in their work and applauded their master.

"Where's Gibbs? Tell him to come and bring my will. We'll have a reading," Billy Roy said.

Mama Eanes protested gently, but Gibbs was fetched nevertheless. The pale secretary unrolled a document and started to read, but Billy Roy, a beaker of cognac clutched to his chest, lifted a hand to stop him.

"You, Calhoun, my dear friend, it's you I charge to build my monument according to the plans I've drawn up," said Billy Roy in a voice hoarse with emotion. I want a big statue of my faithful dog Willard lying at my feet, and I want plenty of giant stone wreaths and a big eternal flame so people can see where I'm resting. I want carvings of the great football games, the heroic battles, beautiful women, some of the great men I've known—Roosevelt, Churchill, Hitler, Mussolini, Sinatra, Lombardi, Lyndon, Ike, old Curt Lemay, Duke Wayne, Peron, old man Hunt, guys like that sitting on their thrones welcoming me to heaven with Shirley Temple giving me an armload of roses. I want my plot to be one hundred yards wide and two hundred deep, with fruit trees and green vines planted all around, and a gazebo for summer concerts. A man ought to be as careful about his tomb as he is about his house, because he'll be in it a hell of a lot longer. Put up a neon sign that says THIS IS BILLY ROY EANES'S TOMB—HIS HEIRS DON'T OWN IT. I'll not be insulted when I'm dead. I want cops day and night. People can visit my tomb, but only if they stay in line and are orderly. Carve me handing out money to the poor. I want airplanes, rockets, ships, trucks and railroad trains on my tomb. Don't forget to put horseys on there, too. My two Derby winners and my Clydesdale, Big Bill.

"On one wall carve a banquet in progress with people having a good time. Put a statue of Mama on my right looking properly sad. Put a clock in the middle with my name on it. For an inscription you might use

> "HERE RESTS BILLY ROY EANES
> LOYAL, BRAVE AND HUMBLE—
> A GREAT MAN WHO STARTED
> WITH NOTHING BUT MADE
> BILLIONS AND NEVER LISTENED
> TO A PHILOSOPHER.
> FAREWELL BILLY ROY
> HAPPY TIMES UP YONDER.
> FAREWELL FRIEND."

At these words, Billy Roy began to weep. Mama Eanes was blubbering, and so were the Calhouns, and then Hamhock and most of the servants and guests took it up. I discovered myself to be snuffling. Albert and Guy-Guy were making sounds that could have been construed as sobs or perhaps not.

"But we know we have to die," Billy Roy said, dabbing his eyes with a napkin. "We might as well die happy." The band had ceased during his speech. He stood up and chopped the air like a conductor. "Let's have happy music, damn you! Let's lay out the gold and silver! The bronze and porcelain! Let's have buckets of stingers! I feel like making a night of it! I'm gonna drink until I hear a rooster crow!"

☆ ☆ ☆ ☆

The leader of the country band consulted hurriedly with his musicians. Then they played a tune called *My Dog Billy's Waggin His Tail in Heaven Tonight*. Billy Roy stretched out atop the table and folded his arms across his chest. Hamhock imitated a trumpet playing *Taps*. Calhoun staggered to his feet and clasped his hands in a gesture of prayer. He placed a broken lily on Billy Roy. Mama Eanes, Mrs. Calhoun and such other guests as were still conscious set up a terrific racket of mourning, which caused dogs to begin howling all over the estate.

Hearing the commotion, the roving fire patrol thought surely there was a disaster at the banquet hall. Without pausing for investigation they smashed open the doors with heavy blows and rushed in spraying foam from their fire extinguishers. That created quite another ruckus. In the noise and confusion, Albert, Guy-Guy and I bolted past a steward who yelled. "This door's an entrance! You'll have to leave through an exit!" But the guards who watched our departure thought we were running from a real fire.

Dan Jenkins

The Social Structure of Claybelle High

DAN JENKINS grew up in the Dallas-Fort Worth area and his best writing is about the metroplex and its people. His career as a journalist took him to New York, however, where he became senior writer for *Sports Illustrated*. His special interests included football, country and western music, and the little world of bars and restaurants (he owns several of the latter). He made free use of these elements in shaping a second career as a novelist. *Fast Copy,* his sixth novel, features Betsy Throckmorton Winton, who has beauty, brains, background, and talent, now returning to Texas with her new husband Ted to take over her father's newspaper and radio empire. What happens to her in her home town of Claybelle, twenty-five miles from Fort Worth, in the year 1935, takes the reader on an exciting trip through Texas in bygone years. In this excerpt Betsy reveals for Ted the pattern of high-school society in the mid-twenties. The pattern is possibly more human than Texan.

From *Fast Copy*. New York: Simon & Schuster, 1988, pp. 108–114.

> "Kick' 'em in the stomach,
> Hit 'em in the head!
> Come on, Jackets,
> Kill 'em till they're dead!"

"Same old yell," Betsy said. "We were cuter, though."

"Wait a second," Ted said with surprise. "You were a cheerleader?"

"Would you rather be married to a cadet sponsor? Dumb."

They sat down on a bench in the square and Betsy revealed that she had been a cheerleader her last two years in high school. She and Eva

Jane McKnight had both been cheerleaders their last two years. Laura Mueller had been the third girl their junior year. Patsy Thornton had been the third girl their senior year. Laura and Patsy had both married beneath them, according to Anna Sue Beaton.

It had been a big deal to be a cheerleader, Betsy explained. You had to be elected by a vote of the student body after all of the candidates had led yells on stage at assembly. If you were elected as a junior, it was almost a foregone conclusion that you'd be re-elected as a senior, unless, of course, you happened to develop a case of acne in between. Such cases had been known of. Billie Renée Cowden, for one.

The Claybelle pep squad had dressed differently in Betsy's years. The girls had worn beanies, sashes around their waists, longer skirts, and long satin cloaks.

Anna Sue Beaton had never forgiven the school for not electing her a cheerleader. She'd had to settle for cadet sponsor.

"How did one get to be a cadet sponsor?" Ted asked.

"Flirt with a colonel in the ROTC. There was gossip that Anna Sue carried it beyond flirting, but I never believed it."

"We don't have girl cheerleaders in the East."

Betsy said, "I know. It's terrible. Girls don't get to do anything up there but sell chrysanthemums."

"Why do you think this is?"

"I've thought about it a lot," Betsy said. "I think it has something to do with the Civil War. In the South, all available boys were expected to go to war. Football is war, so to speak. So all available boys are expected to go out for football, which means you have to have girl cheerleaders."

"There were boy cheerleaders a minute ago."

"They have asthma. It's okay for a boy to be a cheerleader if he has asthma."

The jalopy carrying the cheerleaders had driven around to Thompson's Pharmacy and the kids had stormed the drugstore to make life miserable for Bertha Thompson, a birdlike woman in her sixties. Bertha would not be a happy person as she sat behind *her* register and tried to listen to *her* radio.

The ruckus around the soda fountain and amid the stacks of comic books would no doubt distract Bertha from the plight of Helen Trent, who, when life mocked her and broke her hopes and dashed her against the rocks of despair, fought back bravely, successfully, to prove what so many women longed to prove in their own lives—that the romance of youth could extend into middle life and even beyond. Sitting in her apartment on Hollywood's Palm Drive, Helen would be facing another crisis in her love life, having been caught in another trap set by the beautiful but evil Fay Granville.

There on the bench in the square, Ted asked what bleak fate must have enveloped all of the sad young ladies who had been denied the status of cheerleader or cadet sponsor in Claybelle High.

"Well," Betsy thought, now smoking, "they could be a sophomore favorite, a junior favorite, or a senior favorite, except I was all of those."

"They had nothing, in other words."

"They had lots of things. There was something for everybody—if you weren't a crud."

"A *crud?*"

"You met Fred Astaire and Noel Coward the day we arrived?"

"Cruds?"

"Classic. But Slop and Tommy Jack could get by because they were on the football team."

"A girl crud didn't have it so easy, I gather."

"No, they didn't," Betsy admitted. "I can tell you it was pretty rough sailing for Dalilla Roper and Evelyn Miellmier."

No one to go out with, other than cruds. And cruds always had to sit in the middle when riding in cars.

"I think Still Norris had to sit in the middle," Betsy mused. "That's why he butchers copy."

"Beware of people who had to sit in the middle, that's your advice?"

"Many become mass murderers."

Betsy went into all of the activities that were available to those students who were less fortunate than cheerleaders, cadet sponsors, class favorites, or athletes.

They could be officers in the YMCA or the YWCA. They could be in the Home Economics Club and learn to make pie crust. They could be Meliorists. Nobody knew what the Meliorists did, but they wore glasses and carried tin lunch boxes. People who were smart had passes to go home for lunch so they could not go home at all but go to the soda fountain at Thompson's or the lunch counter at B's, or hide in the bushes and smoke, as had often been the case with Betsy.

They could join Los Hidalgos if they had a fondness for Spanish. They could be in the Dramatics Club. This was if the boys were named Dorcas and the girls were named Helga. They could be in the Parabola Club if they were math nuts. They could be a member of the Brushes if they appreciated art as much as Bob Walker had.

Bob had been taken into the art club because Old Lady Ziegler had liked his drawings of soldiers and football players, but he had been kicked out of the art club because the teacher had lacked a sense of humor. Assigned to make a sculpture out of soap, Bob had carved a nice set of tits and a lady's ass out of a bar of Woodbury.

"And what is this supposed to be?" Old Lady Ziegler had asked.

"It's for the skin you love to touch," Bob had said.

He had been sent to the principal's office where Old Man Byers was supposed to punish him, but Old Man Byers had only laughed, primarily because Bob Walker was Claybelle's best quarterback.

Betsy continued. The less fortunate students could be in the Natural Sciences Society if they wore thicker glasses than the Meliorists. They could be in the band, which was one of the neatest deals around. The band got to travel. The band went to Fort Worth and marched in the Armistice Day parade, and went to Dallas and marched in the State Fair parade, and went to Tyler and marched in the Rose Festival parade.

They could be in the Choral Club if their mamas wanted to make them a white vestment out of a bedsheet. And finally, they could be in Alpha Chi, the national honor society, in which case they were either Marguerite Whitehouse, who always waddled around with an armload of books, or Elmer Otis Kinkel, who did all of the homework for the eleven starters on the football team under the constant threat of having his head shaved and painted yellow and brown.

"The cruds revolted one year," Betsy said.

"I'm not surprised."

"My senior year, somebody called a meeting—we never found out who. All of a sudden, two hundred cruds were in the lunchroom one afternoon, yelling, making speeches. People we'd never seen before were standing up on tables and shouting, saying if they all got together they could run the school—elect cheerleaders, favorites, everything. Bob Walker named it. On page one of *The Yellow Jacket:* "The Great Crud Revolt of 1926.'"

"How could there be students you hadn't seen before?"

"Well, it's a big school, but I think tradition had more to do with it than anything. The best neighborhoods in Claybelle are on the west side of town. So we always hung out in front of the radiator at the west end of the main hall. I don't think I ever had a class on the east side of the building."

The cruds had celebrated what they thought was a victory later in the spring of that year when L. M. Spragins, one of their own, was elected junior favorite. In actual fact, however, the west-siders had stuffed the ballot box for L. M. Spragins, who was a retarded epileptic. Moreover, when the yearbook had come out in May, L. M. was featured in the snapshot section. Someone had taken a picture of L. M. threshing around in a flower bed, having one of his fits, outside of Old Lady Vaughn's homeroom. Bob Walker had sneaked the picture into the yearbook.

Let the cruds revolt again, Bob said.

Shadowlawn Country Club's golf course was considered something of a freak. It consisted of only eleven holes. A wealthy cotton farmer named Jack Wilkinson had built the club and designed the course in 1922. His logic had been that a round of golf didn't have to be nine holes or eighteen holes just because somebody back in Scotland had said so.

The founder had died in 1927 and the members had taken over the club, Ben Throckmorton among them. They someday hoped to have an eighteen-hole golf course that couldn't cause as much laughter among out-of-town guests, but the widow lady in Dallas who owned the farmland surrounding the course was asking a fortune for it. It was the hope of the members that when the widow lady died her heirs might be sympathetic toward golfers.

Betsy explained all this to Ted on the day she took him out to the club for lunch.

The clubhouse at Shadowlawn was a two-story wood-frame house. Thick round white columns on the wraparound porch supported a gabled roof with flaring eaves. Members could sit in rocking chairs on one side of the porch and look at the swimming pool. They could sit on the other side and look at two asphalt tennis courts. They could sit in front and look at the putting green, a little patch of grainy Bermuda set within the circular drive.

Betsy and Ted went out on the porch after lunch, and that's where they noticed Shady Webster sunning himself in a reclining chair by the swimming pool. It was a weekday and Shady was all alone at the pool.

They walked down to say hello to the oilman.

"They like 'em tan," Shady said by way of explaining his presence.

His presence was further explained a moment later when Eva Jane McKnight showed up with her two boys, Billy V. and Robbie D., eight and six.

As Anna Sue had promised, Eva Jane was a hot number, a willowy girl with a sexy walk, shadowed lids, and thick dark hair tumbling down to her shoulders. In a white bathing suit, Eva Jane's deep tan from a whole summer in the sun made Betsy feel anemic.

Eva Jane yelped at the sight of Betsy. They hugged, for this was their first encounter since Betsy's return from New York.

"It's grand to see you, Betsy. I'm so happy you're back in town. What fun! I'm back. You're back. We'll have each other to talk to. Believe me, there aren't too many others around. I want to hear about New York. What are they wearing? Where are they going? Everything."

Betsy introduced Ted while he was being jarred off balance by the flying tackles of Billy V. and Robbie D.

"Y'all get the hell out of here!" Eva Jane snarled at her sons. "Go bother somebody else!"

Billy V. gave his mother the finger.

Eva Jane drew back a fist. "You hear me?"

Robbie D. spit at his mother's foot.

"I said git!"

The kids went racing onto the golf course in their swim trunks.

Eva Jane and Shady exchanged casual hellos as if they were mere acquaintances.

Shady suggested he buy everyone a cool drink. Swell idea, Eva Jane said. Shady jogged into the clubhouse and came back with a rum collins for everyone, and the four of them took a table under an umbrella.

Eva Jane talked non-stop. She said that if Betsy went to Neiman's she should ask for a saleslady named Clara, that she was leaning toward Swedish modern in the bedroom of the Pemberton house she was doing over, that Anna Sue was wasting away in Claybelle, that she, Eva Jane, hadn't divorced Bubba Dean Norwood a minute too soon—he wasn't a lawyer, he was an ambulance chaser—and that she hoped Betsy would do something about the *Times-Standard,* specifically about Carolyn Moseley's so-called society column.

"As a reader, Betsy, I can't tell you how putrid her column is. She has the same names in there all the time. All she cares about is who comes to the tea dances out here on Sunday. Does she even *know* where Fort Worth and Dallas *are?*"

Shady Webster got around to saying he was drilling in Caddo lime out near Strawn. It was prolific, but you might have to go a little deeper than normal.

"What does it cost to drill an oil well?" Ted asked.

"About thirty thousand the way I do it," Shady said. "All you really need's a driller, a roughneck, and cable tools. But I got four goin' at once right now, and I'm afraid my partners are gonna have to come up with more cheese. I ain't rollin' all them dice by myself."

"I hope Daddy's not one of your partners," Betsy said. "I plan to spend his money on the paper."

"Ben?" Shady said with a grin. "Ben Throckmorton wouldn't bet on a big dog to whip a little dog."

Shady's partners were silent. They wanted it that way, he said.

"But you'll hear 'em holler if I make the ocean."

"What does that mean?" Ted asked.

"It means we've done hit saltwater instead of dinosaurs."

Betsy and Ted left Shady and Eva Jane to themselves. But as they walked away, Betsy had slyly glanced back and seen Eva Jane drape her shapely tan leg over Shady's hairy white leg and kiss him in his ear.

Molly Ivins

Ah For The Days When Porn Was About Sex, Not Materialism

A NATIVE OF HOUSTON, Molly Ivins was educated at Smith College, Columbia University and the Institute of Political Science in Paris, France. Her career in journalism began in Houston as the Complaint Department of the *Houston Chronicle* and she "rapidly worked her way up" in her own words, "to the position of sewer editor." Next she became a police reporter for the *Minneapolis Tribune* and was assigned to a beat called Movement for Social Change, where she encountered "militant blacks, angry Indians, radical students, uppity women, and a motley assortment of other misfits, and troublemakers." After a stint as editor of the *Texas Observer,* beginning in 1970, she joined the staff of the *New York Times* and in 1983 returned to Texas for good. She is a columnist for the *Dallas Times-Herald* and has made her mark as free-lance writer and speaker. She has won many awards in her field but says she is proudest of having the mascot pig of the Minneapolis Police Department named for her and for having been barred from the campus of Texas A&M University. Obviously she is able to laugh at herself— the final test of a humorous writer.

From the *Dallas Times Herald,* March 14, 1989.

AUSTIN—TREND, HO! I was reviewing a book when I spotted this trend, breaching through the *haute* trash of the new Michael Korda novel—it's the pornography of materialism. Thar she blows.

I have nothing against good trash and believe it should be pre-scribed for bad colds along with aspirin, bed rest and plenty of fluids. Sex is the only thing that can take your mind off the flu.

The trouble with Korda's book, "The Fortune," is that it's not the kind of soft porn you used to get in some fine old bodice ripper like "Angelique."

This is the real 1980s porn, materialism. The book is more or less a *roman a clef* about the Rockefeller clan, mostly more. It opens when the patriarch of the richest family in America, a former governor of New York who has run for president and who has a strong interest in modern art, dies in the saddle, as it were, at his mistress's apartment. You get three guesses.

The hook here is that the woman in question wasn't just his mistress—he had actually married her and left her everything. And would his trio of neurotic children go to any lengths to keep the bimbette from inheriting? You bet.

OK. Pretty promising material for a trash novel. But right away you start noticing these bizarre generalizations. "She had always been thin—none of the Bannermans was fat, as if being overweight was a problem that did not affect people of their wealth and class."

Has anyone told Bunky Hunt about this? A character announces, "The rich—the *real* rich, I'm talking about, you understand—are selfish and cruel. I went to school with them, so I know."

In the days when pornography was about sex, we used to get a lot of lush purple prose about how "her satin skin became flushed with desire." Great stuff. Now we get a conspicuous consumer's guide disguised as literature. Characters don't have cars, they have erotic objects off which the sun gleams richly: "His silver Porsche 930 Turbo," "his wine-red Maserati Quattroporte."

We know them not by their strength, courage, wit or warmth, but by their accessories: "His Cartier sunglasses and diamond- studded gold wrist chronometer" . . . "He unbuttoned one of his kidskin Hermes driving gloves to give her a pat on the thigh." It's the driving gloves, not the thigh, that are the erotic center of that sentence.

In Korda's book, the billionaire's expression of his passion— in Racine it was called "the avowal"—goes thusly: "She looked at her watch, a thin, flexible band of gold scales, with a face so small that it was almost impossible to tell the time—her first present from Arthur.

It was typical of him that he had not gone to Buccellati or Tiffany to buy her a present, but instead had given her an infinitely more valuable heirloom. The watch was one of a kind, designed by Cartier in Paris, so unique that when she took it to the Cartier service department on Fifth Avenue, the manager himself came over to examine it and offered to buy it back for the Cartier collection if she ever wanted to sell it. She did not ask what it was worth; the bill for cleaning and regulating it came to nearly five hundred dollars, which she herself paid without telling Arthur."

Let me confess right here that I didn't know it was *declasse*, even parvenue, to shop at Buccellati or Tiffany. In fact, I never even heard of Buccellati before. We live in a nation of people who buy things made out of leatherette from K-Mart, but most of us are trying to improve ourselves. For many years, instruction in the right kind of things to drink and to have around your house came from the ads in The New Yorker magazine. That's where a couple of generations learned sophistication—from the ads and the cartoons both.

The first book I can recall that offered this service was the James Bond series, which had a sort of middle-brow upscale quality: Between bedding beauteous dames, Bond was always advising us to stir, not shake, the martinis and the like. There are heavy doses of this kind of thing in Judith Krantz novels like "Princess Daisy" and apparently in Jackie Collins novels as well.

But the tendency became pronounced in the 1985 novel "The Two Mrs. Grenvilles," which pays slavering attention to what the *real* rich wear, what the *real* rich eat, how the *real* rich so effortlessly distinguish themselves from the unreal rich.

And now it has led to this *brennschluss* of idiocy in the Korda book, all of which led me to inquire cordially in my review, "Who gives a rat's butt?"

This pertinent question stirred Dominick Dunne, author of the Grenville book, to send a snippy note reporting that "millions and millions of people" give a rat's butt, presumably as reflected in the sales of his work.

Maybe there are millions of people dying to learn about Porthault sheets by reading bad novels. It's a curious American habit, this social-climbing by the acquisition of prestigious things.

Reminds me of a dreadful book that was a big success several years ago "You Are What You Wear."

You've probably already thought of this, but actually, you aren't. You aren't what you wear or what you eat or what you drive or what you sleep on. But the materialism of our culture has eaten so deep, many of us behave as though it were true.

So I amend my question: "Who with a grain of sense gives a rat's butt?"

Joyce Gibson Roach

A High Toned Woman

JOYCE ROACH grew up in North Texas and now lives at Keller. A woman of many talents, she writes and produces musical drama, collects and sings old-time gospel songs, lectures on Texas folklore and plays a good fiddle. She also teaches English at Texas Christian University. She has won Spur Awards from Western Writers of America for *The Cowgirls* and "A High Toned Woman," reproduced here. Old times and old-timers are important to her and she handles them with love and humor.

From *Hoein' the Short Rows,* Francis Edward Abernethy, ed. Publications of the Texas Folklore Society, no. 47. Dallas: Southern Methodist University Press, 1987, pp. 1–10.

In a song made popular by Tennessee Ernie Ford, the male in "Sixteen Tons" complains that, among other troubles, "ain't no high toned woman make me walk the line." From one hardworking man's point of view, high toned women should be avoided. Such a woman might want to improve upon or change the naturalness of a man who could load sixteen tons. In contrast, and in words from a modern translation of Old Testament sentiment, a good woman of Jack County was laid to rest with these words, "She is a worthy woman, high toned, more valuable than rubies and her husband and family rise up and call her blessed." Who then was this creature, this High Toned Woman, feared and suspected by some, venerated and adored by others? Did she really exist? And when? Can we take her dimensions, test her worthiness, name her parts, examine her, proclaim her riches? And how does the High Toned Woman fit into the great chain of being and on the ladder of other female types—mothers, others, and the liberated who can "bring home the bacon, fry it up in the pan, and never ever let you forget you're a man"? Where do we find her, how do we identify her, rescue her, and name a movement after her? Who or what were High Toned Women? They were those women in every small community who counted themselves as the authorities in matters both temporal and spiritual, but mostly spiritual. They could organize, direct, conduct, and orchestrate feminine matters; could fine tune, refine, regulate, and monopolize the female psyche; and could judge, draw, and quarter unworthy opponents. They were looked up to, respected, and emulated for their clear judgment, their unerring fortitude, their dogged pursuit of truth as they saw it, their unflagging dedication to showing the rest of us how to live. They were the nearest thing a community had to folk heroines, and they strutted in a hen yard just big enough to accommodate them.

High Toned Women were found in rural communities where little contact and influence from the outside world were possible, or else there was just enough contact to get matters all mixed up and to pick out the most glaring faults of the civilized city and cast them in country molds. Churches served as the community clubhouses, so to speak, and were the meeting grounds several times a week for not only High Toned Women but every other variety. Opportunities were many to practice the female arts in Sunday School, which in some churches was an all-female group, Sunday morning worship, Training Union, Sunday evening services, Wednesday evening prayer meeting, women's missionary groups, choir practice, weddings, funerals, Bible study, and class socials.

Although High Toned Women might be viewed anywhere in the community from the post office to the bank to any store around the square, they were on display in all their glory at church. I fellowshipped with the Baptists, but Methodists, Pentecostals, Churches of Christ, and Presbyterians had choice entries in the High Toned category too. They scratched and clucked in their own yards and only rarely got in each other's way, sometimes at a revival. Usually there were not more than three to any given territory. It seemed to be the rule, however, that whatever denomination held a revival, the visiting High Toned Women yielded to the women in the presiding church.

Within the church, High Toned Women were most obvious in the choir, usually in the front row in the soprano section. Sometimes a fine alto got in on the ladder, but altos sat behind the sopranos; therefore the front-row soprano had the upper hand. At times, deep emotion, or perhaps, contrition, during the closing hymn played upon the face of a High Toned Woman as the words (or perhaps the sound of her own splendid voice) moved her to shake her head, close her eyes, take out her handkerchief, let her voice break (for a moment only and never long enough to cause her to lose control or her pitch), and gasp for a moment. Did anyone come forward? Ah well, perhaps another verse. High Toned Women paid no attention to the choir director, but rather let the spirit, through them, lead the choir, the preacher, and the entire flock into ten more verses. High Toned Women always knew best the mood and disposition of the Holy Spirit. I have often wondered if the custom of the "long call" was instituted by a High Toned soprano and not by any pleading preacher.

Personally, I learned early to take the cue from the choir. The long call was unnecessary. I plunged down the aisle at every opportunity at every revival, every church, and gave my heart to whatever cause was pending—missionary work at the stop sign at the edge of town, praying on the street, singing on the curb, teaching on the sidewalk, persuading by the wayside. Religiously, I've been on more street corners than the *Dallas Times Herald*. It became obvious and alarming to my family that by the time I was twelve, I was a High-Toned-Woman-In-Training—a docent in the museum of rural high society.

It was not in the choir, however, that High Toned Women worked the hardest. It was in the congregation on Sunday mornings and "amongst" the masses at revival. Although there were some variations on the grand theme, almost all High Toned Women were large and fleshy women, wore corsets, had hour-glass figures, donned hats and gloves for all religious occasions, and carried black purses with strap handles. When they came into the aisles from the back of the church or arbor, their entrance reminded one of great ships at sea as they turned their bows into the wind, sailing relentlessly on to the front with their summer-weight dresses rippling and flapping like sails in their own breeze. We felt the platform tremble and the planks of the benches moan as their well-staved masts groaned and creaked against the rigging of their underwear.

It was in the church aisles that the real power of a High Toned Woman was sometimes wielded. When the invincible ironsides turned her guns on sin and sinners who ought to be at the altar, the smoke billowed, the air hung heavy with the smell of fire and brimstone, and it seemed indeed that "the earth did shake and the veil of the temple was rent in twain," as a High Toned Woman wrestled during the long call with the devil in the soul of some misguided youth or hardened husband. And no one could keep his head bowed and his eyes closed *too*, for we all wanted to witness the power of a tongue in flames as the High Toned Woman pleaded, exhorted, and called down God Almighty and a few angels to assist her in bringing a lost soul home. Her voice intoned, "Oh, sinner, if just one soul like you is saved tonight, the angels in heaven weep." That was probably no exaggeration. Meanwhile, in the choir another High Toned Woman jumped into another verse of "Almost Persuaded" to assure her sister of a little more time with the stubborn, hardheaded, nasty little sinful son-of-a-saint.

There may have been High-Toned-Women in cities. We often speculated that there might be some in Dallas, but we never knew for sure. We knew Fort Worth was a big town, but still a country town and their ways were not the stranger's ways. But Dallas! Dallas was such a dangerous place and we didn't go—hardly ever. All the women there were Quality, which is not the same as High Toned or the same as Choice or Prime. I had Quality explained to me once in Dallas by my grandmother. Mama Hartman took me once, when I was a small girl, inside the very walls of Neiman-Marcus. We kept to the sides of the store, never venturing into the aisles except to get to another wall. She allowed me to look swiftly at whatever goods were on eye level, but she kept a firm grip on my hand. The ladies who were shopping paid no attention to us, and so I got to look at them all I wanted. What I saw was Quality.

"We are going to hunt the bathroom."

"But, Mama, you told me never to go to the bathroom in a strange house and never, never in a department store 'cause you never knew who'd been usin' the pot. You said, if you were desperate, never to sit on the seat—never—but to hunker above it. And then when you do go, it leaves the seat all wet all over it and you either have to clean up or else not let anybody see you leave because they'd know you were the one who did it on the seat. You said it was better to hold in no matter what; and to always go to the bathroom the last thing before you left the house. Mama, I don't need to use Neiman-Marcus' bathroom." I was pulling back now and whispering so she wouldn't shush me.

"I know all that, Joyce Ann." Now she was whispering so I wouldn't shush her. There was enough rush of noisy air coming from our mouths to have launched a hot-air balloon. "I want you to see something."

We pushed open the door and there was only one Quality woman in the place. She was washing her hands and tucking her hair up. She licked one finger and pushed up her eyebrow. Then she licked another finger and pushed up the other one. Anyone could tell that she was a good, clean woman since she didn't lick the same finger to do the other brow. She was certainly a lesson in Quality. Watching Quality at her toilette was not, however, what Mama had in mind. When the lady left after giving a good tug to her girdle, we went to the first booth. The toilet seat was dry! We made every stall, eight of them, and—they were all dry!

Mama said, "See, Joyce Ann." I shook my head in amazement and agreement, but never till the day she died did I ever have the courage to ask an explanation about the dry toilet seats. The only logical conclusion was that Quality women took a better aim.

Being a High Toned Woman constituted a career of sorts for country women. The career offered many opportunities, good working conditions, selected hours, and executive positions only, but the pay was poor and chances for advancement were limited. After woman's oldest profession, and woman's second-oldest profession of motherhood, being a High Toned Woman might qualify as woman's third-oldest profession.

There was one rare opportunity for a High Toned Woman to advance in the world, unlike women in the first two professions. She could become a missionary. It seemed in my child's mind that every missionary I ever met was female and High Toned. That truth, of course, did not everywhere abound, but we all live by our own assumptions, and for all I knew, to be female was a requirement to being a missionary. What little we knew of geography or the larger world, we knew from mission study. God called upon missionaries and us to feed the hungry and to clothe the naked. I thought the African people needed our kind of food—corn bread and red beans, chicken fried steak, such as that—and I didn't worry about their getting it because good money went regularly to the mission fund and probably some good missionary prepared it herself around a cozy campfire in the jungle. (Another assumption was that Africans were the only ones who needed missionaries, and that they along with Tarzan and Cheetah had about all the bases covered.) But I could see how the missionaries needed help with the clothes. It was a long time, and only after repeated trips to the forbidden *National Geographic,* that I realized that the heathen Africans preferred nakedness and the missionaries preferred to have them cover their nakedness. The logic was clear. You couldn't have naked, brown humans running around disrobed in front of a High Toned Woman. I nearly wept when the truth sank in. Clothing the naturally naked was the high aim of the missionary movement before 1950. Such a work! To be able to gather barrels of clothes so that all Africans, every last naked one of them, might sweat, itch, and pull at tight underwear as I did was worthy of my best efforts. I could help civilize and robe them in a fashion worthy to be presented at the throne of God. I wanted to see every last God's one of them cinched, girded about the loins, trussed up, and covered with Fruit of the Loom, not with merely a fig leaf. Putting clothes on Adam and Eve was almost the first civilized act of God when the pair brought sin and civilization upon themselves, and I intended to make it my life's work by way of the U.S. mail. Wisdom was a long, long time in coming, and if in my mind I had to undress as many Africans as I had sworn to clothe, the job would not have been too great.

If it seems that High Toned Women were found consorting in merely busy business of predominantly religious affairs, it should be pointed out that the same women had a goodness about them unequalled in any period in history. These same women were the ones trusted to hold a dying child, called upon to console a widow, asked to bear sad news in a telegram which no woman should have to read from paper, relied upon to prepare graves, and honored for remembering all the proper rituals of the heart which have never been written down. If they were the authorities in matters of living, they were also the ones enduring enough to accompany us to the edge of the grave and to bring us back again to the land of the living, drawing us after them in footsteps plainly visible. Trained psychologists and psychiatrists would only wonder at the wisdom, the deftness in dealing with the human condition, the splendid appropriateness of their gestures and their words. The professionals should reach back in time and call them "sister."

But there is more: gifts of good, little surprises for the children they knew, gifts for acquaintances; they were peacemakers in family and community. The positive force which emanated from High Toned Women made many of them eligible for sainthood.

I do believe that the clan, High Toned, is universal and occurs in all civilizations from pagan to Christian, from Africa to South America, from Siberia to Australia, and represents a kind of feminine category common to every nationality on earth. The status and importance of High Toned Women were probably felt only in female domains. Males, as far as I could tell, paid no attention to them unless perhaps a preacher had to deal with them from time to time. There does not appear to be a related category known as High Toned Men, for instance. No one questioned a woman's role in male relationships either. It was usually a woman-to-woman thing. Most men probably felt like Ernie Ford, knowing that a High Toned Woman would make them walk the line — maybe.

The decline of High Toned Women began with World War II when women went to work and opened up a whole new classification of types. Radio, which brought the voices of the nation and the world into the living room, did not favor High Toned Women. Movies occasionally captured one or two on film, but High Toned Women were always featured in supporting roles, which is, perhaps, what High Toned Women did best — support. Movies made of them merely Busy Bodies. The Andy Hardy series comes to mind. Aunt Bee in the Andy Griffin television series approached High Toned, but fell short, too. It could be that Schick rehab centers took up High Toned Women's work, and Dear Abby is as close a confidante as modern women can find. Barbara Walters asks questions that real High Toned Women avoided at all costs. When there is no need, High Toned Women, or any other institution of folklore, pass away, and new forms of popular culture rise to fill the gap. I'm not so sure they have been replaced with "something of value."

I shall gladly help bury the High Toned Woman with tenderness, care, and sweet remembrance, but let no one say that I helped dig her grave. Do not forget the type. Go to some exotic, strange, remote, primitive, backward, rural, timeless place, if you can find it, and you will still find the High Toned Woman. She may not speak your language, but you will know her when you see her. If you would, perhaps, care to form a club, please meet me later. I am already the president, and so you need not apply for that job. And just as soon as I can get my corset laced and my hymnbook out, we shall stand outside on the corner and sing the anthem of High Toned Women, always done as a solo, "The Ninety and Nine," the last verse of which goes:

> And all through the mountains thunder riven
> And up from the rocky steep
> There arose a glad cry from the gates of heaven
> Rejoice I have found my sheep
> And the angels echoed around the throne
> Rejoice for the Lord brings back his own.
> Rejoice for the Lord brings back his own.

Works Excerpted

Dillon Anderson, "The Windmill Fixers," *I and Claudie*. Boston: Little, Brown, 1951.

Ed Bateman, "The Old West Blows Out," *Western Horseman*, May 1989.

William Brammer, "Arthur Fenstemaker in Action," *The Gay Place*. Boston: Houghton Mifflin, 1961.

Bill Brett, "The Way It Was: Southeast Texas, 1915," *This Here's a Good'un*. College Station: Texas A&M University Press, 1983.

J. Mason Brewer, "The Palacious Rancher and the Preacher," *Dog Ghosts and Other Negro Tales*. Austin: University of Texas Press, 1958.

_____"The Preacher and His Farmer Brother" *The Word on the Brazos: Negro Preacher Tales from the Brazos Bottoms of Texas*. Austin: University of Texas Press, 1953.

Joe Bob Briggs, "Is the National Geographic in Zambooli Land?" *Dallas Times-Herald*, August 31, 1984.

Alex Burton, "Just One Kiss, Baby," *Just One Kiss, Baby*. Austin: Eakin Press, 1983.

George Dolan, "I Gonna Be a Artist," *Slightly Left and Right of Center*. Fort Worth: Branch Smith, Inc., 1967.

John C. Duval, "The Wild Texan Comes Home," *The Adventures of Big Foot Wallace*. Austin: The Steck Company, 1935.

A. W. Eddins, "Austin Wheeler's Dream," *Southwestern Lore*. Publications of the Texas Folklore Society, no. 9, 1931, J. Frank Dobie, ed. (reprint edition, Hatboro, Pennsylvania: Folklore Associates, Inc., 1965).

Max Evans, "Booger Boggs Pitches for the Lord," *My Pardner*. Boston: Houghton Mifflin, 1963 (reprint edition, Albuquerque: University of New Mexico Press, 1984).

John Henry Faulk, "Cowboy Dick's Last Ride," *The Uncensored John Henry Faulk*. Austin: Texas Monthly Press, 1985.

Ben K. Green, "Maniac Mule," *Horse Tradin'*. New York: Alfred A. Knopf, 1967.

A. C. Greene, "The Ominous Journey," *A Personal Country*. New York: Alfred A. Knopf, 1969.

Leon Hale, "Aunt Lizzie's Snuff," *Turn South at the Second Bridge*. College Station: Texas A&M University Press, 1985.

Laura V. Hamner, "Ellen Carter and the Black-Eyed Peas," *Light n' Hitch*. Dallas: American Guild Press, 1943.

Ellen Bowie Holland, "A Scotsman Comes Courting," *Gay as a Grig: Memories of a North Texas Girlhood*. Austin: University of Texas Press, 1963.

Molly Ivins, "Ah For the Days When Porn Was About Sex, Not Materialism," *Dallas Times-Herald*, March 14, 1989.

Dan Jenkins, "The Social Structure of Claybelle High," *Fast Copy*. New York: Simon and Schuster, 1988.

Elmer Kelton, "Hewey Arrives," *The Good Old Boys*. Garden City: Doubleday, 1978.

Larry L. King, "My Hero, LBJ," *Warning: Writer at Work*. Fort Worth: Texas Christian University Press, 1985.

James Lehrer, "General Max Takes the Alamo," *Viva Max*. New York: Duell, Sloan & Pearce, 1966.

Randolph B. Marcy, "Frontier Settlers," *Thirty Years of Army Life on the Border*. New York: Harper & Brothers, 1866.

Amado Muro, "Cecelia Rosas," *The Collected Stories of Amado Muro*. Austin: Thorp Springs Press, 1979.

Paul Patterson, "Best Old Feller You Ever Saw," *Pecos Tales*. Austin: Encino Press, 1967.

George Sessions Perry, "Under the Bridge," *Walls Rise Up*. New York: Doubleday, Doran, 1939.

Shine Philips, "Put Your Little Foot," *Big Spring*. New York: Prentice-Hall, 1942.

Bill Porterfield, "Juneteenth with Sassmouth," *Texas Rhapsody*. New York: Holt, Rinehart and Winston, 1971.

Lloyd E. Price, "Hanging Was Good Enough For My Father," from "Anecdotes about Lawyers," in *Backwoods to Border*. Dallas: University Press [Southern Methodist University], 1943, Publications of the Texas Folklore Society no. 21.

Cactus Pryor, "The Ballad of Billie Sol," *Inside Texas*, Bryan, Texas: Shoal Creek Publishers, 1982.

_____ "The Law South of the Belt," *Inside Texas*. Bryan, Texas: Shoal Creek Publishers, 1982.

Joyce Gibson Roach, "A High Toned Woman," from *Hoein' the Short Rows*. Publications of the Texas Folklore Society no. 47, Francis Edward Abernethy, ed. Dallas: Southern Methodist University Press, 1987.

T. T. Robinson, "Pidge the Humorous Ranger," *Daily Democratic Statesman*, September 24, 1874. Quoted by Chuck Parsons in *"Pidge": A Texas Ranger from Virginia*. Wolfe City, Texas: Harrington Publishing Co., 1985.

Edwin Shrake, "Billy Roy Eanes's Roman Banquet," *Peter Arbiter*, Austin: The Encino Press, 1973.

H. Allen Smith, "The Silent Treatment," *The Best of H. Allen Smith*. New York: Trident Press, 1972.

Alex E. Sweet, "The Typical Texan," *Texas Siftings*, May 9, 1886. Reproduced in *Alex Sweet's Texas*, Virginia Eisenhour, ed. Austin: University of Texas Press, 1986.

Alex E. Sweet and J. Armoy Knox, "John Wesley Hardin at Cuero," *On a Mexican Mustang through Texas*. Chicago: Rand, McNally, 1891.

Edward Swift, "Cowgirls for Christ," *Principia Martindale*. New York: Harper & Row, 1983.

Frank X. Tolbert, "Cowboys: A Bunch of Sissies," was first published in *A Bowl of Red*, Garden City: Doubleday, 1966. Reprinted here from *Tolbert of Texas,* Evelyn Oppenheimer, ed. Fort Worth: Texas Christian University, 1986.

_____"Father Casey Speaks His Mind," *Tolbert's Texas.* Garden City: Doubleday, 1983.

Elizabeth Wheaton, "A Quiet Tuesday Night at Mr. George's Joint," *Mr. George's Joint.* New York: E. P. Dutton, 1941.

Owen P. White, "El Paso on the Move," *The Autobiography of a Durable Sinner,* New York: G.P. Putnam's Sons, 1942.

C. L. Sonnichsen—scholar, teacher, folklorist and grassroots historian—was educated in the East but migrated west to the Texas School of Mines (now the University of Texas at El Paso) in 1931. At UTEP he served as chairman of the English department, graduate dean and H. Y. Benedict Professor of English. He retired to Tucson, Arizona, in 1972 to edit *The Journal of Arizona History* and still serves as senior editor of that magazine.

During the forty years Sonnichsen spent in Texas he traveled extensively throughout the state, interviewing pioneers and their descendants for books and articles. His interests ranged from notables like John Wesley Hardin and Judge Roy Bean to the history of El Paso and the literature of the Southwest. Sonnichsen's experiences left him with a special fondness and understanding for Texans and Texas institutions and a keen eye and ear for the frailties and foibles of his subjects—observations and research that led naturally to *The Laughing West* (Ohio University Press, 1988) and to *Texas Humoresque*.

Known affectionately to his students and friends as "Doc," he is the author of over twenty-five books, numerous articles and hundreds of book reviews. He has received prestigious awards from Western Writers of America, the National Cowboy Hall of Fame, the Texas Institute of Letters and Harvard University (his alma mater). Sonnichsen's books include *Roy Bean: The Law West of the Pecos* (1943), *Cowboys and Cattle Kings: Life on the Range Today* (1950), *Tularosa: Last of the Frontier West* (1960), *Pass of the North* (1968), *From Hopalong to Hud* (1978), *The Ambidextrous Historian* (1981) and *Tucson: The Life and Times of An American City* (1982).